TEACH YOURSELF BOOKS

CARD GAMES

To
Albie Fiore

CARD GAMES

David Parlett

TEACH YOURSELF BOOKS

For UK orders: please contact Bookpoint Ltd, 78 Milton Park, Abingdon, Oxon
OX14 4TD. Telephone: (44) 01235 400414, Fax: (44) 01235 400454. Lines are open from
9.00–6.00, Monday to Saturday, with a 24-hour message answering service.
Email address: orders@bookpoint.co.uk

For USA and Canada orders: please contact NTC/Contemporary Publishing, 4255 West
Touhy Avenue, Lincolnwood, Illinois 60646–1975, USA. Telephone: (847) 679 5500,
Fax: (847) 679 2494.

Long renowned as the authoritative source for self-guided learning – with more than 40
million copies sold worldwide – the *Teach Yourself* series includes over 200 titles in the
fields of languages, crafts, hobbies, business and education.

A catalogue record for this title is available from The British Library.

Library of Congress Catalog Card Number: On file

First published in UK 1994 by Hodder Headline Plc, 338 Euston Road, London, NW1 3BH.
This second edition published 1999.

First published in US 1994 by NTC/Contemporary Publishing, 4255 West Touhy Avenue,
Lincolnwood (Chicago), Illinois 60646–1975 USA. This second edition published 1999.

The 'Teach Yourself' name and logo are registered trade marks of Hodder & Stoughton Ltd.

Typeset by Transet Limited, Coventry, England.
Printed in Great Britain for Hodder & Stoughton Educational, a division of Hodder
Headline Plc, 338 Euston Road, London NW1 3BH by Cox & Wyman Ltd, Reading,
Berkshire.

Impression number   10 9 8 7 6 5 4 3 2 1
Year   2005 2004 2003 2002 2001 2000 1999

CONTENTS

INTRODUCTION

This book has several aims. The main ones are to introduce you to the delights of card-play if you don't already enjoy them, to draw your attention to some games you may not have played before, and to act as a reference source in case you've forgotten some of the finer points, or can't agree on the exact rules of play.

Cards have been a popular source of enjoyment for over 600 years, and remain so largely because they are cheap and sociable. For less than a pound you can buy a pack of these pretty pasteboard objects and assure yourself of hours of entertainment. Unlike telly, it's an entertainment that puts you in the active role and credits you with a modicum of intelligence. And there's as much variety in the programmes as you want: the games described here just scratch the surface of the wealth available.

People sometimes wonder how there come to be so many different games to choose from. There are several answers to this. One is that the gaming material is so ingenious and versatile that you can do almost anything with it – unlike, say, a Chess set, with which you can only play Chess. (There are Chess variants, but they are still varieties of Chess, not significantly different games.) Given this inherent versatility, another is that different nations and communities have developed their own particular favourites, and there has been plenty of time (historically speaking) for them to have diversified and evolved. Another is that people of different temperaments develop different types of game: there are games of pure fun, for children; games of pure chance, for gamblers; and games of great intellectual skill, for people who like games to be the mental equivalent of strenuous physical exercise.

Another wellspring of variety is that there are games designed for specific numbers of players, which is another advantage of playing-cards over board games like Chess, Backgammon, Scrabble™, and the like. There are games for just one player, generically known as Patience or Solitaire. (There are so many of these that, rather than include any in this book, I have made a separate selection of them in *Teach Yourself Card Games for One*). There are some excellent card games for two, such as Cribbage, Piquet, Gin, and Bezique. Card games for three are less well known in Britain than elsewhere, but the German game of Skat is outstanding in this respect, and, if you find it too mathematical, you might instead try Five Hundred, Ninety-Nine, or some form of Rummy. Four players are well served by partnership games such as Whist, Bridge and Canasta; but if you prefer to play on your own account you can hardly do better than Solo Whist. Then there are games designed for an indefinite number of players from three to about seven, such as Knockout, Crazy Eights, Newmarket and Poker. There are also casino games played with cards, which I do not cover in this book. (If this is your interest, see instead *Teach Yourself How to Win at Card Games*, by Belinda Levez.)

Poker, unlike most casino games, is a game of skill, contrary to the vague misapprehension of those who have never played it; and perhaps this is the point to address an equally common and related misapprehension – namely, that cards are 'just' a form of gambling, and offer little scope for intelligent play because they are randomly distributed to start with.

First, gambling. This has two meanings, one of which is 'playing for money'. Any game *can* be played for money, even Chess and Scrabble™, so it is nonsense to single this out as being a defining characteristic of card games. The other is 'wagering money on the outcome of an event over which you have no control', such as Bingo, the National Lottery, or racetrack betting. Here it is necessary to point out that *some* card games are indeed gambling games by this strict definition of the term: they are the ones played in casinos, and in which most serious card-players have little interest. Others, however, do not fall into this category. Generally speaking, the more skilled and less chancy a card game is, the more interest derives from the actual play of the game rather than from basing monetary transactions on the outcome. Poker is a game of skill because money itself (or chips or counters representing it) are the actual instruments of play, and players have complete control over how they manage their investments. It is only a gambling game in the first sense of the term, not in the second.

Other games involve different types and degrees of skill. The fact that you get a random distribution to start with, and don't know which cards are in other players' hands, is not of itself antithetical to the application of skill. On the contrary, one of the skills of a game like Whist and Bridge is that of deducing or inferring other players' holdings from the cards they play and the order they play them in, or from spoken information conveyed in an 'auction' that precedes the play.

Other types of skill may be involved as well, but what they are must be left to emerge from the individual games themselves. Some, like Rummy, involve memory; others, like Cribbage, don't. Skat and Piquet involve a lot of counting; Newmarket and Crazy Eights practically none at all.

One other misapprehension must be dealt with before you set off on your exploration, and that is the myth of 'official rules'. The vast majority of card games are folk games: they do not have official rules of universal applicability, but are played in slightly different ways from town to town, from club to club, from home to home, sometimes even from day to day by the same group of players. The relatively few games that are equipped with universal rules, such as Bridge and Skat, have them because they are played at national or international level in clubs and tournaments, where it is obviously necessary for everyone to know in advance exactly which rules they will be following, and for which there are well-organized clubs and federations who co-operate in formulating and promoting such rules. Other games, such as Cribbage and Piquet, have them because they are 'book' games: they have been played for so many centuries by generally literate players that the actual play of the game has been influenced by their descriptions recorded in books.

The basics of card play

The standard British and international pack contains 52 cards plus one or more Jokers. Jokers are used only for a few odd games and can be ignored till you come to them.

The 52 cards are divided into four series of thirteen. The series are called *suits* and their individual members are *ranks*. Each suit is distinguished by its suitmark, a symbol of a particular colour, namely:

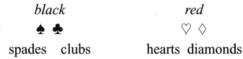

black	*red*
♠ ♣	♡ ◇
spades clubs	hearts diamonds

All suits are equal. None is inherently higher or better than another, but individual games may attach more importance to one than to another, or even arrange all four in an order of importance.

The individual members of each suit, its 13 ranks, are basically the numerals 1 to 10, plus three face cards or 'court' cards ('courts' for short), namely King, Queen and Jack (formerly Knave). The numeral One is called Ace. In trick-taking games, and some others, it is not the lowest but the highest card, outranking even the King. The normal ranking of cards – albeit with frequent exceptions – is therefore usually one of the following:

in non-trick games (low to high):   A 2 3 4 5 6 7 8 9 10 J Q K
in trick-taking games (high to low): A K Q J 10 9 8 7 6 5 4 3 2

It is usual to describe trick-taking games in high–low order because most of the important play takes place with the high cards (just as most of the play at snooker takes place at the black-ball end of the table), and the low cards are often so unimportant that they can just be referred to as 'x'.

Each card is thus uniquely identified by rank and suit, as for example 'Two of clubs', 'Queen of hearts', 'Ace of spades', though they are generally printed with the suit first: ♣2, ♡Q, ♠A. Its identity by rank and suit is marked as an 'index' in the top left-hand corner, so that you can readily identify all the cards in your hand without having to fan them out too widely.

The skill and fun of card games is based on the fact that individual cards are identifiable only from the front and not from the back. Invariably, the cards are first randomized by shuffling, then dealt face down to players, who then pick them up and hold them in such a way that you can only identify the cards you are holding yourself and have no idea of who else holds what. For this reason, card games are technically described as games of 'imperfect information'. Intelligent card games, however, as opposed to simple betting games, hinge on the process of acquiring information by a variety of methods, including observation, inference and deduction. (Yes, by cheating too; but this complicates the issue.) They are therefore better thought of as games of 'developing information', for this is precisely what they are all about.

What to do at the card-table

Players. Most games are designed for a specific number of players, or at least have variants designed for specific numbers. If played by the wrong number, the balance of a game will be upset, and its enjoyment spoilt. Patience is played by one, and many good games by two or three. Four may play alone or in two partnerships of two, in which case partners sit opposite each other across the table. Games for five or more tend to be more chancy and less skill rewarding

Seating and partners. In case of disagreement as to who sits where, players may each draw a card at random from a pack spread face down in a row, the highest rank drawn conferring first choice of seat, and so on downwards. Two or more tied cards will draw again to break the tie. The same draw may be used to establish partnerships. In Bridge, for instance, those drawing the two highest cards play as partners against those drawing the lowest. In games for four or fewer, it is usual to refer to the players by their compass positions at the table – North, East, South, West.

Rotation. In Britain, the turn to deal and play usually passes to the left, or clockwise around the table as viewed from above. However, this varies from country to country, and serious players prefer to play whichever way round is appropriate to the country of origin of the game being practised. As the exact rotation makes no real difference to the play, I will only mention in passing which way round is customary for any particular game, and leave you to do as you please.

Game structure. Depending on the game, the play of a single hand or deal may last anything from less than one minute to ten or more.

To make the play worthwhile, and to balance out the receipt of 'good' and 'bad' hands, a game therefore consists of several deals. It may be played:

■ for an agreed length of time,

■ up to a target score set either by the rules of the game or by prior agreement,

■ for as many deals as agreed beforehand or specified by the rules of the game.

Shuffle and deal. Whoever drew the highest card usually deals first, and the turn to deal passes to the left. Before dealing, the dealer shuffles the cards in order to randomize the pack. You can't learn shuffling by words, only by observation and practice. In most card games (other than Bridge, which has a lot of silly rules of its own), anyone has the right to shuffle on demand, but the dealer has the right to shuffle last. The dealer then offers the pack to his right-hand neighbour, who initiates a 'cut' by lifting the top half and placing it on the table. The dealer then completes the cut by placing the bottom half on the top. The purpose of this rigmarole is to ensure that no one can have seen the bottom card of the pack and so identify a card held by another player. It will of course be frustrated if the dealer is careless enough to hold the pack at an upright, outward angle when dealing.

The deal is made by distributing cards face down one at a time around the table, the first card of each round going to the player at Dealer's left (variously called 'eldest hand', 'forehand', etc.) and the last to himself. Some games specify that cards be dealt not singly but in batches of two or three at a time. Such a rule makes a significant difference and should not be ignored. In some games, the whole pack is dealt out. In some, for various purposes, a few neutral cards may be dealt face down to the table as a spare hand or 'widow' or 'talon'. In some, a batch or stock of cards will be left face down, from which players draw additional cards in the course of play so that all are eventually used. In others, the undealt cards are left untouched and play no part at all, except to increase the chance factor by making the acquisition of 'perfect information' impossible until it is too late to do anything with it.

Tricks

The vast majority of western card games involve playing cards to tricks. A *trick* consists of one card played by each player in turn face up to the table. It therefore consists of as many cards as there are players. The leader – the first to play – is normally allowed to play any card he likes. The others are then normally required to furnish a card of the same suit as the one led, if possible, until the trick is complete. Whoever played the highest card of the suit led wins the trick, turns it face down in a squared-up pile before him, and then leads the first card to the next trick.

Normally, a card of a different suit from that led cannot take the trick. However, many games permit one suit to be designated *trump* (from 'triumph'). In such games, a player unable to follow suit to a plain-suit (non-trump) lead can beat the suit led by playing a trump. The rule of trick-winning therefore becomes: 'The trick is taken by the highest card of the suit led, or by the highest trump if any are played'.

Most trick games follow this rule, though slight variations will be encountered.

Here is an example of normal trick-play. Of four players, assume that North leads clubs, and that two players have no clubs to play:

North ♣9, East ♣Q, South ◇K, West ♡2.

If the game is played at no trump, East's Queen wins because it is the highest card of the suit led. South's King, though ranking higher, is of the wrong suit.

If hearts are trumps, West's Two takes the trick, as it is the highest (only) trump played. If diamonds are trumps, South's King is the winning card. And if clubs are trumps, East wins again, because a trump suit cannot itself be trumped.

Of many ways of selecting a suit for trump, the commonest are these. In older and simpler games the last card of the pack is turned face up and its suit becomes trump automatically. In more highly developed games a trump suit (or 'no trump') is nominated by the player who contracts to win the greatest number of tricks in return for so doing. Such games are usually preceded by an 'auction' in which players 'bid' to nominate trumps by increasing the number of tricks they offer to win. For greater interest the suits may be graded in a specified order of superiority, so that a bid can be overcalled not necessarily by raising the number of tricks but by bidding the same number of tricks in a higher-ranking suit, or at no trump, which beats every suit. This is the distinguishing feature of Contract Bridge.

Scores and payoffs

The amount you win or lose is particularly interesting in card games, most of which produce more varied results than the simple '1 for a win, 0 for a loss, 1/2 for a draw' of Chess. Card games fall into two types as to the way in which scores are made or recorded; first are 'hard-score' games and second are 'soft-score' games.

Hard-score games are played directly for cash, or for objects representing cash, such as chips or counters. Settlements are made at the end of each deal, so that each deal is a complete game in itself. A session of play has no overall game structure, and can end at any point.

Soft-score games are played for notional points recorded in writing on suitable scoresheets. In this case a game consists either of a specified number of deals, or of as many deals as it takes for a player or partnership to reach a specified target score. This gives the game an overall structure, to which additional scoring interest may be attached – for example, bonuses for reaching the target score soonest, or penalties for failing to reach a minimum level. Additionally, scoring considerations may influence one's strategy ('playing to the score').

All gambling games are played for hard score, and games of chance usually for cash, but it does not follow that all games played for hard score are 'gambling games' in the popular sense of depending more on chance than skill. Solo Whist, for example, is almost invariably played for hard score, and for cash at that, but it can be a game of great skill and only an accident of social history has deprived Solo of the sort of highly developed scoring system that has contributed so greatly to the success of Bridge.

Most games of skill are played for the 'soft score' of points recorded in writing. At end of play, these may or may not be converted into the 'hard score' of cash settlements between the players. The more skill-demanding the game, the greater the tendency for interest to attach to the play itself rather than to its capacity for determining cash settlements. Many play such games 'for small stakes' as a matter of temperament or tradition. Others will not play for money at all. Whatever one's attitude to playing for money, it must be admitted that it is the gambling origin of card games that has led to their fascinating scoring systems, and, consequently, to the unique feature of card games where one's strategy is often governed by the various scoring possibilities of a given hand.

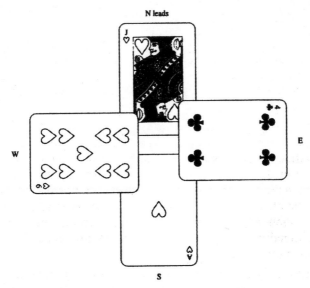

Figure 1.1   Playing tricks
(1) Playing at no trump, North leads the Jack of hearts. The others, playing in clockwise rotation, must follow suit (play hearts) if they can. East cannot follow, and discards a club. South wins the trick with his Ace, it being the highest card of the suit led. (2) With clubs trump, the trick is now won by East, who is permitted to trump (or 'ruff') by virtue of having none left of the suit led. Had West been unable to follow, he might have won the trick by 'overtrumping' with a club higher than the Four.

Choosing your game

What shall we play?

First, decide how many of you there are. In the following table, games are primarily arranged according to the number of players for which they are suitable. Those noted in brackets can be played by the number in question, but are not ideally suited to it.

If there are four of you, decide whether you prefer to play in fixed partnerships, or as individuals ('solo'), as these two groups are listed separately.

Next, decide whether or not you want to play a trick-taking game. On the whole, trick games include some of the deepest and most skill-demanding, while those more designed for fun and sociability tend to be of the non-trick variety. Games that are particularly easy to pick up are asterisked. Special attention is also drawn to gambling games, here defined as those played for coins or counters rather than for a written score.

Finally, remember that different games appeal to different temperaments – for example, players generally divide into those who favour fixed partnership games like Bridge, and those who prefer solo games like – well, Solo. Some prefer matching games to trick games; some like playing for coins or counters and others for a written score; and so on.

Deciding which game to play according to number of players

	Tricks	Non-tricks
2 players	German Whist*	Cribbage*
	Piquet	Gin Rummy*
	Elevens	
	Sixty-Six	
	Bezique	
	Klaberjass	
	(Ninety-Nine)	
3 players	Bismarck*	Rummy*
	Knockout*	Crazy Eights (etc.)*
	Oh Hell!*	Newmarket*†
	Nap*	Pontoon*†
	Ninety-Nine*	Brag†

	Euchre Skat Twenty-Five (Five Hundred)* (Hearts)*	Poker† (Cribbage)* (The Bum Game)
4 players (partnership)	Whist* Bridge Spades Euchre Five Hundred Don (Twenty-Five)	Canasta (Cribbage)*
4 players (solo)	Solo Whist* Dutch Whist* Knockout* Oh Hell!* Nap* Hearts* Twenty-Five	Rummy* The Bum Game* Crazy Eights (etc.)* Newmarket*† Pontoon*† Brag† Poker†
5 or more players	Knockout* Oh Hell!* Nap* Twenty-Five (Ninety-Nine*)	Rummy* (The Bum Game) Crazy Eights (etc.)* Newmarket*† Pontoon*† Brag† Poker†

* *particularly easy to learn*
† *gambling games (best played with coins or counters)*

Part One
VARIETIES OF WHIST

1 | WHIST

The classical partnership game

Many games are called Whist for short, their full names being Solo Whist or Knockout Whist or whatever it may be; but the only one to which the single word rightly refers is that more fully describable as the classical partnership game.

This game is nowadays mostly encountered in fund-raising events called Whist drives, in which capacity it remains (with Brag and Cribbage) the basic English folk game that it has been for most of its over 400-year long history. Before the advent of its natural descendant Bridge, Whist passed through a phase of being the foremost intellectual and social card game of its day. What makes it a great game is the fact that it has extremely simple rules of play, yet can give rise to considerable depth of skill.

If you are want to learn Bridge, you can hardly do better than to start with partnership Whist.

How to play

Whist is played in two forms: the home game and the tournament or 'drive' game. (A third form, Duplicate, is probably extinct. The sort of people who played it now play Duplicate Bridge.) The following description is of the home game. The drive game differs in minor details, as specified after the main description.

Players. Four play in two fixed partnerships. Partners may be determined by drawing cards from a shuffled pack. Whoever draws the highest card has first choice of seats and is partnered by the person drawing the second highest, who sits opposite.

Cards. Fifty-two. It's best to alternate between two packs, one being shuffled while the other is dealt. This ensures thorough shuffling without wasting time.

Object. A rubber is won by the first side to win two games. A game is won by the first side to score 5 points over as many deals as it takes. (But you may find it more logical to follow American practice and play up to 7 points.)

Deal. Whoever drew the highest card deals first, and the turn to deal and play passes to the left. Deal 13 each in ones. The last card goes face up to the table to establish trumps.

Play. The player at Dealer's left leads to the first trick, and the dealer adds the trump turn-up to his hand as soon as it is his own turn to play. Suit must be followed if possible, otherwise any card may be played. A trick is taken by the highest card of the suit led, or by the highest trump if any are played. The winner of each trick leads to the next. All tricks won by a partnership are stored in front of whichever member of it first wins one.

Revoke. A player who fails to follow suit though able to do so may correct his play without penalty before the next card is played. If a revoke is discovered later, 3 points are deducted from the current score of the revoking side, or, if this makes less than zero, are added to the other side's score.

Score. Whichever side took a majority of tricks, seven or more, scores 1 point per 'odd trick' – that is, for each trick won in excess of six. Winning all 13 tricks would therefore score 7 points.

After scoring for tricks, it is possible to score for honours. Honours are the highest trumps (A–K–Q–J). If one partnership held all four trump honours, either in one hand or divided between them, they add 4 for honours. If they held any three, they add 2 for honours. Honours are not scored, however, if the side concerned is 1 point short of game, i.e. standing at 4 points under English rules. (The Americans dispensed with honours entirely, and modern players may wish to do the same, as they depend entirely on chance and obviously form too large a proportion of the total.)

Game and rubber. On winning a second game, a partnership adds 2 points for the rubber. Their margin of victory is the difference between both sides' scores.

Drive Whist. In tournament play, the last card is not turned for trump. Instead, the first hand is played with hearts trump, the second with clubs, the third with diamonds, the fourth with spades, and the cycle is repeated thereafter. Sometimes the cycle is five deals, the fifth being played at No Trump. It is not unheard of to play a six-deal cycle, the sixth being Misère. This is played at No Trump, and the side that wins the smaller number of tricks scores 1 point for each trick taken less than seven. A leg or rubber is 24 deals, or any other fixed number, after which the partnerships move round to the next table. It is possible to buy pre-printed Drive Whist score-cards for this purpose.

Notes on play

Unless you are exceptionally strong in trumps, your normal strategy as a partnership is to establish and bring home your longest plain suit or suits. To establish a suit means to force out the high cards which your opponents hold in it (preferably by winning them in tricks, though not necessarily) so that those remaining in your hand are the highest left in play. Bringing it home means subsequently leading and winning tricks with those cards without having them trumped.

Consider the underlying principle first. Since there are 13 cards in each suit, each player will be dealt an average of $3\frac{1}{4}$ of them. Any suit in which you hold four or more is therefore 'long' as far as you are concerned, since you have more than the average number. Those cards of it which are certain to win tricks (disregarding the possibility of trumping for the moment) are described as 'long cards'.

Suppose you have been dealt ♠A K Q 2, spades not being trumps, and the other players have an even three each. How many of these are long cards? At first sight only the top three. But on closer inspection:

Ace draws	3, 4, 5
then King draws	6, 7, 8
then Queen draws	9, 10, J

and now no one has any of the suit left, so your Two is bound to win if led (and not trumped). You have thus established the suit, and if you can reach a position from which you can lead the Two without having it trumped, you will have brought the suit home.

Since few holdings are so clear cut, you and your partner will generally need each other's assistance in bringing home your respective best suits. Your best suit will, normally, be your longest; but if you have two long suits it will be the one with the most likely trick-winners. Clearly, a holding of A K Q 2 in one suit is better than one of 6 5 4 3 2 in another, even though it is normally better to play a five-card than a four-card suit.

Opening lead

The best opportunity you have for declaring your suit is at your first lead to a trick, especially when sitting immediately left of the dealer and so leading to the first trick of the hand.

Lead from your best suit, so that your partner will know which one to return to you when he or she gets the lead. Of that suit, lead a card which will indicate to him what sort of holding you have in it, so that by deducting his own holding in the suit he will be able to start building up a picture of where the key cards lie.

In the days when Whist was regarded as a 'scientific' game, the club experts and analysts devised all sorts of ingenious and elaborate leading conventions. Nowadays that sort of brain-power goes instead into devising bidding systems at Bridge, and the tradition of elaborate Whist leads has been lost. In fact, most players tend to follow principles similar to those used at Bridge, which can be summed up as follows:

- lead the Ace if you have it, otherwise
- top card of a high sequence (such as K Q J, Q J 10, etc.)
- top card from an interior sequence (J from K J 10, 10 from Q 10 9)
- fourth highest from a suit with one or two honours (e.g. 5 from K J 6 5 2)
- highest from any other long suit ('top of nothing').

Following your partner's lead

Given these leads, you will get some idea of your partner's holding in his best suit, and by comparing this with your own holding in the suit can get some idea of how the suit is distributed overall.

What you play to it depends on whether or not you need to contest the trick. For example, if he leads the Queen, your right-hand opponent plays the King, and you have the Ace, you will play it for obvious reasons. If there is no such urgency, such as when he leads the Ace, you can choose a discard that will convey some information about your own interest in that suit. In this case it is usual to play high if you want to encourage further leads in the suit, and low if you don't.

If your partner leads low, indicating weakness, take the trick if you can, and with your best card – there's no point in trying to be clever. In this case, however, there are other things to take into account.

The first one illustrates the basic principle of the finesse. Suppose he leads a small card, the second player does likewise, and you hold the Ace and Queen. It is strictly correct to play the Ace, but perfectly acceptable to play the Queen instead. If your left opponent now wins with the King, you will have the benefit of having cleared out a high adverse card while still retaining control of the suit (in the shape of the Ace); if not – there being a fair chance that the King is held by the other opponent, or even your partner – you will have made a trick with the Queen and will still retain control of the suit with the Ace. To finesse is to attempt to win a trick with a card lower than necessary. If the Queen does win, the finesse will have succeeded.

A low lead may actually be that of the fourth best card of his long suit. The reason for choosing the fourth best is that it enables you to gather some useful information by applying a device called the Rule of Eleven. The rule says: deduct from eleven the number of pips on the card led, and that will tell you how many higher cards lie against the leader; deduct the number of higher cards held by yourself, and that will tell you how many are held between the opponents'. For example, suppose your partner leads ♡7, and second-hand plays low. Seven from eleven is four, so there are four cards higher than Seven which are *not* held by your partner. Now suppose you have two of them – say, Queen and Nine. Then your opponents between them hold two of the following ranks: A K J 10 8. Your partner doesn't hold the Ace, or he would have led it; nor does he hold K J 10 or he would have led the Jack; so he is pretty certain to have led from K J 8 7, leaving the others with the Ace and Ten. You accordingly play the Queen, knowing that it will either win the trick or, more probably, force the Ace from your left and so leave your partner in command of the suit.

Returning your partner's lead

If your partner led to a trick before you did, and you subsequently win a trick, then you in turn have your first lead and are immediately faced with the question whether to declare your own suit by leading from it – in accordance with the same conventions applicable to the opening lead – or to return your partner's suit.

Sometimes you can more or less do both. For instance, if your best suit is headed by A K you can lead the King and then follow with your partner's suit. The fact that the King won is enough to let him know that you also have the Ace. Thus you will have gained a trick, conveyed useful information, and kept command of your own suit, which is now known to both of you.

When you first get the lead and can return your partner's suit, a useful rule is to play the higher card if you have only two of the suit, otherwise the lowest. If you have two, and play high before low, your partner will know by convention that you have none left in the suit. Furthermore, if your higher card is significantly high – say Ten or better – then playing it removes the risk of blocking his suit and so preventing him from establishing it. On the other hand, if you have three or more, you must have been dealt the suit long to start with (having already released one to the trick he led in it). In this case the suit is good for both of you, and the need to unblock is less urgent – though you can still do so by playing high to a subsequent trick as required

If your partner led from trumps, return your lowest.

Playing second to a trick

Play low, unless you know for certain that you can win the trick. Don't try to compete for it, but leave it to your partner, who will have the advantage of playing last and knowing what he has to beat, whereas you would be playing speculatively. If, however, there has as yet been no sign of the Ace, and you hold the King and Queen, you can reasonably try the Queen, which will either win the trick or force the Ace out and leave you in command of the suit. If you can't follow suit and don't know whether your partner can win it, should you ruff it, to be on the safe side? Much depends on your trump holding. If it is weak, then the best use you can make of your small trumps is to attempt all reasonable ruffs; if strong, pass it up. You can afford to lose the trick if you have strength in trumps for later play, where trumps come into their own, and discarding from a side suit not only gets rid of a useless card but may also convey potentially useful information to your partner about the rest of your hand.

Playing third to a trick

The traditional rule is 'third hand plays high'. The reasons are obvious. It's your side's last chance of winning the trick if your partner's lead is not a known winner, and, assuming the lead comes from his strong suit, your high card will serve one of several useful purposes: it may force out a higher card from the left, leaving your side in command of the suit; it may unblock the suit for your partner to run through; or, failing either of these, it may even win the trick. Even if you have nothing but losers, at least playing the highest of them will give your partner *some* useful information about your hand.

Questions arising in third position are: whether to finesse, if the opportunity exists, and whether to trump or discard if unable to follow suit. There's no easy answer to the first question, as a lot depends on how much you can deduce about the position of the card that would beat it, and how badly you need the trick. (You obviously won't play Queen from Ace-Queen if your side has six tricks and needs a seventh.) As to trumping when void, a general rule is to do so if you are weak in trumps and are reasonably certain that your left-hand opponent can follow suit and possibly win the trick.

Playing fourth to a trick

In this position your only job is to take the trick if your partner has not already won it, and the only logical requirement for you is to play the lowest you can for either purpose. Remember that the rule about winning a trick as cheaply as possible applies even when you are playing from a sequence. For instance, if you are playing fourth to a trick containing (improbably) the Two, Three and Four of a suit, and you hold (say) Seven, Eight and Nine, play the Seven. It is true that any card of a sequence is as good as any of its fellows for trick-taking purposes, but for the purposes of conveying information, the fact that you are known to be playing the lowest is a useful piece of information.

Discarding

When you are void and prefer not to trump, choose carefully which suit to discard from. Don't just look for you lowest card regardless of suit, and certainly don't weaken your longest suit or the one you are trying to establish. Prefer to throw the lowest card from your weakest suit. But consider this example: you have the choice of discarding from A Q 2 in one suit or 10 9 3 in another. Here it is better to throw the Two, for reasons which you should be able to work out for yourself.

Trumps

It is reasonable to lead trumps if you have five or more, and possibly from four trumps if they include two honours and you have no other clear lead.

If you have strength in trumps but haven't got the lead, you may still find an opportunity to call for them by the way in which you play to other tricks. The call for trumps – a signal known as the Blue Peter – consists in playing an unnecessarily high card in a given suit, and then following it with a lower one when next playing to that suit. We have already seen something similar at work in the situation where, holding two of your partner's suit, you return the higher of them first: when you play the second, you thereby indicate that you are void in the suit, and are in a position to trump if it comes round again. The very fact that you play high then low should notify an alert partner that you are ready to play in trumps.

There is also the question of forcing trumps, which means leading a suit in which you know somebody else is void. You should always force if you know your opponents are strong in trumps, as this may reduce the power left against the eventual establishment of your own suits as well as against your own trumps when trump tricks are led. If the opponents refuse to be drawn, keep on forcing until they dare not do otherwise.

You may also force your partner, but only if you are strong in trumps yourself.

Sample game

West deals and turns the following hands, turning ♡K for trump:

North	♡Q 10 ♠Q ♢A Q J 9 8 5 ♣Q 10 4 2
East	♡J 9 7 6 3 2 ♠J 10 9 8 ♢K 2 ♣J
South	♡A ♠K 7 5 4 3 2 ♢10 4 3 ♣9 5 3
West	♡K 8 5 4 ♠A 6 ♢7 6 ♣A K 8 7 6

North makes the opening lead. Winning cards are underlined.

	North	*East*	*South*	*West*
1.	<u>♢A</u>	♢2	♢4	♢7
2.	♢J	♢K	♢3	♢6
3.	♡10	♡6	<u>♡A</u>	♡5
4.	♢5	♣J	♢10	<u>♡4</u>
5.	♡Q	♡2	♠2	<u>♡K</u>
6.	♣2	♠8	♣3	<u>♣A</u>
7.	♣4	♠9	♣5	<u>♣K</u>
8.	♣10	♡3	♣9	♣6
9.	♠Q	♠J	♠3	<u>♠A</u>
10.	♣Q	♡9	♠4	♣8
11.	♢8	♡7	♠5	♡8
12.	♢9	♠10	♠7	♣7
13.	♢Q	♢J	♠K	♠6

East-West win five odd tricks and the game (5 points), thanks to East's trumping with ♡9 instead of ♡7 at the tenth. This enables West to lead the last club, to which East can discard a losing spade, followed by West's own losing spade, which East can trump to yield the extra trick necessary for game (5 points). Had East ruffed with ♡7 at trick ten, South would eventually have made his King, thus denying East-West their game-winning trick. This was not a matter of luck or guesswork. East knew that West held the last remaining trump, from the previous play of trumps; that he held a losing spade (because he played ♠A instead of ♠K at trick nine); and that his other card was the last club because there was nothing else for it to be.

2 | SOLO

Whist for individualists

Solo Whist crossed the Channel from Belgium in the late 19th century and rapidly became one of the most popular of British card games. In its early days it almost rivalled Bridge as a potential successor to partnership Whist in clubs, homes and 'polite society'. In the event, Bridge won out, but Solo went on to secure an alternative niche as a game of home and hearth, of public house, and, up to the death of the railway system in the 1960s, as the quintessential commuter game. Incidentally, it should not be thought of as an adaptation or perversion of partnership Whist. It is a game in its own right and with its own pedigree.

As a social activity, Solo differs from Bridge in a number of significant and related respects. The main one is that it has no overall structure. Each deal is complete in itself, and the result can be settled up immediately in cash or hard score, enabling players to cut in and out of a game without disturbing its flow, and a game can last for as many deals as there remain four people round the table, even though (as well befits a commuter game) they may not be the same four that started the session going. For all these reasons, it is by nature a far less formal game than Bridge – chatting and ragging is not merely permitted but virtually required as an integral part of the proceedings. A more unfortunate consequence of all these circumstances is the fact that Solo is regarded by some as a rough and ready gambling game, and so not credited with the attention and respect it deserves as a game of skill.

Solo also has the rare merit of being one of the few trick games designed for four players in which the participants play for themselves and not in fixed partnerships. This makes it ideal for those who dislike partnership games and prefer to play on their own account, beholden to no one for their mistakes or their bouts of creative experimentation.

How to play

Cards and players. Four players, 52 cards. The turn to deal and play passes clockwise around the table.

Shuffle and deal. Shuffle the cards thoroughly at start of play, but not between deals until a slam or abundance has been played and won. Deal twelve cards to each player in batches of three at a time, followed by a single card to make thirteen. The final single card, which belongs to Dealer, is dealt face up to the table and not taken into hand until after the auction. Its purpose is to fix a suit of first priority for trumps.

Auction. There is a round of bidding to decide whether the contract to be played will be a partnership one or a solo against three opponents. The player at Dealer's left bids first, and each subsequent player must either pass or make a higher bid than any gone before. From lowest to highest, the bids are:

- Proposal ('Prop'): An offer to win eight tricks with the aid of anyone willing to form a partnership, with the turned suit as trump.
- Acceptance ('Cop'): An offer to partner the player who made a proposal, provided no higher bid has supervened.

The following are all higher and all independent (non-partnership) bids:

- Misère ('Mis'): An offer to lose every trick, playing at no trump.
- Solo: An offer to win at least five tricks, with the turned suit as trump.
- Abundance ('a bunny', 'a bundle'): An offer to win at least nine tricks, with a trump suit of one's own choice, other than that of the turned card.
- Royal abundance: An offer to win at least nine tricks with the turned suit as trump. This is actually announced as 'Abundance': at this stage it is only

necessary to specify 'Royal' in order to overcall an
earlier player's bid of abundance.

■ Misère ouverte ('Spread'): An offer to lose every trick,
playing at no trump, and with one's hand of cards
exposed on the table.

■ Abundance declared ('Slam'): An offer to win all 13
tricks, playing at no trump but with the advantage of
the opening lead. (Some schools allow slam with a
personal trump suit, which may be overcalled by slam
with the turned suit as trump. If this is followed, the
soloist does not need the advantage of leading to the
first trick.)

A contract is established when a bid is followed by three
consecutive passes. The dealer then takes the turn-up into hand.

If the first player passes, and a subsequent player makes a proposal
which no one accepts or overcalls, the first player (only) is
permitted to accept the proposal, but not to make a higher bid.

If the only bid made is a proposal, and no one accepts it, the
proposer may raise his bid to a solo. The cards are gathered up and
formed into a new pack without being shuffled and the next dealer
deals them out. (Alternatively, some form of 'general misère' may
be played. In the simplest form, all play at no trump and the winner
of the last trick loses an agreed amount.)

Play. The opening lead is (normally) made by the player at
Dealer's left. Players must follow suit if possible, otherwise may
play any card. The trick is taken by the highest card of the suit led,
or by the highest trump if any are played, and the winner of each
trick leads to the next.

Particular contracts have particular rules as follows.

In *Prop and cop*, partners do not change positions or go out of their
way to play alternately. If they are sitting next to each other, they
play consecutively.

At *misère,* if the soloist wins a trick he loses the contract without
further play.

In *abundance*, some schools do not require the soloist to name
trumps until the first trick has been played and won.

In a *spread misère,* the soloist's hand is laid face up on the table only after the first trick has been played and won.

In a *slam* played at no trump, the soloist leads to the first trick, regardless of position.

Note that, following a successful abundance or slam, the cards are thoroughly shuffled before the next deal.

Hard score. Typical pay-offs in a British game are as follows (use similar small amounts in other currencies):

- ■ Prop and cop wins a basic 10p plus 2p per overtrick. One opponent pays this to one partner, the other opponent to the other partner. If lost, each partner pays an opponent 10p, plus 2p per undertrick.
- ■ Solo pays the same as prop and cop, but to the soloist by each opponent, or, if lost, to each opponent by the soloist.
- ■ For abundance, the rate is 30p for the contract, plus 3p per over-or under-trick.
- ■ Misère wins or loses a flat 20p, spread misère 40p, a slam 60p.
- ■ A general misère, if played, requires the loser to pay 10p to each opponent.

Some schools keep a separate kitty for slams and abundances. Everyone contributes an agreed amount to the kitty at start of play and after it has been won. The player of a slam or abundance wins the kitty if successful, or, if not, increases it by the amount of his original contribution.

Soft score. Notional scores may be kept in writing. I recommend the following schedule, in which scores are made only by bidders – plus if successful, minus if not:

- ■ Solo won: 10 basic plus 1 per overtrick.
- ■ Abundance won: 20 basic plus 5 per overtrick.
- ■ Solo or abundance lost: 10 per undertrick.
- ■ Misère, spread, slam: win or lose 20, 40, 50, respectively.

Notes on play

Solo Whist is a subtle game in which it is easy to err in either of two directions – that of excessive caution, and that of extreme recklessness. The over-cautious player will never take a chance on a reasonable but not foolproof bid which the more experienced or imaginative player will undertake promptly; the reckless player will undertake too many long-shot hands and come off worst. If all players are cautious, as usually happens with beginners, the game is dull because there are few bids. This danger is best overcome by playing a competitive misère when all pass, as those who lose by taking the most tricks will thereby learn to recognize strength in hand when they see it. If one player is reckless, the game is dull because he hogs the limelight, preventing others from taking a hand with their more reasonable bids, and his frequent losses will be a foregone conclusion. (What makes any game exciting is the fight, not the defeat.) Since dullness can therefore be caused by one reckless player, though not by one cautious player, some argue in favour of playing for money in that the expense incurred discourages reckless overbidding. The point is arguable, in both senses of the word.

Before considering the individual bids that may be made, note first the one important respect in which Solo differs from Bridge, Whist and the majority of other trick-taking games in English card tradition. This lies in the fact that cards are rarely shuffled and are always dealt in batches of three, with the result that a balanced distribution of cards among the four players is the exception rather than the rule. In Bridge and Whist you normally expect to find the cards of your own hand distributed 4–3–3–3 or 4–4–3–2 among the suits, so that any suit longer than five or shorter than two gives you a hand well worth thinking about. In Solo, a hand of the pattern 7–4–2–0 may well give you a good bid, but should not be regarded as anything out of the ordinary. Whether or not a given hand is biddable depends on its overall strength rather than on its distribution.

This makes it easy to indicate the difference between a slightly risky bid and an out-and-out long shot. A slightly risky bid is one which you will only lose if the remaining cards are unfavourably distributed against you in your opponents' hands. Such a bid is worth making. A long shot is one which you can only win if the remaining cards are distributed among the others in your favour. Such a bid is not worth making.

When you are not the caller, remember that you are playing as a member of a partnership of three, and not just for the pleasure of making as many tricks as you can yourself (or losing them, in the case of a misère). It is always to the advantage of the caller's opponents – who, in accordance with card tradition, but in defiance of logic, are known as the defenders – to lead through the caller rather than up to him. In other words, the lead to a trick is always best made by the player on the caller's right, so that he has to play second. Caller's preferred position to a trick is either first (leader) or fourth; the others should therefore play as far as possible to deny him this advantage. When defending a positive (non-misère) bid, lead low through the caller, and try as much as possible to weaken his hand either by leading trumps or by forcing them out of him by leading suits in which he is void. If playing from a sequence (e.g. from Q J 10, etc.) always take with the lowest but lead with the highest – though, if you hold Ace, King, lead the King. By following these and other principles derived from partnership Whist your co-defenders will be able to deduce useful features of your hand and play accordingly.

Keeping track of the cards played is important. You need not remember them all, but try at least to count the trumps as they appear, to keep track of the Aces and Kings, and to note when anyone else has a void suit.

Proposal and acceptance

Some schools do not allow the bids of proposal and acceptance, admitting nothing lower than a solo, possibly on the grounds that 'it is too easy to make'. This view is mistaken. If a particular school does find 'prop and cop' too predictably successful, it means they are playing too cautiously and passing up hands on which more experienced players would go solo. The whole point of aiming for eight tricks between two players is that neither rates their individual hand good enough for five on its own.

It is to be generally understood – as a matter of convention, but born of common sense – that the player who proposes has some strength in trumps, though not necessarily enough to justify a solo bid. It follows that a player who accepts need not himself have strength in trumps, but should be able to offer further support, especially in side-suits. If neither partner feels strong enough to lead trumps the bid was probably risky, and the defenders will take advantage of this reluctance, when they spot it, to lead trumps themselves.

Position is of some importance in the bidding, and especially so in respect of 'prop and cop'. The best position from which to accept is as fourth hand, as the fact that the proposal has not been overcalled by a solo bid bodes well for the partnership contract. It is risky to accept eldest hand's proposal as second hand, as the third and fourth to bid may well let the contract stand for the sheer pleasure of beating it.

As eldest hand (first to bid) do not feel obliged to propose if your cards are only just biddable. If your hand is not strong enough for an independent bid, you may safely pass, since you still retain the opportunity to accept should one of the other players propose – a circumstance which automatically suggests that your hand may be stronger than you think. Alternatively, you may well propose on a hand which may or may not be quite good enough for a solo. If a later player accepts, you have a playable game; if not, and all pass, then you may reasonably consider raising your bid to a solo, knowing that it cannot be overcalled.

Here's a hand on which eldest passed, but subsequently accepted a proposal (spades trump):

♠K Q 10 4 ♡K 2 ♣10 8 5 4 ◊8 5 2

The proposer's hand was:

♠8 7 6 5 3 ♡A ♣A 9 7 6 ◊10 9 6

This is the sort of combination that makes it criminal to abolish 'prop and cop'!

If you and your partner are sitting adjacently, the ideal position is for one of you to be leading to a trick to which the other is playing fourth. As the contracting side, with presumed strength in trumps, you should lead trumps early in order to draw them from your opponents and so establish your side-suits. Against this, however, you should avoid forcing your partner to play trumps if you are weak in them yourself. As in partnership Whist, note what suit your partner leads first, and return it when convenient to do so. Lead from strength – either trumps or from your strongest suit, whichever you want returned. It is not particularly desirable to lead a singleton.

Solo

For a solo bid, you need to be sure of winning at least five tricks with the turned suit as trump. This may sound so obvious as to be trivial, but nevertheless in defiance of all probabilities there are players who will quite happily bid solo, in spades, on a hand such as:

♠K Q 9 4 ♡8 ♣A K Q J 3 ◇10 9 8

The idea is to make two trumps, one of them on a heart lead after the Eight has gone; at least the top two clubs; and one for luck, in either trumps or clubs. Without the lead, a probable outcome is the win of two trumps as anticipated, the possible win of ♣A when led and, if very lucky, the possible win of ♣K, for a final result of four or even only three tricks. 'Yes,' says one commentator, who shall be nameless; 'Solo is easy enough; just look for five near-certain tricks.'

At the other extreme, there are players so mesmerized by Aces that they will pass up a perfectly feasible solo bid for lack of them – as, for example, on the following hand, again with spades turned trump:

♠K J 9 8 7 5 2 ♡5 ♣J 9 4 ◇Q 3

Given the lead, this is a good example of the 'slight risk' which we defined previously as being worth taking. With seven trumps in hand, you can afford to lose two of them in the not unreasonable hope that those same two tricks will clear the defenders out of their three top trumps (Ace, Queen and Ten). Correct strategy, therefore, is to lead the King.

Even without the lead, you could safely bid solo (spades, again, for convenience) on:

♠K Q 10 8 7 6 ♡K 10 9 8 ♣K 4 2 ◇–

The side-suit Kings should produce two tricks, the void in diamonds brings in a low trump, and the remaining five trumps are good for the outstanding two.

What, in general, are the minimum requirements for a biddable solo? The first merit is length or strength in trumps, counting as part of this assessment any void or singleton side-suit which can be ruffed with a low one at the appropriate time. On trumps alone, the borderline between a doubtful and a feasible solo is finely drawn.

For instance, a holding of A K Q 9 and one lower is risky, whereas A K Q 10 and any might be expected to succeed without inducing gasps of astonishment. When holding five trumps, always calculate on the pessimistic assumption that at least one defender may hold five as well. Even a seven-card suit should be headed by nothing less than K J 9.

In side-suits, the chief merit is strength and shortness (not length). The expected failure of the first hand quoted above lies in the undue length of the club suit – A K Q J 3, five in all. The most favourable possible distribution of the outstanding eight is 3–3–2, which means that someone will certainly be trumping by the time you have drawn the odd two with the Ace and King. A more probable distribution is 4–3–1, giving you the Ace but not the King, while there is a strong chance (given the unbalanced distribution of your own hand) of one defender's being void, thus depriving you even of the Ace.

With strength and universal shortness – that is, an unusually even distribution of suits – you may even dispense with strength in trumps. The fact that spades is the turned card does not prevent the following holding from offering a good solo:

♠5 4 3 2 ♡A K 2 ♣A K 2 ◇A 3 2

Of course, it will be beaten if any defender is out of diamonds or holds only one heart or club, but the evenness of the suit distribution in your own hand is good enough to lower the probability of such an event to the acceptable level of 'slight risk'.

Some hands make acceptable solos only if you have the lead; others really require to be led up to. For example, consider the trump holding A K Q 10 2 in a hand which does not include a void or easily voidable (singleton) suit. The problem card is the Jack. If you have the lead, you can play out the top trumps in order and without undue optimism hope that the Jack will fall by the time the Queen is out, leaving Ten high and a certain trick with the Two, and giving enough for solo even without side-suit support. Without the lead, the missing Jack is a permanent nuisance. By the time you have voided your short suit you run the danger of ruffing low with the Two and finding it overtaken by a higher trump. On the other hand, a holding that lacks Aces but can place reliance on guarded Kings in short suits will work best if you do not have the lead.

In defending against a solo it is good practice to lead a singleton to the first trick (in which respect the game differs from partnership Whist and also from the play at a 'prop and cop' contract in Solo, where a singleton lead is not to be recommended). With a fairly even distribution, a low trump is also not a bad lead. Otherwise, lead your best card – from not too long a suit – and the highest of a sequence, unless you hold Ace, King, in which case play the King.

Abundance and royal abundance

An abundance is a solo, only more so. As before, you must have length and strength in trumps; in addition, you should have a strong, lengthy side-suit and at least one void. Because the dealing system, 3–3–3–1, produces uneven distributions easily, double voids are not uncommon, and a strong two-suited hand is often a must for abundance.

Since your aim is to make at least nine tricks, one way of assessing the hand is to identify the four cards you can afford to lose – and to make sure there are not five of them. Otherwise, you make what is known as an 'eight-trick abundance', which comes expensive.

Given two suits of equal length, do not automatically entrump the stronger. Quite often the apparently weaker suit not only makes a better trump, but actually proves the only way of avoiding loss. On this hand, for example:

♠A K Q J 10 9 ♡10 8 6 5 3 2 ♣A ♢–

you can certainly 'go a bundle', but must do so in hearts, not in the apparently stronger spade suit. The reason is perhaps easiest to see if you examine the hand from the viewpoint of the four losers rather than the nine winners. If you make spades trump, how are you going to avoid losing more than four hearts? With hearts trump, however, you can afford to lose four for the sake of extracting the adverse trumps and thereby safely establishing the spade suit. You will make one heart by ruffing a diamond lead, and a second either by a ruff in diamonds or clubs, or by virtue of finding your Ten high when the top trumps have gone.

Defending against an abundance, lead from your longest and strongest suit. Remember that the defenders need five tricks to win, and lose no opportunity to make five as soon as possible – that is, before caller can get in with his trumps and dictate the rest of the play. By all means lead suits in which caller is void, thereby forcing him to trump and so weaken his hand. Sometimes caller will be relying on a 'bum card' for a lucky trick: if you can spot this coming you can defend against it. He may, for instance, lead Ace, King of a side-suit, then switch to another line of attack in pretence of being void. By retaining the odd Queen, Jack or even Ten, instead of discarding at the earliest opportunity, you may well find it winning a low one at the thirteenth trick, led to by caller after extracting all the trumps. Again, if caller is hoping to make a risky King or Queen he may be hoping to do so on a bad lead by the defenders, in which case he will be trying to lose the lead – which you can give him back by forcing him to trump.

Declared abundance (Slam)

This is a bid to win all thirteen tricks at no trump, and as the sort of hand which will enable you to do so is unmistakable there is no point in describing it. Or even playing it; for you only declare abundance on a cast-iron hand, and if it really is cast-iron you simply lay it face up on the table and claim your winnings. If any defender can find a way of beating it then the game must be played, and if he is right you will have learnt a valuable lesson.

It will be worthwhile explaining why a declared abundance is properly played at no trump, even though many seem to accept it as a trump game. The reason is, quite simply, that if you can safely make thirteen tricks with a trump suit, then you can safely make thirteen tricks without a trump suit. But don't you need a trump suit if you have a void? No. Take the following:

♠A K Q J 10 ♡A K Q J ♣A K Q J ◇–

Since the rules of play allow the slam caller to make the opening lead, your void in diamonds is irrelevant.

Misère and open misère

Beginners may be forgiven for imagining that a misère, the winning of no tricks at no trump, is what you bid when you have no good trick-winners but only a general miscellany of dribs and drabs. In fact, this is the sort of hand on which you do not bid at all. The misère bid is a positive undertaking to successfully defend yourself against all efforts on the part of your opponents to force you to take a trick. For this purpose you need a very good hand – 'good', that is, from the point of view of beating off such attacks.

Many card-players, especially those who know nothing but Bridge, tend to look down on misère as a sort of jocular substitute round, played when no one has a good enough hand on which to make a 'real' bid. Nothing could be further from the truth. Both attack and defence at misère call for, and often receive, some of the finest play that can be observed at the card table.

To business: in contemplating a misère, there are two good features to look for. One is low-ranking cards, and the other is a void suit. Note that the length of any suit you hold is irrelevant so long as it contains low cards. For example, in this hand

♠5 3 2 ♡A Q 10 8 6 4 2 ♣7 3 2 ◇–

the hearts are just as safe from attack as the spades, for no one can force you to take a trick in either suit. As for low ranks, in a holding of five or more you must have the Two (you may escape without it, but the risk is great); with fewer, you may get away with nothing lower than Three or even Four. Note, too, that a holding of alternating low ranks is just as good as a sequence. In the hand quoted above, for instance, the A Q 10 8 6 4 2 of hearts is as strong as would be 8 7 6 5 4 3 2. To prove it, imagine that the Three is led; you play the Two, and your Four is then the lowest of the suit. If the Five is then led, you play the Four and your Six is lowest. And so on.

The advantage of a void is obvious: when it is led, you can throw out your potentially dangerous cards. The recognition of potential dangers can be a subtle affair. Take the hand quoted above. Because the hearts are safe from attack, as we have seen, it contains no dangerous cards, so you need not rush to throw out the Ace or Queen when diamonds are led. Clubs, however, are a different matter, for ♣7 is the most dangerous card in the hand. With three clubs (6–5–4) out against you, you can successfully defend against the lead of only two of them (with 3–2), and by the time the third is led you may find the other two players void, thus forcing you to take the suit with the Seven. This won't be just a case of bad luck, for experienced opponents will inevitably discover your weak suit and exploit it.

You therefore need the void in diamonds as a means of discarding your dangerous Seven. In general, then, you cannot bid misère with dangerous cards unless you have saving voids to accommodate them, and even then the device may only be expected to work once. Remember, too, to look at things from your opponents' viewpoint. If your hand is good enough for a misère but not good enough for an open misère, then by definition it contains a weakness, and the strategy of your opponents will be to find out where this weakness lies. They need to force you to take only one trick to win; once you have done so, the contract is lost and there is no point in playing further.

In defending against a misère a good lead is any singleton, or, failing that, a middling card from a short suit. Do not play from a long suit, as there is a chance that caller will be void and will immediately throw any dangerous card he may hold. Do not play too low, as you must give your partners an opportunity to get rid of their own high cards in that suit. If you hold a Two, especially in a short suit, you may well hold the means to beat the contract. Save it until the top cards are out, then get the lead and play it – for which purpose retain an Ace or other master card to ensure ability to enter when you judge the time ripe.

3 | VARIETIES OF WHIST FOR TWO TO SEVEN PLAYERS

Relatively simple trick-taking games

The name 'Whist', by itself, properly denotes only the four-player partnership game; but there are games for other numbers of players that might be regarded as varieties of Whist because, with minor exceptions, they exhibit the following Whist-like features:

- ■ Played with 52 cards ranking A K Q J 10 9 8 7 6 5 4 3 2.
- ■ The aim is to win most tricks.
- ■ A game may be played with a trump suit or at no trumps.
- ■ Some games include a no-trump deal called *misère* in which the aim is to lose tricks instead of winning them.
- ■ Any card may be led to a trick.
- ■ Players must follow suit if possible, otherwise may play any card. The trick is taken by the highest card of the suit led, or by the highest trump if any are played, and the winner of each trick leads to the next.

German Whist

There is nothing particularly German about this game, and different books give different rules of play.

Players. Two.

Cards. From a 52-card pack deal 13 each, in ones, and stack the rest face down. Turn the top card of the stock face up to establish trumps.

Object. To win most of the 26 tricks, or (if preferred) most of the last thirteen.

Play. The are two phases to the game: the first lasts so long as any cards remain in stock, and the second begins when the stock is empty. Non-dealer leads to the first trick. In Phase 1, the follower may play any card, but may only trump if unable to follow suit. The winner of each trick, before leading to the next:

■ draws the top (faced) card of stock and adds it to his hand,
■ waits for the loser to draw the next (which need not be shown),
■ turns the next stock card face up so that both can see which card the next trick-winner will get, and then
■ leads to the next trick.

(Note: the trump suit remains unchanged throughout.)

Phase 2. When no cards remain in stock, the last 13 tricks are played to normal Whist rules, it being obligatory to follow suit if possible.

Score. The winner scores 1 point for each trick taken above thirteen. If tied, the winner of the next deal scores double.

Alternative scores.

1. To prevent ties, score only for the last 13 tricks.
2. Alternatively, score 1 point for each of the first 13 and 2 points for each of the remainder.
3. Score minus 1 point for each of the first 13 tricks (so you are playing to lose instead of to win) and plus 1 for the last 13.

Bismarck

Bismarck is a 'compendium' game, consisting of a number of different games strung together in a particular order. The exact components and the exact order varies from school to school. This one is typical.

Players. Three.

Cards. Fifty-two, in their usual Whist order.

Game. A game consists of 12 deals. Each player in turn deals four times in succession, the deal passing to the left after the first four have been played.

Deal. The dealer distributes 16 cards to each player, takes the last four himself, and discards any four unwanted cards face down before the opening lead is made by the player at his left.

Each of the four deals is a different game, as follows:

First deal. The aim is to win tricks, playing at no trump. Dealer scores 1 point for each trick he wins above eight, each opponent scores 1 point for each trick he takes above four.

Second deal. The aim is to win tricks, with a trump suit selected at random (such as by turning the last card, or cutting another pack). Score as above.

Third deal. The aim is to win tricks, with a trump suit declared by the dealer after examining his hand but before the first card is led. Score as above.

Fourth deal. The aim is to lose tricks, playing at no trump. Dealer scores 4 points less the number of tricks he took, and each opponent 6 points less the number taken by himself.

It is very easy to create more interesting variations on this simpler game.

Dutch Whist

The equivalent of Bismarck for four players in partnerships. Each player deals in turn and each receives 13 cards from the 52-card pack.

Deal 1. Show the last card to establish trumps. The side taking most tricks scores 1 point per trick taken above six.

Second deal. No card is turned, and the game is played at no trump.

Third deal. No card is turned, and a trump suit is announced by the player who leads to the first trick.

Fourth deal. Trumps are established by cutting the pack before the deal.

Knockout

A children's or gambling game, however you prefer to regard it, Knockout is widely played in schools and pubs, and appears to be of surprisingly recent origin. The name is actually short for Knockout Whist, and by younger players who have never heard of the real game of Whist it is often known simply as 'Whist', which can make life very confusing for card-game researchers.

There are many variations, but the underlying theme goes like this: Everybody places a single stake in the pot. On the first deal each player receives seven cards, on the second six, the third five, and so on, reducing by one card on each occasion. Dealer turns the next card for trump and leads to the first trick.

Anyone who fails to win a trick is knocked out of the game and has no further part to play. Those who remain contribute another stake to the pot. Whoever won most tricks (or, if equal, the tied player who cuts the higher card from the pack) gathers the cards up and deals to the next round.

This continues until one player wins the pot by winning every trick played – usually on the last deal of one card, though it can happen earlier.

Oh Hell!

This game first appeared in the 1930s under the name Oh Hell! and has since been recorded under dozens different names – such as Blackout, Jungle Bridge, Botheration, and various bowdlerizations of its original title. At the time of writing, it is most often referred to as Nomination Whist, which is a pity, as this title more properly denotes an interesting variety of Solo. Its principal feature is that of bidding to take an exact number of tricks rather than a minimum number, a concept more thoroughly explored in the game of Ninety-Nine.

Players. From three to seven. One of them must be appointed scorekeeper, who will rule up a scoresheet into as many columns as there are players. A game consists of a number of deals with one card fewer dealt each time, so the last is always a one-card, one-trick hand.

Cards and deal. Whoever cuts the lowest card (from a standard 52-card pack) starts by dealing all the cards round until everyone has the same number, which means (unless four play) a smaller number will be left over. For example, if seven play, each receives seven cards and three remain. The top card of the undealt batch is faced for trump. If none remain, play at no trump.

Object. To win exactly as many tricks as you bid, neither more nor fewer. The players look at their cards and each in turn, starting with the player at Dealer's left, announces how many tricks he proposes to win. If seven are dealt on the first round, for example, each player bids any number from none to seven. The scorekeeper notes each player's bid in his column on the scoresheet.

In some circles the Dealer, who bids last, is prohibited from bidding a number which would bring the total of bids to the number of tricks played. The purpose of this is to ensure that at least one player will fail. Decide in advance whether or not to follow this rule.

Play. The opening lead is made by the player at Dealer's left, and tricks are played to normal Whist rules.

Scoring. This varies from school to school. It has become much simplified with the passage of time, but the original schedule is as follows. Each player wins 1 point per trick taken, whether bid or not, and adds a bonus of 10 for fulfilling his bid. In any deal of five or more cards, a bonus of 50 is awarded for bidding and winning every trick played (grand slam) or 25 for bidding and winning all but one trick (small slam).

The winner is the player with the highest score at the end of the last deal, or the first to reach 100 points if this happens sooner.

In some schools the first deal is one card and each subsequent deal is one card more. In others, the number starts low and rises to the maximum, then goes back down to one again – or it starts high and goes down, then goes back up again. Either version is called Up the River, Down the River.

Nap

Nap, short for Napoleon, was a staple amusement of British family life before television took over the world, since when it has lost ground. Though full of Napoleonic associations, it was certainly invented too late to have been played by the original emperor, and was probably named with some sort of reference to Napoleon III, a well-known card-player of Victorian England.

Nap is more of a gambling than an intellectual game, but you can (if you like) increase the 'think' factor by stripping the pack according to the number of players.

Players and cards. Three or four play with a 25-card pack containing nothing lower than the Eights, five with 36 or 40 cards, i.e. respectively Sixes and Fives low.

The cards are shuffled before the first deal, and are cut before each subsequent deal, but are not shuffled again until a player has won a bid of Nap or higher.

Deal. Five cards each, either one at a time or in batches of three and two, and stack the rest face down.

Bidding. Each in turn either passes or makes a higher bid than any gone before. A bid is an offer to win at least the number of tricks stated, using a trump suit of the bidder's choice, which is not yet stated. From lowest to highest, the bids are:

Two
Three
Miz (no trump; lose every trick)
Four
Nap (five)
Wellington (five, for doubled score or stakes)
Blücher (five, for redoubled score or stakes).

Wellington may only be called over a previous bid of Nap, and Blücher only over a previous bid of Wellington.

Play. The highest bidder leads to the first trick, and the suit of that card is automatically trump, except when playing miz. Play as at Whist.

Score. The bidder, if successful wins from each player two, three or four units for the relevant bids, three for Miz, 10 for Nap, 20 for Wellington, 40 for Blücher. If unsuccessful, he pays to each opponent the amount he would have won, though penalties are usually halved for lost bids of five.

Optional Joker. If a Joker is added, it counts as the highest trump. In Miz, it is the only trump: it may only be played when its holder cannot follow suit, and, if led, belongs to whatever suit its holder declares, which must be one in which he is otherwise void.

Part Two

TWO'S COMPANY . . .

4 | CRIBBAGE

Ye old Englysshe pubbe game

Cribbage, mostly called Crib, has been the English national card game for some 400 years – perhaps even 500, if you count its immediate ancestor, Noddy – and is widely played throughout the English-speaking world. Originally favoured by royals and aristocrats, it sank down the social scale in the 19th century, and for most of the 20th century remained the archetypal pub game. It remains, in fact, the only game legally playable in public houses without special licence from the local magistrates, and is played on a league and championship basis in many parts of the country. However, the recent advent of computerized games has led to a resurgence in popularity, and it is now taken seriously enough to be one of the four card games featured in the annual Mind Sports Olympiad. (The others are Bridge, Poker, and Skat.)

Crib is a game of adding up and scoring for making card combinations. It is easy to learn and fast to play. The skill involved is largely that born of experience rather than of brain-busting strategic calculation, and the most experienced player will usually win consistently. It is an excellent way of introducing children to card games.

How to play

Players. Two, but there are versions for three and four, and partnership Crib is the usual pub game.

Cards. Fifty-two. The ranking order is A 2 3 4 5 6 7 8 9 10 J Q K. Ace is always low. Numerals Ace to Ten count at face value, courts 10 each.

Scoring. A game is won by the first player to reach 121 points, and play ceases the moment this happens. For failing to reach 91 in play the loser is said to be 'lurched' or 'in the lurch' (or, in American parlance, 'skunked'), and loses double; but as this rarely occurs between experienced players it is rather theoretical. Because scores are made in continuous dribs and drabs throughout play, it helps to record them mechanically rather than in writing. The traditional scoring device is illustrated in Figure 4.1 and will probably be familiar even to non-players. How to use it is explained in the caption.

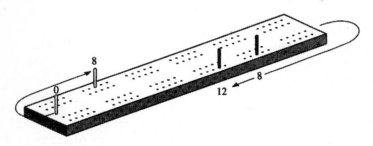

Figure 4.1 Cribbage board

Using the 61-hole Crib board. Each player starts from zero at each short edge and records scores by moving two pegs alternately 'up the outside' (from 1 to 30) and 'down the inside' from 31 to 60. Two such circuits are made in the standard game to 121 points. As illustrated here, White has evidently pegged nothing in play and 8 in hand, while Red must have made 8 in play and hand followed by 4 in the box.

Deal. Each in turn cuts the pack and shows the bottom card of the top half. Whoever cuts the lower card deals first, Ace being lowest of all. (Some players count Ace high and play high card deals. This is probably due to the influence of trick-taking games like Bridge, but in Cribbage is non-traditional, irrelevant, and illogical.) The dealer is said to be 'in the box', and has several advantages which should normally yield him or her a higher score. The deal therefore alternates, to even this advantage out.

Deal six cards each, face down, one at a time, starting with non-dealer, and stack the rest face down.

Laying away. Both of you now examine your hands and make any two discards face down. These four discards form the crib, which is placed in front of the dealer. Once they have been laid away, neither player may examine them before the end of the hand. Each player's aim is to retain four cards that will be of most use in the play and will score best for the combinations described below. As to the crib, it is of course the dealer's object to lay aside cards that promise to combine well, such as a pair, fifteen, or two-card sequence, and non-dealer's aim to contribute unrelated cards designed to be useless for combinations.

Cribbage combinations. The combinations and their scores are:

combination	definition	examples	score
Fifteen	Two or more cards totalling 15	9–6, K–5, A–6–8, A–2–3–4–5, etc.	2
Pair	Two cards of the same rank	A–A, 9–9, Q–Q, etc.	2
Prial (pair royal)	Three of the same rank	9–9–9, etc.	6
Double pair royal	Four of the same rank	K–K–K–K, etc.	12
Run	Three or more cards in sequence	A–2–3, 5–6–7–8, 10–J–Q–K, etc.	1 per card
Flush	Four or five cards of the same suit		1 per card

Note that any individual card may be counted as many times as it forms part of a distinct combination. For example, 7–7–7 scores 6 because the prial consists of three distinct pairs of two cards, scoring 2 each. Similarly, the combination 8–7–7–7 would score 12, counting 6 for the prial of Sevens, plus another 6 for the three different fifteens that can be made by attaching the Eight to each of the three Sevens in turn.

The starter. When both have discarded to the crib, non-dealer cuts the pack (without revealing the bottom card of the top half), and dealer takes the top card of the bottom half and places it face up on top. This is called the starter, or turn-up. If it's a Jack, dealer scores 2 'for his heels'.

The play. Non-dealer leads to the first play by placing any card face on the table and announcing its value, e.g. 'One' if an Ace, 'Ten' if a court, and so on. Dealer responds by playing a card face up and announcing the combined value of the first two cards. If these form a pair, or total 15, dealer announces that fact and pegs two points immediately.

Note: Play your cards face up in front of yourself, taking care not to muddle them up with those played by your opponent.

This continues, with each in turn playing another card, announcing the new total made by all cards so far played, and pegging for any combination they may make when considered in conjunction with those immediately preceding it in unbroken succession (other than a flush, which doesn't count in this part of the game).

Example

North	South
◇4 'Four'	
	♠4 'Eight for 2' (pair of Fours)
♡7 'Fifteen for 2'	
	♡6 'Twenty-one'
♠5 'Twenty-six for 4' (4–5–6–7)	
	◇3 'Twenty-nine for 5' (3–4–5–6–7)
'Go'	
	'And one'.

Here note that North's Five made a sequence of the previously played 4–7–6, and that South's Three extended it by another one. Neither player could go beyond 31 without busting, and South scores 1 for the last card. Had either of them held a Two, it could have been played for a score of 8 – that is, 6 for the run of 2–3–4–5–6–7, plus 2 for making 31 exactly.

The 'go'. Neither player may bring the count beyond 31, but each must play if able to do so without busting. If you can't play without busting, or run out of cards, you say 'Go', and your opponent then continues the series alone by playing as many more cards as possible scoring for any combinations they make with one another.

Whoever plays the last card pegs 1 point, or 2 points if the final total is 31 exactly.

If either of you has a card or cards left in hand, those played to the first series are turned face down, and a second series started by the opponent of the player who scored 1 for the go or 2 for making thirty-one. Play continues as before, and a third series played if any cards still remain. When one player runs out of cards, the other continues playing and pegging alone.

If either player reaches 121 in course of play, the game ends. If not, continue as follows.

The show. You both now pick up the four cards you played and score for whatever combinations they contain. For this purpose, however, you also include the starter as if it were a fifth card in your own hand.

Non-dealer shows and scores first, counting for each and every combination that can be made from the five cards concerned. A run may therefore contain up to five cards, and pegs as many points. A four-card flush in hand pegs 4, or 5 if it matches the suit of the starter. Finally, if your original four-card hand includes the Jack of the same suit as the starter, you peg an extra '1 for his nob'.

As dealer, you score in exactly the same way for your own hand when non-dealer has finished, unless non-dealer reached 121 and thereby won. If this doesn't give you 121, you then turn the crib face up and score for that in almost the same way. The only difference is that a four-card flush does not count. If the crib cards are all of a suit, you only score for the flush if the starter is of the same suit, enabling you to peg 5 points.

Note: If the starter is a Jack, neither player can claim 'one for his nob', as this is precluded by the dealer's original score of 'two for his heels'.

Points of order. The correct procedure for making the starter is as follows. Non-dealer lifts off the top of the pack a packet of cards numbering at least six, and leaving at least six on the bottom half. To prevent the bottom card of the top half from being seen, they should not be tilted or lifted any higher than necessary to enable dealer to extract the next card down. Non-dealer then places the top half squarely atop the bottom half, and dealer places the starter face up on top of that.

Disputes sometimes occur about the validity of combinations pegged in play. The main thing to notice is that the cards of a run need not have been played in numerical order, as illustrated in the playing example given above. A run is, however, broken by a pair. For example, if the cards played in order are 3–4–6–5, the Five makes a run of four, but if they are 3–4–6–6–5, then it does not. However, they could be followed by a Four or Seven, making a three-card run with the last-played Six and Five.

The following is true even if apparently illogical. Suppose the cards played are 7–2–7. The last Seven does not make a pair, as it is separated from the first by the intervening Two. But if the cards played are 7–7–7, the third Seven is not regarded as being separated from the first, so all three of them peg 6 for the prial.

For the sake of discipline, and to ensure that players keep track to their own and the other's rightful score, combinations should be reckoned in this order: fifteens, pairs, runs, flushes, and his nob. Score are announced cumulatively as you go along.

Example. Suppose you have ♠5 ♡5 ♣6 ◇J and the starter is ◇7. Then you announce 'Fifteen 2, fifteen 4, pair 6, seven–eight–nine, ten–eleven–twelve, and one's thirteen.' Note that the two Fives, besides scoring 2 for a pair together, each make a fifteen with the Jack, as well as a three-card run of 5–6–7. The final 'one' is for the Jack of the turned suit. Sadly, one must report that the traditional phrase 'one for his nob' is unknown to many modern players.

Tips. There are fifteen different ways of discarding two cards from a hand of six cards, and the knack of Crib lies in choosing the best two. To add to the interest, the best two discards from any given hand usually depends on whether it's you or your opponent in the box. A perennial problem is that many hands are easier to split 3–3 or 5–1 than 4–2, and it's in the handling of these that you'll need all your wits about you.

In throwing to your opponent's crib, you will naturally avoid discarding Fives, Tens, courts, pairs, and two sequential cards, though you needn't worry about offering two of a suit, as the chances of making a five-card flush are remote. There are, however, two circumstances in which you can ignore these dangers. One is if the four cards left in hand give you higher-scoring combinations than the dealer is likely to get, bearing in mind that he may not be laying aside cards that fit in with yours. The other is when you're close enough to 121 to stand a chance of getting there first, either in the play, or by virtue of being first to score for the show. In either of these cases it hardly matters which two cards you lay aside.

Throwing to your own crib is not so nerve-racking. Given a hand rich in combinations, just work out which of the possible 4–2 splits give you the most points for certain, and go for that. Given the opposite, just keep the cards that are likely to be most useful in the play to 31. Obviously, these will include low cards like Aces and Twos, and adjacent or nearby ranks that may enable you to score for runs.

In leading to the play, you'll want to avoid a Five, Ten or court, which runs the immediate danger of offering a fifteen. Any card lower than Five is a good lead, as it makes an immediate fifteen impossible. Having passed fifteen, the worst thing you can do is to let the other player go out with a pair to 31. For example, avoid playing a Ten or court to a count of 21, Nine to 22, and so on.

Auction Crib

Deal six cards each as in the standard game, and discard two to the crib. In this case, however, neither player knows for certain which of them will be in the box. Whoever it is will have the advantage not only of counting the crib, but also of counting for hand and crib before the other counts his hand. This privilege goes to whichever of them bids higher in the auction. A bid is a number of points that the bidder is prepared to deduct from his current score before starting play. Non-dealer may pass or make an opening bid of 'One' (or more). Dealer may pass or bid higher, and bidding continues alternately until one of them passes. The other then deducts the amount of his bid by moving his forward peg backwards by the stated number of holes, and the dealer cuts the pack for the starter, scoring 2 for his heels if it is a Jack. The final bidder plays first, and, after play, counts hand and crib before the other counts his hand. The deal alternates, regardless of who took the box in the previous deal.

Losing Crib

This is played exactly like the parent game, but the first to reach 121 is the loser. This may sound trivial, but a little practice will prove there's more to think about than meets the eye at first. At least one Cribbage software program offers the Losing game as an option, and it is an interesting challenge to see how low you can get your final score. The lowest I have ever managed is 36 – can you get lower still?

Five-card Crib

The original five-card game is still current in pubs and clubs, having been superseded by the six-card game only in domestic play. The differences are as follows.

A game is 61 points (once round the board), and the loser is lurched with 30 or less.

The non-dealer to the first hand starts with a score of 3 as compensation for the initial dealer's advantage.

Deal five cards each instead of six, and discard two each to the crib.

There is only one play-off up to 31, even if both have cards remaining in hand.

Each hand consists of four cards including the starter, and the crib five including the starter. As in the six-card game, a flush in the crib requires all five to be of the same suit, but a flush in hand is either 3 without the starter, or 4 with.

Three-hand Crib

Deal five cards each and one face down to the crib, which belongs to the dealer, and to which everybody then contributes one card, leaving a playing hand of four. The player at dealer's right cuts the pack, the dealer turns a starter, and the third player leads to the first round of play. After play, the player at dealer's left counts first, then the player at dealer's right, and finally the dealer, who counts for hand and crib.

Partnership Crib

Partners sit opposite each other and play alternately. Everyone receives five cards and discards one to the crib, which belongs to the dealer. A starter is turned and the player at dealer's left begins the play, which proceeds as at two-handed Crib. Then each in turn, starting with the player at dealer's left, counts their hand, and finally dealer counts the crib. Each side scores the total made by its two members, but it is usual for individual players to receive from everyone else side-payments for special occurrences, such as dozens (a hand scoring 12 or 24), or 'nineteens in the box'. A 'nineteen in the box' is a crib that pegs no points at all – so called in allusion to the fact that no possible combination of five cards can ever score exactly nineteen. (Try it and see !)

5 | GIN RUMMY

From the great days of Broadway

Although Gin first appeared in the early 1900s, it wasn't until the 1930s that it struck gold in the annals of popular culture by revealing itself to be the game of the great movie stars, as you may readily see if you set your video to record the films of this period. There's a simple explanation for this. Gin is easy to learn and fast to play, requires no fiddly in-deal scoring, can be performed on mental auto-pilot, and can be picked up and dropped out of at a moment's notice in between takes or walking-on parts. In the writings of Damon Runyon, the characters are often found to be playing Klob or Klaberjass; however it is worth remarking that his characters are far more frequently encountered playing Gin.

So what is it, exactly? Well, exactly, it is not greatly different from the earliest known form of Rummy, which can be traced back to the mid-19th century Mexican game of Conquian. Conquian was a simple win-or-lose game for a fixed stake, and if Elwood T Baker, the supposed inventor of Gin, can be credited with anything, it is most probably with the refined scoring system, which made it more interesting to play for money, and gave an edge to players who could think and calculate just that little bit faster than their opponents. The great thing about Gin is that everyone thinks they can play it well, so, if they lose, they can blame it on card distribution. Those who really can play it well keep quiet about it, and just pocket their winnings.

Gin is the classic two-player member of the Rummy family. As in all Rummy games, your object is to collect cards which 'go together', either being of the same rank, like ♠7 ♡7 ♣7, or forming a sequence in the same suit, such as ◇7 ◇8 ◇9. Such a matching collection is called a *meld*.

Any unmatched cards left in your hand at the end of a deal are called *deadwood,* and incur penalties equivalent to their combined face values. The method by which cards are collected for this purpose will probably be well known even to non card-players. At each turn you draw a card from a stockpile and throw out an unwanted card to a discard pile, and you keep doing this until all the cards you hold can be arranged in matching sets, or melds.

Gin Rummy is very easy to learn and the rules are clear, simple and fairly well standardized.

How to play

Cards. One standard 52-card pack.

Game. The game is won by the first player to reach 100 points, which normally takes several deals.

Rank and value of cards. Cards rank A 2 3 4 5 6 7 8 9 10 J Q K and are worth their face value, with Ace 1 and court cards 10 each.

Deal. Whoever cuts the higher card chooses whether to deal first. Thereafter the winner of one hand deals to the next, and the winner of a game deals first to the next. It is important that the cards be thoroughly shuffled before play, dealer having the right to shuffle last. Deal ten cards each, one at a time. Place the remainder face down to form a stock. Take the top card of the stock and lay it face up beside it to form the first 'upcard'. This will form the base of a gradually constituted waste pile of faced cards, the topmost of which is always known as the upcard.

To start. Non-dealer starts by either exchanging the upcard for any unwanted card from hand, or passing. If he passes, dealer has the same option. If either player takes the upcard, that constitutes the first turn and the game continues from there. If both refuse it, non-dealer must start the game by drawing the top card of the stock and discarding any card face up on the original upcard to continue the waste pile.

Play. Thereafter, each player in turn must draw either the top (face-down) card of the stock, or the faced upcard at the top of the waste pile, and finish by making one discard face up to the waste pile. It is *not* permissible to draw the upcard and discard it on the same turn.

Object. The object is to collect cards which together form one or more melds. A meld is either

■ three or four cards of the same rank, or

■ a sequence of three or more cards in the same suit.

Aces and Kings are not consecutive: the lowest possible sequence starts A–2–3, and the highest ends J–Q–K.

As soon as your hand consists of enough melds so that your deadwood counts 10 or less, you can end the game by knocking, and you win if your deadwood counts less than your opponent's. A hand consisting entirely of melds, with no deadwood, is described as 'gin' and carries a bonus. In Gin, unlike other Rummy games, you do not lay your melds out as you make them, but keep them secret until one of you goes out.

Knocking. When satisfied with the low value of your deadwood, you can end the game by (theoretically) knocking on the table after drawing an eleventh card and before making a final discard. Actually, it is now usual to close the game by laying your final discard face down on the waste pile, an action still referred to as knocking.

Having knocked, you spread your hand of cards face up on the table, arranged in melds and with any deadwood clearly separated from them. Your opponent then does the same, but also has the privilege of 'laying off' any cards of his own deadwood which may be matched with any of your own melds, in order to reduce the penalty value of his deadwood. He cannot do this, however, if you went gin, having all melds and no deadwood.

The stock may not be reduced to fewer than two cards. If neither of you knocks by the time only two remain, the result is a no-score draw, and the same dealer deals again.

Score. If the knocker has the lower count for deadwood, he scores the difference between the two deadwood values. Going gin attracts a bonus of 25.

If the opponent has an equal or lower value of deadwood, he scores the difference (if any) plus a bonus of 25 for *undercut*. But he cannot undercut a gin hand, for which the knocker still counts 25, nor may he himself score the bonus for gin, whether he had it already (in which case he should have knocked) or acquired it by laying off.

The two players each keep a running total of their scores, so that it will be clear when one of them has reached or exceeded the game target of 100.

Game score. As soon as either player reaches or exceeds 100 points, the game ends and a line is drawn beneath both totals, beneath which various bonuses are recorded. The winner first records a bonus of 100 for game, then a 25-point 'box' bonus for each hand that he won. Finally, if he won every hand he adds a bonus for 'shut-out'. This is equivalent to twice the basic amount he scored plus another 100 for game. (In some circles, the box bonuses are also doubled. Other bonus systems may be encountered, but the one described here is usual American practice.) The difference between the two final totals is the margin of victory.

Hollywood scoring system. For those who can't get enough of it, this is a method of playing three or more games simultaneously. Three sets of double columns are drawn up, each double column headed by the initials of the players. When you win your first hand, you record your score in the first set only. The score for your second won game is recorded in the first and second sets, and that for your third in all three, unless and until any of them has been ruled off with a win. As soon as a player reaches 100 in any of the three (or more) sets of columns, that set is ruled off and bonuses noted in the usual way. Play continues until all games have been completed and scored.

Oklahoma variant. In this version the maximum count of deadwood with which you may knock is not necessarily 10, but is determined by the value of the initial upcard. For instance, if it is a Six you must have six or less to knock; if a King, ten. It is usually agreed that if the first upcard is an Ace, you must have a gin hand to go out. This adds some much-needed variety to the game.

Notes on play

Managing your hand can be a somewhat mechanical affair, in the sense that for any given situation there is a fairly calculable best move. It is because there is a 'best' move that observation is the foremost aspect of skill required. What you do is:

■ *observe* what your opponent is discarding and which of your discards he is drawing; then, from that:

■ *infer* what sort of cards he has, assuming that he is either making the best moves or following a habit of play that you are used to; and, thereafter:

■ *remember* all the key cards that have gone, and the changing contents of your opponent's hand as the play proceeds.

As to the play of your own hand, the first thing to note is the inadvisability of going all out for gin. The bonus of 25 isn't usually enough to compensate for the times when you should have knocked instead of waiting around for glory, and thereby found yourself more knocked against than knocking. And, worse still, being undercut for your pains. A typical game ends about half way through the pack, so if you get a knocking hand much earlier than that do not hesitate to go down for all you can get.

It is generally better to draw the stock card than the upcard. The more upcards you draw, the more transparent your hand becomes. Drawing upcards also means you are taking cards your opponent doesn't want (except when he is bluffing), while drawing the next card of stock may well prevent him from going gin. The best exception to the rule is when you need to take the upcard to convert two matching cards into a meld of three, thus eliminating three pieces of deadwood (including the discard) – or, of course, when it enables you to knock immediately. It may also be useful to expand a meld, especially if you thereby eliminate a high unmatched card; but this should be done with caution rather than as a matter of course, as it can do more harm than good. If, for example, you hold

♠K ♡K ♣K, ♢7–8–9, ♠5, ♢5, ♡2, ♣2

it isn't worth taking ♢10 as the upcard, as you must then throw one of a pair and so halve the number of draws that will enable you to knock. One other conceivable reason for taking the upcard might be to reduce your deadwood when you suspect an imminent knocking from the other side of the table. The lower the rank discarded, the worse the danger would appear to be.

Because it is desirable to throw high cards instead of low ones, in order to keep your deadwood down, it is also reasonable to retain high-ranking pairs and two-card sequences acquired early in the game, in the hope that your opponent will discard a matching third in exchange for a lower-valued draw. But this should not be kept up too long. When to give up such expectations and start reducing deadwood is a matter for fine judgement.

Keeping track of discards is fundamental to the play. Suppose your opponent throws ♣J. The easy assumption is that he is 'not collecting Jacks', so you discard ♡J at the next opportunity and are surprised to see him pounce on it. Too late you spot the ruse. He might have held ♡9 ♡10 ♣J and thrown the Jack to draw one of the proper suit for the sequence. Even more cunningly, and perhaps at greater risk (depending on how well he knew the contents of your hand) he might have discarded from ♠J ◇J ♣J. Why, then, should he run a risk to bluff the fourth out of you? Because he thereby not only reforms his meld, but also prevents you from laying off a Jack when he goes out on the next turn, and perhaps undercutting him.

Of course, what's sauce for the gander is sauce for the goose, and you are at liberty to practise such stratagems yourself. And here's another. Suppose your opponent throws a Jack and you have two Jacks. You are tempted to take it immediately and complete a meld. But resist! He might have been playing from a pair. If so, leave it. He will be bound to throw the other Jack, and then you can take it and be certain he cannot lay off against that meld of yours and be in a position to undercut. For this to work, you must be pretty sure that he was playing from a pair to start with, and that he is not retaining the other Jack as part of a sequence. If all the Tens and Queens have gone, there is no danger of the latter; and if you have held your Jacks for some time, there is a fair chance that his discard was made from two. If it does go wrong, there is still the chance that either you will draw the other Jack or he will draw and discard it before too great damage is done. Unless he knows every card in your hand, he would be unlikely to draw it and keep it.

So much depends upon observation and remembrance of the contents of the waste pile that you must clearly be very careful in your choice of discard. The first card *not* to throw out is the one you have just drawn from stock and are still holding in your hand: if it really is useless don't let him know. Hang on to it for a turn or two before getting rid of it. On general principles, as we have seen, it is desirable to throw out a high unmatched card in order to reduce deadwood. The time not to do so is when you suspect that it may be of use to your opponent. In particular, he may be deliberately forcing a card out of you by one of the bluffing stratagems described above, in which case you must hold it back for a turn or two. Check this by matching your proposed discard against the current upcard. The less relation it bears to it, by rank and suit, the better. One player of my acquaintance insists that the ideal discard is different in suit from, but adjacent in rank to, the existing upcard.

It is possible to select a discard in such a way as to elicit useful information. Suppose you have to split up ♠K ♡K, ♠Q ♣Q. In this case throw ♠K. If it is picked up, it can only be to go with another King (in which case you keep yours to lay off if necessary), since your own holding of the Queen shows that it can hardly be wanted for the sequence.

In arranging your melds after knocking, prefer to attach a card to a set of four rather than a sequence if it could equally well go with either. In this way you certainly prevent your opponent from laying off against it, whereas with a sequence there is the danger that he may hold (and therefore lay off) an odd card attaching to one end of it.

In brief, play your own hand with methodical accuracy, and devote all your thinking to the constitution of the waste pile and the probable structure of your opponent's hand. Above all, remain flexible. Don't select a hoped-for meld at the start of play and concentrate upon it fixedly: circumstances may require you to change plans at any time.

6 | SIXTY-SIX

A snappy little counting game

One of the most delightful and varied two-handers ever devised, Sixty-Six has been popular in Germany for some 200 years, and, under the name Schnapsen, remains one of Austria's national card games. It is the snappy little ancestor of the more sedate and elaborate games of Bezique and Pinochle.

In case you find its arithmetical aspects daunting at first sight, you may want to try leading up to it gently by playing its even simpler ancestor, Elfern (German for 'Making Elevens').

Elevens (Elfern)

How to play

Cards. Use a 32-card pack ranking A K Q J 10 9 8 7 in each suit. Deal six cards each and stack the rest face down.

Object. To win, in tricks, 11 or more of the 20 honours. The honours are all the Aces, Kings, Queens, Jacks, and Tens.

Play. Non-dealer leads to the first trick. There is no trump, and suit need not be followed. The trick is taken by the card led unless the follower plays a higher card of the same suit, and the winner of each trick leads to the next. Before doing so, the winner draws the top card of the stock and the loser draws the next, so long as any remain.

When none remain in stock, the last six tricks are played to a different rule, in that it is now obligatory for the second player to follow suit if possible.

Score. Score a single win for capturing 11 to 14 honours, a double for 15 to 19, a treble for all twenty.

Variant 1. Elfern becomes more interesting with the addition of trumps. After the deal, the top card is turned face up and slipped half under the stock to indicate the trump suit. It will eventually be drawn by the loser of the tenth trick. A trick can now be taken by playing a higher card of the suit led or by trumping a non-trump lead. In the last six tricks the follower must follow suit if possible, otherwise must trump if possible, and only otherwise may play anything else.

Variant 2. It becomes even more interesting if the honours are given point-values as follows:

each	Ace	counts	11 card-points
	King	counts	4
	Queen	counts	3
	Jack	counts	2
	Ten	counts	10

Since the total number of card-points is 120, the object now is not to win one more than half the honours (eleven out of 20) but one more than half the card-points, namely 61 or more. Score a single for doing this, or a double for 91 to 120, or a treble for winning every trick regardless of points.

This card-point system is common to a wide range of games played throughout central Europe. If you get used to it early on, you will be able to pass with ease to such great card games as Sixty-Six, Skat, Belote, Pinochle, and Klaberjass.

Sixty-six (and Schnapsen)

How to play

Cards. Twenty-four, ranking A 10 K Q J 9 in each suit. Note that Tens rank higher than Kings – a logical consequence of having a higher card-point value. Deal six each in two batches of three and stack the rest face down. Turn the top card of the stock for trump and slip it half under the pack so as to remain identifiable. Whoever holds the Nine of trumps may exchange it for the trump turn-up so long as it remains beneath the stock. The exchange may be made at any time.

Object. The aim is to be the first to reach 66 by counting as follows. For capturing in tricks:

each	Ace	11 card-points
	Ten	10
	King	4
	Queen	3
	Jack	2

Scores may also be made for holding and showing the King and Queen of the same suit at the same time, known as a marriage:

trump marriage	40
non-trump marriage	20

For winning the last trick: 10

The significance of 66 is that, disregarding marriages, it is one more than half the total number of points available in play, since 30 for the card-points in each suit, plus 10 for last, makes 130.

Throughout play, you must count and remember the total number of points you have gained so far, as the deal is not necessarily won by the first player to reach 66 but by the first to claim (correctly) to have done so. The hefty scores for marriages make it possible for both players to pass this total, hence the importance of announcing it.

Play. Non-dealer leads to the first trick, and the winner of each trick leads to the next. Any card may be led, and, so long as cards remain in stock, any card may be played second, it being unnecessary to either follow suit or trump. The trick is taken by the higher card of the suit led, or by the higher trump if any are played. The winner of each trick draws the top card of the stock, waits for the other player to draw the next, and then leads.

Marriages. If at any time you hold a King and Queen of the same suit, whether dealt or drawn from stock, you may declare and score for the marriage upon leading to a trick. You do this by showing both cards, announcing 'and 40' if it is in trumps or 'and 20' otherwise, and leaving one marriage partner on the table as the lead to the trick. Since you may only do this upon leading, it follows that, as Dealer, you will have to win a trick before you can declare a marriage.

Endgame. The first half ends when the loser of the sixth trick draws the trump turn-up, which will be the trump Nine if it has been exchanged. The last six tricks are played to different rules. You may lead any card, but the second to play must now play a higher card of the same suit if possible, otherwise a lower card of the same suit if possible, otherwise a trump if a non-trump was led. A marriage left over from the first phase of the game may still be declared. For winning the last (twelfth) trick, count an extra 10 'for last'.

Quite often, however, the game never gets as far as the last trick, for the following reason.

Shut-out. If, before the stock runs out, you think you can reach 66 from the cards left in hand, you may shut the stock by turning the trump turn-up face down. You may do this before or after drawing a sixth card, but, if you do draw a sixth, you must allow your opponent to do so as well. The last tricks are played in the same way as described above (follow suit, head the trick, trump if unable to follow), except that '10 for last' does not apply, as this specifically applies to winning the *twelfth* trick, and there will not have been that many played.

Score. The first player to claim correctly to have reached 66 scores 1 game point, or 2 if the other player is *schneidered* ('snipped') by failing to reach 33; or 3 if the other player is *schwarz* ('blackened') by not having won a single trick.

The following special notes apply.

    1. If non-dealer declared a marriage upon leading to the first trick, but failed to win that trick or any other, the marriage does not score, and its declarer is accounted schwarz.

    2. If one player claims to have reached 66 but is proved wrong, the other scores 2 game points, or 3 if he or she had not yet won a trick.

    3. If one player shuts the stock and fails to win, the other scores 2 game points.

    4. If both make 65, or neither claims to have reached 66 by end of play, the game point is held up and goes to the winner of the next deal.

Game. Play up to 7 game points.

Schnapsen

The Austrian game differs from Sixty-Six only in that it is played with 20 cards, the Nines being omitted. In this game it is the Jack of trumps that may be exchanged for the turn-up.

Notes on play

For a game based on so few cards and simple material, Sixty-Six offers extraordinary scope for tactical and strategic skill.

The most important strategic requirement is to decide whether and when to shut the stock and foreclose the game. Between experts, few games are played out to the bitter end. The time to foreclose is when you have a majority of the trumps remaining in play, including the Ace and Ten (unless either has already gone), and can be sure of reaching at least 60 from the winners in your own hand. You can reckon on gaining an average 2–3 card-points from each losing card played by your opponent, but don't expect to capture an Ace or Ten that you have not yet seen in play, as it could well be lying in the undrawn stock.

Before the shut-out, or the last six tricks, an average safe lead is the Nine or Jack of a plain suit, especially if you hold the Ten, as your lead will probably force the Ace out and leave your Ten high. If, however, you hold the Ace, keep it for as long as the Ten remains unseen, as you may thereby manage to catch it with the Ace in the play of the last six.

Don't lead plain-suit Aces in the first half of the game unless you want them trumped in order to weaken your opponent's trump holding. You might do this, for example, if you know you have three trumps each and want to enter the end-game with a majority of trumps. More often, it can be a good move when you yourself are weak or void in trumps and want to prevent the other player from enjoying a clear run of trumps in the end play. If you find yourself short of trumps and holding such a long suit that it is unlikely your opponent can follow, lead low from that suit as often as possible. Either you will pick up points from castaways thrown to them, or you will force out trumps with little loss to yourself.

Obviously, you will keep single Kings and Queens in the hope of marrying them. But if your opponent plays to a trick the partner of a King or Queen in your own hand, you will know there is no point in keeping it and thus be given a spare discard or good lead.

Sixty-Six calls for much concentration to be played successfully. Always be aware of how many of the six trumps you have, and how many have been played to tricks, so that by the time the last six are played you will know pretty well what the trump division is between you and play accordingly. It is a tremendous advantage to go into the last six with one trump more than your opponent.

Keep track of Aces and Tens, in order to assess your chances of capturing a Ten with an Ace, and how to avoid losing a Ten to an Ace. Keep track of Kings and Queens, so that you will know whether or not it is safe to discard an unwed marriage partner.

Finally, keep count not only of your own point-score to date but also of your opponent's. This takes practice, and you will probably have to start by just concentrating on your own.

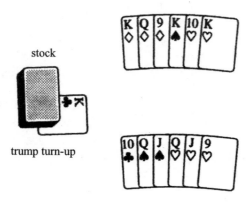

stock

trump turn-up

Figure 6.1   Sixty-Six

The turned King makes clubs trump. North will start by showing the diamond marriage, announcing '20 to score', and leaving the Queen on the table as the opening lead. North's 20 does not come into effect until he has actually won a trick. South, having nothing to declare and seeing no reason to cash the trump Ten so early in the game, will pass this by throwing a worthless card (Nine) from his longest suit. North then draws from stock and will lead again when South has also drawn.

7 | BEZIQUE AND PINOCHLE

Romantic games of marriage and intrigue

A more substantial derivative of Sixty-Six, Bezique became a world-wide classic over a hundred years ago. It has been played in many different forms, and in America gave rise to Pinochle in all its varieties. Although no longer played as a club or tournament game, it maintains a devoted following among all true card-lovers. Indeed, as it has long since been abandoned as a serious gambling game, Bezique could nowadays be well described as a game for lovers. Much is made of 'marriages' between Kings and Queens, and the name of the game itself (only fancifully derived from *besico*, supposedly Spanish for 'little kiss'), denotes an irregular liaison between a Queen and Jack of different suits.

The form of Bezique described below is for two players using two 32-card packs shuffled together. Other versions were invented for various numbers of players and involving greater numbers of cards, but are not now much in evidence – probably because few people nowadays are likely to keep out of circulation eight or even six 32-card packs shuffled together for the rare occasions on which they have the time and inclination to embark on such exotic monstrosities.

Bezique

How to play

Equipment. Two 32-card packs shuffled together, neither containing any card lower than a Seven. It doesn't matter if they are of different back designs or colours, so long as they are the same size.

Scores are made continually throughout the game, and can be kept on paper, though some sort of mechanical scorer is useful. Patent Bezique markers, of the same design as Whist and Piquet markers, are now antiques, but dial-type scorers are still produced from time to time. Even a Cribbage board will do. All Bezique scores are in tens, so twice round the crib board at 10 per hole gives a maximum of 1210 points, enough to be getting on with.

Rank. In each suit, cards rank: A 10 K Q J 9 8 7. Note the position of the Ten. It counts higher than King both in play and in cutting for the deal.

Deal. Whoever cuts the higher-ranking card may choose whether or not to deal first. Deal eight cards each in batches of three, then two, then three. Turn up the next card – the seventeenth – and lay it to one side between the two players. The suit of this card is the trump suit for the current deal and, if it is a Seven, the dealer immediately scores 10 for it. Place the undealt cards face down across this card to form the stock, so that the turn-up projects from beneath it.

Object. The winner is the first player to reach 1000 points, which may take several deals. Points are scored for capturing *brisques* (Aces and Tens) in tricks, counting 10 points each, and, through drawing and discarding, acquiring certain combinations of cards scoring anything from 20 to 500 points each.

Tricks. Non-dealer leads to the first trick. The follower to a trick may play any card with complete freedom. A trick is taken by the higher card of the suit led, or the higher trump if any are played, or by the first played of two identical cards. The winner of a trick lays the won cards on the table before him- or herself (not necessarily face down), shows and scores for any scoring combination that may be contained in the hand, then draws the top card of stock to restore the hand to eight. The trick-loser draws the next card of the stock, and the trick-winner then leads to the next trick. This continues until the stock is exhausted, when the rules of play change.

The purpose of winning a trick is not primarily to capture any brisque it may contain, as these score relatively little, but to declare a scoring combination if you have one, as this may only be done upon winning a trick.

Scoring combinations. Upon winning a trick, you may declare
and score for any one (not more) of the following combinations, by
removing its constituent cards from your hand and laying them face
up on the table before you.

combination	definition	score
Sequence	A 10 K Q J of trumps	250
Royal marriage	K–Q of trumps	40
Common marriage	K–Q of plain suit	20
Hundred Aces	any four Aces	100
Eighty Kings	any four Kings	80
Sixty Queens	any four Queens	60
Forty Jacks	any four Jacks	40
Bezique	♠Q–♢J	40
Double bezique	♠Q–♠Q –♢J –♢J	500

Having declared a combination, you leave it face up on the table,
but its cards continue to form part of your hand, and you can play
them to tricks as and when you wish. Cards won in tricks remain
out of play and can no longer be used to form combinations.

Combinations on the table, and their remnants when one or more of
their constituent cards have been played off, may be used in new
combinations made by rearranging them on the table or adding to
them from the hand, though in each case it is necessary to win a
trick before scoring for any such rearrangement or addition.

Special rules govern the formation and re-formation of
combinations. The basic principle is that a card which has already
been used as part of a scoring combination (and is therefore still
lying on the table) may subsequently be used in another
combination, provided that it is a combination of a different type.

Examples of re-use. Having declared a marriage in spades, you
could subsequently add three more Queens to score Sixty Queens,
or ♢J to score a bezique, or both on different occasions, so long as
the ♠Q remains on the table throughout and is not played to a trick.
If you declare a royal marriage for 40, then so long as both cards
remain on the table you can later add A–10–J of trumps to score 250
for the sequence.

Restrictions on re-use. Having declared a marriage in spades, you may not remarry either partner by adding another King or Queen to it, though there is nothing to stop you declaring a second marriage in the same suit if you happen to get one. Similarly, having declared a quartet (four Aces, Kings, Queens or Jacks), you cannot use any of them to form another quartet. Most importantly, you cannot declare a trump sequence for 250 and subsequently claim the royal marriage it contains. You may, however, score the marriage first and then add the other three cards to score the sequence later. Similarly, you cannot score 500 for double bezique and subsequently count each constituent bezique for 40, but you are allowed to declare first a single bezique, then another single bezique, and finally the double bezique, for a total of 580, provided that you win a trick before making each declaration, and that all the relevant Queens and Jacks remain on the table throughout.

Some maintain that a combination is scorable only if at least one of its cards is played directly from the hand; but this is untrue. For example, it is perfectly proper to declare Kings for 80, Queens for 60 at the next opportunity, and then, so long as the appropriate cards remain on the table, a marriage upon winning each of the next four tricks. Or: suppose Kings have been declared for 80, and two have been played out, leaving ♠K ♡K on the table. At a later turn, you can legally play ♠Q ◇J from the hand and announce 'bezique for 40, and a marriage to score', subsequently counting the spade marriage when you win another trick.

Seven of trumps. If you hold or draw the trump Seven, you may declare it at any time – usually upon winning a trick – and score 10 points for it. Alternatively, you may, upon winning a trick, declare it for 10 and exchange it for the turn-up. This, however, counts as a declaration, and prevents you from declaring any other combination at the same time. (There are conflicting rules on the use of the trump Seven. This one is a recommended compromise.)

Endgame. When the loser of the 24th trick has taken the turn-up into hand, and no more cards remain in stock, the rules of play change. Both players take up all eight cards into hand and the last trick-winner leads to the first of the last eight tricks. The second to a trick must follow suit if possible and must win the trick if

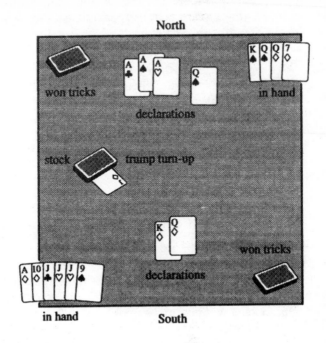

Figure 7.1 Bezique

A game in progress. North has evidently scored '100 Aces' earlier on and since played one to a trick. Rules of play forbid the same combination to be re-formed and scored again by the addition of another Ace.

Similarly, North's ♠Q on the table is left over from either a marriage for 20 or a bezique for 40. Drawing another Queen would enable the addition of three Queens from hand to that on the table to score '60 Queens'. If North has just won a trick, the ◊7 may now be exchanged for the turned Jack, enabling it to be added to the ♠Q for bezique.

South, who has scored 20 for a diamond marriage, would also very much like to get the turned Jack. It could be combined with the marriage and the Ace-Ten in hand to yield 250 for the trump sequence, and then, on a later trick, the other three Jacks in hand could be added to it for '40 Jacks'.

possible, by trumping if unable to follow suit. No combinations may be declared after the last card has been drawn. The winner of the last trick scores 10 points for it.

Score. If neither player has yet reached the target score of 1000 points, both then sort through their won cards, counting 10 points for each Ace and Ten captured. If neither player has still not yet reached 1000, the next player deals and another hand is played. The game ends when one or both players have reached 1000. The winner is the player with the higher score, and the win is doubled if the loser fails to reach the 'Rubicon' of 500 points.

Notes on play

It is generally not worth winning a trick unless it contains a couple of brisque or you have something to declare. Otherwise it is usually best to lose a trick and play second to the next one, as this gives you more latitude. For example, a brisque is a good card to win a trick with if you are playing second, but not a desirable one to lead. On the other hand, situations often arise in which you suspect that your opponent has a valuable declaration to make, in which case you may attempt to keep winning tricks until the stock is exhausted in order to prevent them from being made. Bearing in mind that the same will be done against you, try to keep back trumps, especially high ones, to ensure that you will be able to declare a combination when you get one.

The best cards to throw to worthless tricks, or to lead when you have nothing to declare, are obviously Sevens, Eights and Nines. Often, however, you find yourself with none in your hand, which seems to consist of part-combinations and valuable cards. In this case don't hesitate to treat Jacks as dispensable (other than the bezique Jack), as Forty Jacks is not a very high scoring combination and not worth spoiling the hand for. Keep hold of a diamond Jack, however, so long as there is the possibility of making bezique. Also be prepared to play a Ten if it wins the trick, as Tens cannot form part of scoring combinations except in trumps, and are therefore not worth keeping from this point of view.

When it comes to breaking up part-combinations you must weigh the value of each against the probability of making it, to which end you will be guided by what you can see among your opponent's declarations and what has already been played to tricks. For example, if he has declared a marriage in spades and you hold both Jacks of diamonds, it is impossible to make double bezique, and so one more Jack becomes available for discarding – unless, of course, you have seen so few of the eight Jacks to date that there seems a fair chance of forming a Jack quartet.

Cards still lying on the table after being declared are suitable candidates for playing to tricks, on the principle that you give your opponent less information about the state of your hand by playing a card he knows you have rather than one he hasn't seen. Marriage partners and quartetted Jacks are particularly good candidates for this purpose. At the same time, however, it is important to retain those which stand a fair chance of being re-used in other combinations, and those which belong to the trump suit and may therefore be needed for trick-winning. In particular, never break up (by playing a card from) a single bezique so long as the possibility remains of forming a second and scoring the double, as double bezique is the most valuable combination in the pack and will nearly always win the game.

Given a choice of combinations, it is naturally better to score the more valuable ones first. But there is an exception to this rule, in that given a sequence, you may score 40 for the royal marriage first and then 250 for the sequence for a total of 290, but if you count the higher combination first you are restricted to 250, as the marriage may not then be scored. The same applies to beziques: you may declare, on three successive turns, a single, a single and a double, for a total of 580, but you cannot score for a single after counting the double. In these cases you score more for starting with the lower combination and working upwards. If, however, it seems unlikely that you will have time to make these scores the long way, in view of the number of tricks left to play and the state of your own hand, it may be better to score the higher combination first and be prepared to skip the lower.

In the last eight tricks, the ideal is to play worthless cards of a suit in which your opponent is void, in order to weaken his trumps. Experienced players will know what cards their opponent holds and play accordingly. Experience, in fact, is essential to success at Bezique, as it is a game of judgement rather than analysis. The practised player soon develops an instinctive feel for the state of his opponent's hand, and will know when he can safely lose tricks and when he must keep winning in order to prevent a high combination to be scored against him.

Pinochle

The American equivalent of Bezique derives from the German rather than the French branch of the family, and has closer resemblances to Sixty-Six. It is mostly played as a three-hander or as a four-player partnership game, but two-handed Pinochle also has its devotees. The mechanics of play are exactly as for Bezique, but the cards and scoring features differ as follows.

Cards. Use a 48-card pack consisting of A 10 K Q J 9 in each suit, doubled. Deal 12 cards each in ones, turn the next for trump, and place the remainder face down as a stock half covering the turn-up. Whoever has a Nine of trumps (called *dix* or 'deece') may exchange it for the turn-up for a score of 10.

Object. To be the first to reach 1000 points over as many deals as necessary, points being scored for (a) melds and (b) counting-cards won in tricks.

Melds
standard melds

meld	definition	score
flush	A 10 K Q J of trumps	150
royal marriage	trump K Q	40
plain marriage	non-trump K Q	20
Aces around	four Aces, one of each suit	100
Kings around	four Kings, one of each suit	80
Queens around	four Queens, one of each suit	60
Jacks around	four Jacks, one of each suit	40
pinochle	♠Q ◊J	40
dix *or* deece	trump Nine	10

additional melds used by agreement

double flush	2 × A 10 K Q J of trumps	1500
double pinochle	♠Q ♠Q ♢J ♢J	300
roundhouse	four marriages, one per suit	240
K and Q flush	A 10 K K Q Q J	230
K or Q flush	A 10 K K Q J or A 10 K Q Q J	190
grand pinochle	♠K ♠Q ♢J	60

Counters

Individual cards taken in tricks count as follows at end of play:

	A	10	K	Q	J	9
traditional	11	10	4	3	2	–
intermediate	10	10	5	5	–	–
modern	10	10	10	–	–	–
simplified to	1	1	1	–	–	–

Agree beforehand which card-point system to follow. The traditional is now largely restricted to two-handed play. When the simplified system is used, the meld scores are also divided by 10 (flush = 15, royal marriage = 4, and so on).

Special rules. Grand pinochle (♠K ♠Q ♢J) may be declared at one trick for 60, or 80 if spades are trump. Game is 1000. The first to reach that total calls 'out' to end the play, but loses if mistaken. If both have over 1000, play up to 1250, and increase the target by 250 each time this happens.

8 | KLABERJASS (CLOBBY)

A game of many names

Klaberjass is Dutch for 'club Jack', and the game first known under that name originated in the Low Countries some 200 years ago. It has become a particularly Jewish game, and has spread far and wide under a variety of different names – many of them versions of the original, such Kalabriasz, Kalaber, Clobiosh, Clobby, Clob, etc., others taken from its varied vocabulary, including Bela or Bella, and the French national card game Belote.

If you haven't played a card-point game before, such as Sixty-Six, Pinochle or Skat, you may find this a bit daunting at first sight, but it well repays the effort of learning, and it really is very widely played.

How to play

Cards. Thirty-two, consisting of A K Q J 10 9 8 7 in each suit.

Deal. Whoever cuts the lower card deals first, and the deal then alternates. Deal six cards each in two batches of three. Place the remainder face down to form a stock. Turn the top card face up and place it beside the stock. The suit of this card is the preferred suit for trumps, though it will not necessarily be accepted as such.

Object. After the bidding each player will receive three more cards and play nine tricks. Whoever accepts or nominates the trump suit (the 'maker') thereby undertakes to win the greater number of points for tricks and melds. Trick-points are scored by capturing certain counting-cards, as shown below. A meld is a sequence of three of more cards in the same suit, or the King and Queen of trumps, known as *bella*.

Rank and value of cards. In non-trump suits cards rank A 10 K Q J 9 8 7. Note the high position of the Ten. In trumps, the highest card is the Jack, called *Jass* (with J pronounced Y); second-highest is the Nine, called *Menel* (accent on the second syllable); and these are followed downwards by Ace, Ten, King, Queen, Nine, Eight, Seven. Certain cards have point-values, credited to the player winning them in tricks, as follows:

Jass (trump Jack)	20
Menel (trump Nine)	14
Ace	11 each
Ten	10 each
King	4 each
Queen	3 each
Jack	2 each (except in trumps)
Nine	0 each (except in trumps)
Eight, Seven	0 each

Melds. A sequence of three cards in the same suit counts 20, a sequence of four or more counts 50. The sequential order of cards is A K Q J 10 9 8 7 in every suit including trumps. (Thus Q–J–10 is a sequence of three even though the ranks are not adjacent in trick-taking power.) The King and Queen of trumps together *(bella)* score 20. Melds are not counted until both players have nine cards, and only the player with the best sequence may score for sequences.

Bidding. The rank and value of cards and melds are described first because bidding can only be carried out on the assessment of one's chances of winning more points than the opponent. Note that the total value of all the counters in the pack is 152 (though they may not all be in play), and that an extra 10 points go to the winner of the last trick, bringing the trick-points to 162.

Non-dealer has the first choice of accepting the turned suit as trump, thereby becoming the 'maker', and undertaking to win more points for tricks and melds than his opponent. If elder passes, younger may either accept the preferred suit or turn it down (literally).

If both turn it down, elder may nominate another suit as trump, thereby becoming the maker, or pass this opportunity to younger.

If both pass again, the hands are abandoned and a new deal made.

Play. When one player becomes the maker, the dealer deals another batch of three cards to each player from the top of the stock, so that each has nine, then takes the bottom card of the stock and places it face up on top. This card is for information only and has no part in the play. (Its only function is to ensure that neither has had the unfair advantage of being the only one to know what the bottom card is in case it was observed during the deal.)

Dix, pronounced *deece,* is the Seven of trumps if the preferred trump was accepted. If either player has this card he may exchange if for the turned trump card at any time before the first trick is led. This privilege cannot apply if a different suit was entrumped.

Scoring melds. Before elder leads to the first trick, scares are made for sequences if either player holds any. Only the player who holds the best sequence may score, and he is thereby entitled to score for as many as he shows. (The relevant cards must be revealed.) The best sequence is the one of greatest length; or if equal in length, the one with the highest card; or, if still equal, the one in the trump suit; or, if neither is in trumps, that of elder hand. Note that the dix may be exchanged either before or after melds are declared, depending on whether the Seven or the turn-up is required for a sequence; but you cannot both score a sequence with the dix, then exchange it and score another one with the turn-up.

Tricks. Elder leads to the first trick and the winner of each trick leads to the next. The second player must:

- if trumps are led, play a higher trump if possible, otherwise a lower;
- if a non-trump is led, follow suit if possible (not necessarily a higher one); or,
- if unable to follow to a non-trump lead, play a trump if possible.

Bella. If you hold both King and Queen of trumps you may count 20 by announcing 'bella' upon playing the second of them to a trick.

Last trick. Whoever wins the last trick counts 10 for it.

Score. Each player announces the total he has counted for cards, melds, bella and the last trick (as appropriate). If the maker has more than his opponent, each counts towards game exactly the amount he has made. If not, the maker scores nothing, and the opponent scores towards game the combined total made by both players in that deal, unless he tied, in which case he scores just the tied figure.

Game. The game ends when either player, at the end of a deal, has reached or exceeded a previously agreed total, usually 500.

Variants. Among the variations and additional rules followed in different countries and localities, the following may be adopted in whole or part.

- Schmeiss (rhymes with mice). Instead of turning it down or passing, elder hand may bid *schmeiss*. This is an offer either to accept the turned suit and become the maker, or to annul the deal, as younger chooses. If elder passes instead of accepting the trump or passing, younger also has the option of declaring *schmeiss*. In effect, it is a way of preventing the other player from choosing a different trump.

- In making trumps, first preference is always on clubs and second on the suit of the turn-up, if different. This variant increases demands on good judgement and is in keeping with the name of the game – which, as we have seen, means 'Jack of clubs'.

- If both players reject the turned suit, either of them may bid No Trump *(sans atout)*, which takes precedence over a bid in suit and may be used to overcall it. In this case there is no Jass or Menel, cards rank A 10 K Q J 9 8 7 in every suit, and each player's final score for the deal is doubled. This makes it attractive to bid no trump on a safe hand, but expensive to fail on a bad one. If one player bids No Trump, the other can overcall by bidding 'grand' *(tout atout)*. In this case there is a Jass and Menel in every suit – in other words, cards rank J 9 A 10 K Q 8 7 in each suit, and all Jacks are worth 20 and all Nines 14. Otherwise it is played as no trump, and also scores double. Grand may only be bid to overcall a previous bid of no trump.

■ If both tie for best sequence, the result is a stand-off. Elder's does not have priority.

■ A sequence of five or more may be valued at 100 points instead of 50.

■ One source refers to a bonus of 40 for winning all the tricks. It seems reasonable to recognize some sort of bonus for this feat, though the figure quoted would appear to be lifted straight out of Piquet.

■ In Belote, the French game, additional melds may be scored. Sequences of three count 20, of four 50, and of five or more 100. Also, whoever has the best four of a kind (a *carré* or quartet) may score for any and all quartets they may show, valued thus: four Jacks 200, Nines 150, Aces, Tens, Kings or Queens 100, lower ranks not valid. Game is usually at least 1000 points.

■ If, during the course of play, you think you have reached the target score by counting melds or card-points so far captured in tricks, you may claim 'out' and end the game immediately – provided that you have already won at least one trick (Belote rule). If you are mistaken, you lose the game; otherwise you win, even if your opponent has a higher total.

Notes on play

Nearly all points are scored for cards won in tricks plus 10 for last. A whole game may pass without the appearance of a bella or of more than two or three small sequences, so it is hardly worth taking them into account in the bidding unless you are dealt one to start with.

Although the theoretical maximum number of trick-points is 162, it is impossible for all 20 counters to be in play in one deal. In practice, the average number of points in play per deal lies between 100 and 120, of which the maker, if successful, should expect to score 80–90 against the loser's 20–30. If the game were played with a compulsory trump and no opportunity to pass, each player would expect to take an average of 50–60 points per deal. Since you are called upon to bid on only two-thirds of your final hand, you ought to hold 30–40 points in high prospective trumps and supporting Ace-Tens before accepting the preferred suit or choosing another.

It is possible to bid successfully on a hand containing as little as a singleton Jass and two Aces or an Ace-Ten. But this does not mean that all hands are playable. The more expert players become, the more hands they tend to throw in. It does not take more than a few rounds of the game to discover how easily some weak-looking hands win while others, apparently quite promising, fall at the first fence. It is easy enough to recognize a strong hand when you see one, but it takes practice to know whether or not to pass or play on something less clear cut. Beginners, I think, should play boldly. You will learn much more from bidding and losing than from passing and never knowing.

In assessing the hand look first for the dix (Seven) of the turned card, unless the latter is an Eight, which is not worth having. In any prospective trump suit it is imperative to hold either the Jack or an accompanied Nine, preferably with an Ace or Ten for company. Don't play a trump suit containing the Ace or Ace-Ten as highest cards, unless they are accompanied by at least two others of the suit, as there is too great a chance of losing one or more big ones to Jass or Menel in your opponent's hand. Nor be tempted into entrumping a suit just because you have been dealt the King and Queen of it, worth 20 for the bella. If you have a mediocre hand including bella, or a sequence in any suit, the extra value may be just enough to make up either for weaknesses in the hand, or a stout opposition. But never bank on being dealt the marriage partner to a King or Queen already in hand, or a specific card required for a sequence. The odds are more than 7 to 1 against.

A two-card prospective trump including Jass or Menel is sufficient if adequately supported in plain suits, as the odds favour the appearance of a third trump in the last part of the deal.

In non-trumps the best holding is an unaccompanied Ace or Ace-Ten, and there is even a goodish chance (4 to 3 in favour) of winning a trick with an Ace-less Ten provided that the suit is not held so long as to risk being trumped. A long plain suit, say four or more, is not good for tricks unless it contains low cards which can be used to weaken the opposing trumps – bearing in mind the obligation to trump a suit in which one is void. A void suit in the prospective bidder's hand is a mixed blessing for the same reason. It must, for safety, be accompanied by long trumps, otherwise it will be used to weaken the trump holding.

Younger hand may always bid with greater boldness than elder, since elder's pass suggests some weakness.

If you have the lead as maker, your normal strategy on a reasonable hand will be to draw trumps first, partly to test the situation and partly to clear the way for Aces and Tens in plain suits. With a short trump suit, or one headed by a Ten-Ace (Jack-Ace or Nine-Ten) it is preferable to lead a short plain suit with solid top cards. If you feel that your opponent might hold too many trumps, force them out by leading worthless cards from a long plain suit.

When leading trumps, it is worth starting with the Jack if there is a chance of seizing the Ace or Ten thereby, but (of course) it is dangerous to lead the Nine, Ace or Ten if you lack anything higher. Much of the interest of the game derives from the peculiar positions – third and fourth highest – of the high-scoring Ace and Ten of trumps.

With an average holding of two cards in each suit, it is desirable to win with Aces and Tens as soon as the opportunity arises. If (say) an Eight is led into your Ace-King, it is best to bring the Ace home while you safely can, rather than hold it back with a view to catching the Ten.

Sample deals

First deal. Benny deals to Annie and himself the hands shown below and turns the ♡A for suit:

    Annie   ♠K ♡9 7 ♣10 J ◇A

    Benny   ♠7 ♡J 10 8 ♣Q 7

As elder, Annie holds the Menel of the turned suit and can swap the dix for the Ace. Her hand is worth 38 in card-points (assuming hearts trump), and she accepts the turned suit. After three more cards are dealt, and ♠8 turned for information, the hands are:

    Annie   ♠A K ♡9 A ♣A 10 J ◇A 9

    Benny   ♠7 ♡J 10 8 ♣K Q 8 7 ◇10

Neither player's trump holding has improved, and it is interesting to note that Benny was dealt three trumps including the Jass. With a short trump suit headed only by the second highest, Annie leads clubs in the hope of retrieving her Ace and Ten before drawing trumps. She takes 21 points on the first two tricks, but then loses her

Jack to Benny's King (worth a point more than taking it with the Queen). Given the initiative, Benny now aims to make the most of his relatively long trumps. He starts aggressively with the Jass, drawing ♡A for 31 points and the certain knowledge that Annie has only the Menel in hand, which he next forces out by leading ♡8. Now lacking trumps, Annie plays her Aces, gaining 32 card-points in the process, and continues with ◇9. This Benny trumps with his Ten, and concludes with ♣Q, drawing ♠K plus 10 for last. Annie has just succeeded in her bid, taking 67 to Benny's 64. The latter was lucky to hold not only more trumps than his opponent, but also more cards in the same long suit.

Second deal. Annie turns up ♠10, having dealt:

Benny	♠K 9 7 ♡A K ◇10
Annie	♠J 8 ♡10 9 8 ♣A

Benny has three trumps and access to bella by means of the dix. He therefore accepts the turned suit, in which, it will be noted, Annie holds the top card. The information card, after completion of the hands to the following, is ◇K:

Benny	♠9 K Q ♡A K ♣10 K ◇10 9
Annie	♠J 8 ♡10 9 8 ♣A 8 ◇Q 8

After hearing Annie declare her heart sequence for 20, Benny leads. He must allow his clubs and diamonds to be led into, as either Ten could fall needlessly to an Ace if led. He therefore decides to force out any high trumps by means of ♠Q, and is fortunate enough to bring the Jass down, leaving his Menel in charge. He can be sure that the Ace and Ten are not in play, otherwise Annie would have played one of them and held back the Jass for better things, such as catching the Menel or winning the last trick. Annie continues with ◇8, taken by the Ten. The maker now returns ♠K, announcing 'bella' for 20. This draws ♠8, which Benny can be certain is the last trump in the other hand. The remaining tricks are played like bat and ball. Benny wins his game, scoring 49 in tricks plus 10 for last and 20 for bella, making 79 in all, to Annie's 53 in tricks plus 20 for the sequence, 73 in all. The round totals after two deals are Annie 140, Benny 143. And it's anybody's game.

9 | PIQUET

The aristocrat of card games

Piquet, pronounced 'P.K.' the French way or 'Picket' if you prefer English, has long been regarded as one of the great card games and certainly the best for two – assuming that 'best' means a game requiring and rewarding the greatest skill in play. For a game that has been played in so many countries for so many centuries it is remarkable in having undergone little variation in its basic material, thereby indicating how brilliant that material is. It is a game of tremendous depth and variety, and I never tire of it.

The little variation it has undergone relates chiefly to overall structure. The version described here is English Rubicon Piquet, as standardized by London's Portland Club in the late 19th century. 'Rubicon' denotes the target score of 100 points. In the older form of the game, called *Piquet au cent,* Anglicized to 'Saunt', the game was won by the first player to reach 100 points over as many deals as it took. In the Rubicon game, the *partie* (equivalent to the rubber at Bridge) is six deals, and the loser is heavily penalized for failing to reach the 'Rubicon' of 100 points.

Piquet is very easy to follow once you have got the basic idea, but the rules are subject to so many niceties of detail as to make it look at first reading far more complicated than it really is – a classic case of not being able to see the wood for the trees. You may therefore find it helpful to go through the following introductory exercise, either alone or with a prospective partner, before plunging into a thicket of detail.

A sample hand

Take a 32-card pack, or make one by discarding all ranks below Seven from a 52-card pack. Deal out two hands of 12 cards each as follows:

Elder (non-dealer)							*Younger (dealer)*						
♠	.	.	Q	.	.	8 7	A K	.	.	.	.	.	.
♡	A	.	.	J	.	. .	. K	.	.	10 9	.	.
♣	A	.	.	.	.	8 7	. K	Q	J	10	.	.	.
♢	A	.	Q	J	. 9	. .	.	.	.	10	. 8 7

Arrange the remaining cards in the following order:

♡Q ♡8 ♡7 ♣9 ♢K ♣9 ♠J ♠10

Spread them face down in a row, overlapping one another, with the back of the ♡Q on top. This row is called the talon. In real play, of course, no one knows what these cards are.

What will happen is this. Elder (non-dealer) will first discard up to five cards and draw the same number of replacements from the top of the talon, then younger will discard as many as remain (typically three) and also draw replacements. They will then seek to score points for declaring certain card combinations in their new hands, and finally seek to win a majority of 12 tricks played at no trump. The purpose of the draw is therefore partly to compose winning combinations and partly to ensure a good playing hand. Before you can do this, you have to know what the scoring combinations are. They fall into three classes.

> ■ *Point.* This is scored by the player holding the longest suit, or, if equal, the suit of greater point-value after counting numerals at face value, 10 per court, and 11 for the Ace.

> ■ *Sequence.* This is scored by the player holding the longest suit-sequence, or, if equal, the one with the highest top card. That player may then score for any other sequences contained in the hand.

> ■ *Sets.* A set is three or four Aces, Kings, Queens, Jacks or Tens. Lower numerals don't count. A *quatorze* (set of four) beats a *trio* (three). Whoever holds the highest quatorze, or, if none, the highest trio, is entitled to score for it and any other sets held in the same hand.

Now examine the two hands with these combinations in mind. Elder's best chance of making point and sequence lies in keeping all his diamonds. He therefore discards his Sevens and Eights and ♡J, drawing in their place ♡Q–8–7, ♠9 and ◇K.

Younger will obviously keep her high cards and club sequence, and will hope to draw the fourth King or Ten, either of which would give her a winning quatorze since she has one of each Ace, Queen, Jack. Making the obvious discard of three low numerals, she draws in their place ♠J–10 ♣9.

The playing hands are now:

♠	.	.	Q	.	.	9	.	.		A	K	.	J	10	.	.	.
♡	A	.	Q	.	.	.	8	7		.	K	.	.	10	.	.	.
♣	A	.	.	.	.	.	.	.		.	K	Q	J	10	9	.	.
◇	A	K	Q	J	.	9	.	.		.	.	.	10	.	.	.	.

Both players have a 'point of five', elder in diamonds and younger in clubs. But elder's five comprise 50 card-points and younger's only 49, so elder scores one per card, 5 points in all, for holding the better point.

For sequences, elder's four to the Ace is beaten by younger's five to the King. Younger therefore scores for the sequence, and would be entitled to score for any other sequences if she had any. Sequences also score 1 per card, but those of five or more carry a bonus of 10, so in this case younger scores 15.

For sets, elder's trio of Aces is beaten by younger's quatorze of Tens, which also entitles her to reckon her trio of Kings. Quatorzes count 14 and trios 3, so younger scores 17 for sets.

Elder now leads to the first trick with the scores so far at 5 to 32. He cashes his seven winners immediately – there is no point in messing about – and scores a bonus of 10 for winning a clear majority of tricks.

There is far more to it than that, of course; but if you take this sample deal as illustrating the wood you will find it much easier to pick your pathway through the following trees.

How to play

Game. A game or *partie* is six deals, each dealing alternately. The winner is then the player with the higher total. If the loser fails to reach 100 he or she is 'rubiconed', and the winner gets a hefty bonus.

Cards. Use a 32-card pack ranking A K Q J 10 9 8 7 in each suit. Whoever cuts the higher card chooses which player should deal first. Dealing first is sometimes advantageous, and never disadvantageous, so the choice is usually a foregone conclusion.

Deal. Shuffle the cards lightly, have them cut, and deal twelve each. You may deal in batches of two or three, but whichever you choose you must stick to it throughout the partie. Spread the remaining eight face down to form a talon.

Carte blanche. *A* dealt hand devoid of court cards is called a 'blank' or *carte blanche,* and may be declared for 10 points. If you have one, you must declare it immediately, and (if elder) prove it by rapidly dealing your hand of cards one by one face up to the table. If you get one as younger, you declare it immediately but don't prove it until after elder has drawn cards from the talon.

The draw. Elder must discard at least one card, and may discard up to five, drawing the same number of replacements from the top of the talon downwards. If as elder you take fewer than five, you may peep at those you did not take, other than the last three, without showing them to younger.

When elder has drawn, younger may discard up to as many as remain – usually three – and similarly draw replacements from the top of the remaining talon. As younger, however, you are not obliged to draw any if you think it safer not to. Furthermore, as younger, if you leave any card or cards untaken, you may either reveal them to both players or leave them face down. What you may not do is look at them yourself without showing them to elder.

Declaring point. Elder, if he wishes to score for point, states the number of cards in his longest suit – for example, 'Point of five'. Younger replies 'Good' if she cannot match it, 'Not good' if she can beat it. If equal, she asks 'Counting?', and elder then states the total value of its constituent cards, reckoning Ace 11, courts 10 each, and numerals at face value. Again, younger replies 'Good' if she cannot match it or 'Not good' if she can beat it. If she says 'Equal', neither scores for point; otherwise, the better point-holder scores 1 per constituent card.

Declaring sequences. Elder, if he wishes to score for sequences, now states the length of his longest, e.g. 'sequence of four'. Younger replies 'Good' if she cannot match it, 'Not good' if she can beat it. If equal, she asks 'To?', and elder then states the top card of the sequence. Again, younger replies 'Good' if she cannot match it or 'Not good' if her top card is higher. If she says 'Equal', neither scores for point. Otherwise, the holder of the best sequence scores for it and any other sequence he or she can declare. Sequences of three and four score 3 and 4 respectively, of five to eight 15 to 18 respectively. (Sequences of three to eight are called, respectively, *tierce, quart, quint, sixieme, septieme, huitieme.* Quart is pronounced *cart.* The traditional way of declaring a sequence is 'I have a tierce', or whatever it may be. If younger has an equally long sequence and seeks clarification, reply 'Tierce (quart, etc.) major' if it is headed by the Ace, 'minor' if by the King, otherwise 'to the Queen', and so on.)

Declaring sets. Elder, if he wishes to score for sets, now announces his highest-ranking quatorze or trio, e.g. 'Fourteen Queens' (etc.), 'Three Tens', or whatever. A higher-ranking set beats a lower, but any quatorze beats a trio. Younger replies 'Good' or 'Not good', as the case may be. Whoever has the best set scores for it and any other they may hold. Trios score 3 points each, quatorzes 14.

Leading. All such declarations having been made, elder plays a card face up to the table, saying, and scoring, 'One for leading'. Before younger responds, however, the scores so far announced verbally may be noted down, together with any bonus scorable for *pique* or *repique.*

Pique, repique. If either player reaches a score of 30 or more for declarations before the other has scored anything at all in the deal, he adds a bonus of 60 for repique. Here it must be noted that scores accrue strictly in this order: blank, point, sequence, set. If, therefore, either player scores for blank or point, the other cannot score repique for reaching 30 on sequences or sets. Conversely, scoring for sets alone offers no protection from repique if the other player reaches 30 while scoring for sequences. (Some claim that declaring equality for point or sequence prevents the opponent from claiming repique, but, if you intend to follow the official rules drawn up by the Portland Club, this is not the case.)

Pique is a similar bonus, but can be scored only by elder. If elder, by adding to his declarations points made in the play of tricks, reaches 30 before younger has made any score at all, then elder counts an additional 30 for pique. Younger cannot make it because elder's point for leading to the first trick takes effect before younger's score for combinations.

Tricks. Tricks are played at no trump. Suit must be followed if possible, otherwise any card may be played. The trick is taken by the higher card of the suit led and the winner of each trick leads to the next. Score 1 for winning a trick to which you led, or 2 for winning a trick led by your opponent. A convenient way of recording this is to store 1-point tricks face down and 2-point tricks face up on the table. *(The trick-scoring rule is usually stated '1 for leading to a trick, 1 for capturing the lead, and 1 for winning the last trick'. My wording amounts to the same thing, and I think it is easier to follow.)*

For winning a majority of tricks – that is, seven or more – score an additional 10 'for cards'. For winning all 12 tricks, score 10 for cards plus 30 for *capot*.

Game score. Scores are cumulated at the end of each deal ready for the next. Whoever has the greater total normally scores 100 plus the difference between the two final totals. If, however, the loser fails to reach the rubicon of 100 points, then the winner scores 100 plus *both* players' totals. So, for example, if you win by 160 to 110, you score 100 + (160 – 110), making 150; but if you win by 160 to 90, your score is 100 + (160 + 110), making 360. The rubicon bonus applies even if the winner fails to reach 100. If both players have the same score at the end of six deals, another two deals are played to break the tie.

A hand of Piquet

Let's follow a sample hand played by (for the sake of argument) Napoleon and Josephine. Josephine deals, making Napoleon elder hand, and the cards are:

Nap: ♠A K J ♡A Q J 8 ♣J 8 7 ♢9 8
Jos: ♠10 7 ♡10 9 7 ♣K Q 10 ♢A Q J 10

Napoleon has up to five exchanges, and hopes to draw more hearts and the 'fourteenth' Jack. He therefore discards ♠K and the two low clubs and diamonds. Josephine must keep her fourteen Tens, as it is obvious from her own hand that Napoleon cannot have a higher-ranking quatorze, and discards ♠7 ♡9 ♡7. After the draw, the hands are:

Nap: ♠A J 9 8 ♡A K Q J 8 ♣J 9 ◇K

Jos: ♠Q 10 ♡10 ♣A K Q 10 ◇A Q J 10 7

Declarations proceed as follows:

Nap Point of five.
Jos (also having a point of five) Worth?
Nap 49.
Jos (with 48) Good.
Nap In hearts. And a quart major. *(Meaning a sequence of four to the Ace.)*
Jos Good.
Nap That's five for point, four for the sequence, making nine . . . *(Looks for another sequence to count, but fails to find any. His next call is somewhat tentative.)* Three Jacks?
Jos Not good.
Nap (leading ♡A) And one's ten.
Jos I count fourteen Tens and three Queens, seventeen.

Tricks are played as follows, each announcing their score upon winning a trick.

Nap	Jos		
♡A	♡10	(1)	*Nap* Eleven
♡K	◇7	(1)	*Nap* Twelve
♡Q	◇10	(1)	*Nap (playing three hearts at once)* Thirteen,
♡J	◇J	(1)	fourteen,
♡8	◇Q	(1)	fifteen.
◇K	◇A	(2)	*Jos* Nineteen . . . *(then leads four clubs at once)*
♣9	♣A	(1)	twenty,
♣J	♣K	(1)	twenty-one,
♠8	♣Q	(1)	twenty-two,
♠9	♣10	(1)	twenty-three.
♠A	♠Q	(2)	*Nap (capturing the Queen)* Seventeen,
♠J	♠10	(1)	eighteen, and ten for cards, twenty-eight.

Napoleon did right to lose the lead after his first five tricks. If he had led spades immediately, he would only have divided the tricks, and failed to score 10 for cards. Josephine's 'fourteen Tens' served her in good stead. Usually, elder expects to score 28 to younger's 18 or so.

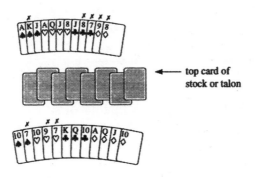

top card of stock or talon

Figure 9.1   Piquet

Napoleon, as elder hand, can discard and draw five cards. Wishing to keep his point in hearts and to draw the fourth Jack, he discards those marked with a cross. This leaves three for Josephine, whose main aim is to retain the diamond point and four Tens.

Notes on play

The difference in strategy as between dealer and non-dealer is more marked in Piquet than in any other two-hand game save perhaps Cribbage. Elder starts with all the advantages, being entitled to five of the eight cards of the stock, having the lead and so determining the point of attack, and being alone able to score for pique. Younger's draw of usually only three cards is rarely sufficient to rescue a bad hand from disaster – it is, in fact, possible for younger to hold all eight cards of a suit and yet lose every trick. For this reason elder is usually in a position to take chances and play an attacking hand, while younger should look first to keeping guards in all suits and not take chances that might weaken them.

To start, then, elder should always seek to exchange his full entitlement of five cards, for to take fewer is to waste his overwhelming advantage and to give younger considerably more room to manoeuvre. If he takes only four cards instead of five, he has reduced his advantage by 20 per cent but increased younger's by 33 per cent. Cards taken in excess of those he feels necessary to his hand are not wasted, as younger does not merely fail to get them but does not even know what they are.

As elder hand, which five cards should you throw out? This is a problem that beginners find hard to solve, as they tend to feel that only non-combinable and non-trick-winning Nines, Eights and Sevens should be discarded, and if they have only three or four such cards will prefer to take fewer than their entitlement. What you should do, however, is to look at it the other way: decide which cards you must retain for the best chances of combining, and throw out the rest.

Of those to retain, the most important are usually those of your potential point – the suit of which you hold the greatest number of cards, or, if equal, that with the highest pip-values or best chances of turning into a sequence. The point in this hand, for example, is hearts:

♠A K J 10 ♡Q J 10 9 ♣A Q ◇K 9

since there are twice as many chances (King or Eight) of converting it to a quint than there are of drawing the Queen necessary for a quint in spades. Furthermore, this quint is 'good against the cards' – meaning that it is obvious from your own cards that younger could not possibly draw an equal or better sequence. The discards from this hand, therefore, are ♠J ♠10 ♣Q ◇K ◇9.

Discards are also made with a view to completing a quatorze, and problems can arise because this combination tends to conflict with the discarding requirements of a point or sequence. The hand above was not complicated by this factor because it contained two each of the valid ranks, thus ensuring that younger cannot score so much as a trio, but not offering strong enough chances of filling a quatorze to allow this hope to influence the discards. Furthermore, the potential quint would have been, if realized, good against the cards.

But this superficially similar hand is far from easy:

♠A K J 10 ♡J 10 9 8 ♣A K 7 ◇K

Again, there are virtually twice as many chances of making a quint or better in hearts (5 to 4 against, or 44 per cent) as a quint in spades (3 to 1 against, or 25 per cent). This time, however it is not good against the cards, as younger might fill, or even have been dealt, an equal or better sequence in diamonds. Furthermore, you have three Kings and would prefer to keep them with a view to drawing the fourth, especially as younger may wind up with fourteen Queens. Since it is vital to restrict younger's entitlement to not more than three cards, you are faced with two possible ways of discarding from this hand. First, keep the heart sequence and the Kings, neither of which is at present good against the cards, and discard ♠A ♠J ♠10 ♣A ♣7. Or, second, keep the Kings and the potential spade quint, discarding the hearts and bottom club and drawing to ♠A K J 10 ♣A K ♢K.

(A third possibility is to forget the Kings and keep both spades and hearts in the hope of making two quints and repique, but the chances of doing so are too remote since only four cards can be exchanged.)

The chances of drawing the fourteenth King are the same in both cases. In the first case there is a 1 in 4 chance of making the quint; in the second there are 4 in 9. But although the latter gives better odds, it would lose if younger had a sequence of six in diamonds, and might tie if he has a quint, whereas the quint major in the former would be good against a diamond quint.

Further, if younger gets only five diamonds instead of six, the retention of spades here stands a better chance of scoring for point because the cards held are higher in value (as it stands, worth 31 against only 27). On the whole, then, case 2 is the safer holding against younger's possibilities, even though case 1 gives better chances on the face of it.

To summarize, elder should nearly always exchange the maximum of five cards, unless the hand dealt is so strong as to contain a quint or quatorze and the chance of (re)pique or capot. The longest suit should be kept intact for point, or, if suits are of equal lengths, then that with the highest count or longest sequence should be retained. A trio should be kept intact with a view to the quatorze, except that a trio of Tens or Jacks may be broken if the cards show that younger may hold a higher ranking quatorze and there are other pressures for discarding from them. If it becomes essential to choose between keeping the point or the trio, go for the point. Having classified cards into those that must be kept for combinations and those that need not, prefer to discard unneeded Aces and Kings rather than discard fewer than five, unless this spoils the chance of capot. If discarding requires it, don't hesitate to unguard Kings or Queens. Discard from as few different suits as possible. Unless it contains a card needed for a combination, it is often as well to throw the whole of a suit as part of it, and sometimes even better.

As younger handed your approach is quite different. Having normally only three cards to exchange, you have considerably less opportunity to draw to high combinations. The question of tricks is also of greater importance, since – to take an extreme case – you can be capoted though holding a handful of high cards, if they are of suits in which elder is void. Whereas elder can usually expect to take more tricks with an average hand and proper play, younger must usually discard and fight to at least divide them.

Your first concern, then, after looking for carte blanche, is to ensure adequate coverage in all suits to avoid the danger of capot. A hand such as this:

$$\spadesuit A\,K\,J\,9\,8\,7 \quad \heartsuit J\,10\,9 \quad \clubsuit Q\,9 \quad \diamondsuit 8$$

will lose every trick if elder has no spade in hand, which seems very likely. Here it is vital, before thinking about combinations, to cover the three weak suits by discarding spades. Even the lowly $\diamondsuit 8$ must be retained, to act as a guard in case the King is drawn. Of course, the probability of drawing one card in each of the three suits is very low, but at least two should be drawn to defend against capot. Even then it may be hard to find the right discards to elder's winning leads. Quite apart from tricks, the potential combinations are not worth much. From the cards, there is every chance that elder will hold seven diamonds, and even six clubs would be worth more than your six spades. (Assess this quickly by noting that your spade suit lacks cards counting 20 in face value, whereas his six clubs would lack only 19.) And if you drew $\clubsuit Q$ for a quart major, he is likely to hold at least a quint in diamonds.

This hand, however, is an extreme case of weakness for tricks, and is introduced only to point out that a good-looking hand at first sight must be looked at very closely before any discarding decisions are made. As far as combinations are concerned, judge your discards in much the same way as for elder hand. Two points must be noted, though. First, don't aim for a particular combination if it means unguarding a suit or losing a vital trick. And second, although it is best for elder to exchange his full entitlement of five cards, as younger you should not hesitate to take only two or even one if it means throwing good cards after bad. In this case (unlike elder's situation) any cards you leave remain out of play instead of going into your opponent's hand.

To summarize: as younger, discard defensively with a view to retaining coverage in sufficient suits to avoid capot. Don't take all cards available if this means throwing out guards or trick-winners, and don't waste good cards in going after high combinations which are not good against the cards. Other things being equal, always keep your point suit, as it is your best and cheapest defence against pique/repique.

The next important part of the game is not the playing of tricks but the announcement of combinations. Practised players often enter the play with a pretty shrewd idea of their opponent's holding, gleaned from what he has announced in declarations together with an estimate of which of the other cards are more likely to be out of his hand than in it. For this reason it is important not to say more about your holding than you really need in order to establish whether or not your declaration is 'good'. Suppose, as elder, you hold:

♠Q J 10 9 ♡A Q J 10 ♣A K 10 ◇10

You call a point of four; younger asks its value, and replies 'not good' to your 40. Your next declaration is 'fourteen Tens', with not a word about the sequence. Why? Because if point of four is not good at 40, younger must have a point of four worth 41, and from your own holding you can see this to be ◇A K Q J. Your sequence of four is bound to be not good, so to mention it at all would only be to give him gratuitous information about your hand. Again, if as elder you held fourteen Kings after exchanging five cards, but had not seen hair nor hide of an Ace, there would be no point in announcing them unless younger took fewer than three cards, as he would certainly not have thrown an Ace with Kings against him.

Similar considerations apply to younger. Suppose you hold:

♠A Q J 10 7 ♡8 7 ♣Q J 10 ◇K 9

Your discards were two diamonds and a club. Elder calls a point of five. Without hesitation you should immediately announce 'good'. Since his point can only be in hearts, it must be worth at least 49 to your 48 in spades, and there is no point in giving away free information.

It is because so many of the opposing cards are known by the time tricks are played that it has been said, in reference to this part of the game, that 'in Piquet, there are no surprises' – which is not quite true, but worth bearing in mind. Elder should normally lead his point suit from the top down, unless headed by a tenace (A–Q or, more especially, K–J); younger, when no longer able to follow, will start discarding from the bottom of his point, unless he is confident of gaining the lead and winning tricks with the whole of his point. A time for elder not to lead his point is when it lacks the top card and there is pique to be made by leading a non-point winner. For example:

♠K Q J 10 8 ♡A K Q ♣A K ◇K Q

Elder has scored nothing for point (younger having 48 in diamonds), but has made 25 from a quart, a tierce, fourteen Kings, a trio of Queens, and 1 for leading. Leading hearts and clubs, instead of spades, gets him to 30 for tricks and 30 for pique.

In defending against elder's point lead, younger must do everything to avoid unguarding suits, even to the extent of throwing out winners from his own point. For example, suppose younger holds:

♠Q 8 ♡Q J 9 ♣K 7 ◇A K J 10 8

Elder has counted point six and three Aces, and then leads his six spades. Younger must throw diamonds from the bottom up after playing his two spades, for if his sixth card is a heart or club he may well be capoted. If possible, of course, younger should keep his point and throw low cards from other suits if this can be done without losing the guard.

The addition of the rubicon has added much interest and excitement to the strategy of the game by sometimes making it vital to play to the score. If your opponent is well in the lead by the sixth deal, while you are still short of the rubicon, you are faced with a nice problem: whether to go all out to reach it, taking chances and playing boldly if need be, or, instead, to go for as few points as possible, by seeking equalities in combinations and playing to divide the cards. (If you are rubiconed, remember, your opponent adds your own score to his, plus 100 for game.)

If elder is trailing at the last deal and feels unable to reach 100, he will do best to sink everything he holds, even if *(especially* if!) this includes a quint or quatorze – in other words, declare nothing and let younger count whatever he holds as good. There is no point in trying to equalize. As elder, you may be convinced that younger has point five and quint major as well as yourself, but if you declare either of them, younger will simply announce good and let you make the score, since it will ultimately be credited to his own account. In trying to divide the cards, elder must not allow younger to manoeuvre him into taking the majority by 'suicide' play to tricks. Younger does not mind who wins the cards, so long as they are not divided.

If the positions are reversed, younger is somewhat better placed for declaring equalities, since elder has to announce first, and younger can sink as much as may be necessary to equalize. For example, suppose you hold a point consisting of K–Q–J–10–7, worth 47. Elder declares a point of four. You ask its value; he replies 'thirty-nine'. You announce 'equal', sinking nine from your face value, and neither scores. Elder next announces a tierce to the Queen. Again, you equalize. By sinking the King, you also have a tierce to the Queen.

(Some players only allow whole cards to be sunk, thus making it illegal to sink nine from K–Q–J–10–7 since that value does not correspond to a card held. This debatable point, not covered by the Portland Club Laws, should be agreed beforehand.)

It is easy to see the value of sinking for the purpose of keeping one's score low when certain of being rubiconed, but some other advantages are less obvious. The author of the following extreme example, 'Cavendish', pointedly adds: 'It is useless to practise this stratagem against an indifferent player who does not count your hand'. In other words, you can't bluff someone who is half asleep. Elder holds:

♠A K Q J 9 8 7 ♡K ♣A K ◇A K

After equalizing on point (younger having seven hearts), elder could next call fourteen Kings. But this would give his hand away. If younger knows he has the singleton ♡K, he will play everything except his red Ace to be sure of taking at least one trick. Elder therefore sinks one King, knowing from his own hand and discards that younger cannot possibly beat it. Younger asks him which King he does not count, and elder (of course) replies 'hearts', which younger may believe or not, as he wishes. This puts younger in the unenviable position of choosing whether to throw all his hearts to elder's lead of spades in order to retain a guard in clubs or diamonds, or to hold back ♡A until the last trick in case elder has not discarded the King. By sinking, elder drops 11 points (counting 3 instead of 14 for Kings), but has a good chance of making capot – except, as Cavendish says, 'against a very acute or very stupid player'.

Part Three
TAKE YOUR PARTNERS

10 | BRIDGE

Not so much a game, more a way of life

Bridge – properly known as Contract Bridge to distinguish it from previous varieties of the game – is basically Whist but with trumps established by bidding rather than by turning the last card. The difference made by this seemingly small point is truly phenomenal. What it means is that most of the information about the lie of cards that in Whist you have to deduce from the play is, in Bridge, largely conveyed before any card is played by means of the auction – a period of play in which players communicate with one another in a highly condensed code. While Whist will serve you in good stead when it comes to the actual play of the hand, a sound grasp of bidding requires much concentrated study and lots of practice before you can safely sit down with regular players. For this purpose it is desirable, first, to study at least one reputable book specifically devoted to Bridge for learners; second, to take a course and get some assisted practice at a local adult education centre; and third, to join a local Bridge club and learn how to learn from playing with (or against) experienced practitioners. There are also private tutors, of course, if you can afford them.

Here it is only possible to offer a general introduction to the game, sufficient to give you some idea of whether or not you are going to find all the above worthwhile. Before you start, you should know that Bridge is played in several different formats. For home and informal play there are two possibilities: Rubber Bridge and Four-deal Bridge, or Chicago. In Rubber Bridge, a rubber is the best of three games, and a game is won by the first side to reach 100 points below the line over as many deals as it takes. As a rubber may take anything from 10 minutes to over an hour to complete, traditional Rubber Bridge is best if there are just four of you.

Chicago, on the other hand, consists of exactly four deals and therefore consistently lasts about 20–30 minutes. This makes it more suitable if you have enough players for two or more tables and wish to change partners or opponents after each game, or if you have an odd number of players so that one or more are sitting out at any one time.

The third format, Duplicate Bridge, is a club or tournament game, in which pairs of players compete with one another by playing the same hands at different tables. The effect of this is to cancel out the 'luck of the deal' so far as any one team is concerned, thus producing (theoretically) a win for the team that played, overall, with the greatest skill.

Rubber Bridge

General idea

Four players, sitting crosswise in partnerships, each receive 13 cards from a well-shuffled 52-card pack. An auction is held to determine what contract shall be played. A contract is an undertaking made by one partnership to win a stated number of odd tricks in return for naming the trump suit, or specifying 'no trump' if preferred. Odd tricks are tricks in excess of six. Thus a bid of 'one club' is an offer to win at least seven of the 13 tricks with clubs as trump, and a bid of 'seven no trump' an offer to win all thirteen without a trump suit.

When no one will bid any higher, the last-named bid becomes the 'contract'. The player who first named the contracted trump suit is the 'declarer', and the members of the opposing partnership are called the 'defenders' – illogically, as they are not so much *defending* anything as *attacking* the contracts. Declarer's partner, after the opening lead, lays his hand of cards face up on the table as a dummy, and Declarer plays from both hands.

If successful, Declarer's side scores 'below the line' (towards game) for the number of odd tricks contracted and won. Any overtricks earn 'premiums' (bonuses) above the line. Premiums for honours and slams also go above the line. If unsuccessful, the defenders make appropriate scores above the line, i.e. not counting towards game.

A game is won by the first side to reach 100 points below the line. This can only be done by winning a contract, not beating one. The rubber is won by the first side to win two games, and the winners score an additional premium which is larger if the losing side failed to win one game. A side that has won one game is described as 'Vulnerable', and is subject to certain extra premiums for success, or extra penalties for failure. The effect of vulnerability, if not its purpose, is to discourage a side that has won a game from deliberately seeking high but unsound contracts for the sole purpose of preventing the other from winning a game.

As befits its social status, Bridge tends to be played with great formality and is accordingly equipped with a multiplicity of procedural niceties amounting almost to ritual. The beginner should learn these from the outset in order to avoid potential embarrassment when playing in formal situations – in other words, as a form of social self-defence.

Preliminaries

Bridge is played with a single 52-card pack, but it is customary to use two such packs distinguishable from each other by the colour or design on the reverse. Both are shuffled, one is spread out face down on the table and each player draws a card from it. The two drawing the highest cards become partners (unless partnerships were agreed in advance), the highest having first choice of seats, right of first deal, and choice of which pack to deal from. For the purpose of drawing and playing, cards rank high–low A K Q J 10 9 8 7 6 5 4 3 2 in each suit. Of drawn cards equal in rank, spades beat hearts beat diamonds beat clubs.

Shuffle and deal

On the first deal, the player at Dealer's left 'makes' (shuffles) the pack to be dealt from while Dealer's partner makes the other. The pack when made is set face down at the maker's right, as his right-hand opponent will be next to deal. Dealer takes the shuffled pack from his left and sets it face down for his right-hand opponent to cut. Having completed the cut, Dealer distributes the cards face down one at a time in clockwise rotation starting with the player at his left and finishing with himself.

The auction

Each in turn, Dealer first, must do one of the following:

■ Pass, which in Britain is normally done by saying 'No
bid'. This does not of itself prevent a player from
bidding later.

■ Make a bid, which must be higher than any previous
bid. The lowest bid is 'one club'. A higher bid is made
by increasing the number of tricks bid or offering the
same number but in a higher suit. For this purpose suits
rank upwards thus: clubs, diamonds, hearts, spades, no
trump. Thus 'one club' can be overcalled by 'one'
anything else, but 'one no trump' only by raising the
level to 'two' or more. The highest possible bid is
'seven no trump'.

■ Announce 'Double' if the previous bid was made by an
opponent. This offers (or threatens) to double whatever
score is won or lost if the last-named bid is established
as the contract.

■ Announce 'Redouble' if the previous announcement
was an opponent's 'Double'. This offers (or threatens)
to quadruple the scoring value of the proposed contract.

A double or redouble is automatically cancelled if followed by
another bid, whether or not in the same suit as the one doubled.

The auction ends when a bid, or a double or redouble, has been
followed by three consecutive passes.

The last-named bid becomes the contract, and its suit, if any, is
trump. The member of the contracting side who, in the auction, first
mentioned the eventual trump suit, or who first bid 'no trump' if
such is the contract, becomes the Declarer.

If all four pass immediately, the cards are thrown in and the next
deal made by the next player in turn to do so.

Play

Declarer's left-hand opponent leads to the first trick by playing any
card face up to the table. Declarer's partner then lays his hand of
cards face up on the table in four columns, one for each suit, each

running from high to low towards the Declarer, and spread just sufficiently to enable each card to be identified. The trump suit (or clubs, if none) should be placed at dummy's right, i.e. Dealer's left as he faces it.

Declarer plays second to the trick from dummy, and fourth to the trick from his own hand. Normal rules of trick-taking apply. Follow suit if possible, otherwise you may play any card. A trick is taken by the highest card of the suit led, or by the highest trump if any are played, and the winner of each trick leads to the next.

Declarer, upon winning a trick, leads from whichever of his side's two hands furnished the winning card. His partner not only takes no active part in the play but may not communicate anything to Declarer by way of advice, suggestion, criticism, query, appeal, horror, apoplexy, etc. The most he may do is call attention to errors of procedure, such as Declarer's failing to follow suit from dummy when able to do so, or leading from the wrong hand upon winning a trick.

The defenders keep all their won tricks together, customarily in front of the partner of the first defender to win one.

Revoke

A player who fails to follow suit though able to do so has committed a revoke. What happens then is too complicated to detail here, and if you are going to play the game seriously you will need a copy of *The International Laws of Contract Bridge*. Briefly, however, if neither the offender nor his partner has yet played to the following trick, the offender may retract the wrong card and play a correct one, and anyone who played after it may retract his card and play another. Furthermore, if the offender was one of the defenders, his incorrect card becomes a penalty card and is laid face up on the table, and so does that of his partner if it is retracted and replaced. If a penalty card is an honour, it must be played at the next legal opportunity; if not, it must be played in preference to any other card of that suit below the rank of an honour. (That is, when that suit is led again, the offender is allowed to play an honour, if he wishes, and to leave the penalty card in abeyance.)

If the offender or his partner plays to the next trick without correcting it (other than to the thirteenth, when it can still be corrected), the revoke is established. In this case, the offending side must concede two tricks to the opposition if they won the trick of the revoke, otherwise one trick. (There are further complications and provisos, but this will suffice for home play.)

Scoring

Each player keeps a scoresheet divided into two columns, one for each side, and divided into an upper and a lower half by a horizontal line. Scores are recorded below the line for tricks contracted and made, and above the line for overtricks, bonuses and penalties.

All scores are recorded individually, not cumulatively. When one side's below-line scores total 100 or more (as can readily be seen 'by inspection'), a second horizontal line is drawn beneath their last score and across both columns. A new game begins, with both sides scoring below this line as before. The side that has won one game is now 'vulnerable', and subject to certain increased rewards and penalties. Another line is drawn when a second game has been won. If it is won by the same side, the rubber ends, and the side with two games gets a bonus before scores are totalled. If not, a third game is played, both sides now being vulnerable, and the rubber ends when either side has won its second game. This carries a smaller bonus.

The rubber ended, each side totals all the scores made above and below the line in its column. The difference between the two side's totals is the margin of victory. The rubber bonus is usually (but not inevitably) sufficient to ensure that the side that won two games will win overall, regardless of above-line scores. Slam bonuses, however, are so great that the scores they attract above the line are capable of outweighing a rubber bonus made by the opposing side.

Details of scoring are presented in the table on page 109. The following notes explain and amplify it.

If the contract succeeds, the declaring side scores below the line a number of points for each trick bid and won. For example, if the contract was 'two' and they made three, they score only for two below, the third counting as an overtrick and so being scored above the line. The actual score per trick depends on which suit was trump, if any, and is affected by doubling or redoubling. Note that a successful contract of three no trump suffices for game, the score

Table of scores at Contract Bridge

tv = trick value (20 or 30), D = doubled, R = redoubled, V = vulnerable

Contract made: *Declarers score below the line for each trick bid and won:*

in a minor suit (♢♣)	20	D	40	R	80
in a major suit (♠♡)	30	D	60	R	120
at no trump, for the first trick	40	D	80	R	160
at no trump, for each subsequent trick	30	D	60	R	120

Declarers may also score above the line:

for each overtrick (if not vulnerable)	tv	D	100	R	200
for each overtrick (if vulnerable)	tv	D	200	R	400
for making a doubled or redoubled contract	–	D	50	R	100
making a small slam	500	V	750		
making a grand slam	1000	V	1500		

Contract defeated : *defenders score above the line:*

for the first undertrick	50	100	200	if not vulnerable*
	or 100	200	400	if vulnerable
for the second and third . . .	50	200	400	if not vulnerable
	or 100	300	600	if vulnerable
plus, for each subsequent undertrick . . .	0	100	200	if not vulnerable

Honours : *scored above the line by either side holding in one hand*

any four of A K Q J 10 of trumps	100
all five of A K Q J 10 of trumps	150
all four Aces at no trump	150

Rubber scores :

if opponents won one game	500
if opponents won no game	700
for winning the only game	300
for being the only side with a part-score in an unfinished game	50

*That is, if the declarers are not vulnerable.

being 40 + 30 + 30 (= 100). Any overtricks they may make are scored above the line. In normal circumstances (undoubled) they score at the same rate as those scored below the line. If doubled or redoubled, however, they each score 100 or 200 respectively, and twice this if the declarers were vulnerable. In addition, any successful contract that was doubled scores a flat bonus of 50, or 100 if redoubled, 'for the insult'.

A successful small slam (contract of six) carries a flat bonus of 500, increased to 750 if made when vulnerable. A grand slam (contract of seven) scores twice these amounts. They are not in themselves affected by doubling or redoubling. Note that slam bonuses accrue only if the relevant number of tricks has been bid – if you win six when you only bid five, you don't score for the small slam. By way of compensation, there is no extra penalty for failing a slam bid: one trick down is one trick down, regardless of the size of the contract.

If the contract goes down (fails), the defenders score above the line a certain amount for each trick by which the declarers fell short of their contract (undertricks). The actual amount per undertrick does not depend on the trump situation, but does vary according to doubling and vulnerability. The rarely occurring bonus for the fourth and each subsequent undertrick applies only in the case of a doubled or redoubled contract, and is additional to that of previous undertricks. Thus, if the declaring side, vulnerable, bid five spades and was doubled, the possible range of scores according to the actual number of tricks taken is then as follows:

Declarers

13: 300 below, 200 above, 50 above ('for the insult')
12: 300 below, 100 above, 50 above
11: 300 below, 50 above

Defenders (above)

10: 200 for first undertrick
 9: 500   = 200 + 300 for the second
 8: 800   = 200 + 300 + 300
 7: 1200   = 200 + 300 + 300 + 400 . . .

and so on.

The score for honours is credited above the line to the side of whichever of the four players was dealt the four or five honours concerned. (Note that honours can be scored by either side, though it is rare for them to be in a defender's hand.) As it is lost if not claimed before the next deal, it is advisable for their holder (if not dummy) to announce 'honours' upon playing the last of them to a trick. The scores are minimal and are not affected by doubling or vulnerability. A rubber can be won only by the declaring side and upon winning its second game. This carries a bonus of 700 if they won two games straight off, or 500 if three were played. If, for any reason, the rubber was not finished, but one game was completed, the side winning that game scores 300 for the rubber. If play ended before a game was completed, and if only one side has made a part-score (less than 100) in that game, then they score a bonus of 50. This is not of itself sufficient to carry an incomplete rubber bonus of 300, but may be made in addition to it if play ended during the second game.

Example of scoring

	WE	THEY	
g	50		
g	200		
f	500	150	c
e	100	60	c
a	30	100	b
a	60	100	c
f	120	80	d
g	80		
h	60		
h	500		
	1700	**490**	
	−490		
	1210		

(a) We bid 2♠, made 3♠, scoring 60 below for the bid of two and 30 above for the overtrick. (b) We bid 3♥, were doubled, and made only two. They score 100 above for the undertrick, doubled. (c) They bid 3NT and made five, scoring 40 for the first and 30 for the other two below the line, plus two overtricks for 60 above. One of them held four Aces, gaining 150 for honours. They win the first game to our part-score of 60. A line is drawn to mark the game, and they are now vulnerable. (d) They bid and make 4♣, scoring 80 below the line. (e) They bid 2♠ and make one, giving us 100 above the line for the undertrick (they being vulnerable). (f) We bid and make a small slam – 6◊, for 120 below the line, giving us a game and making ourselves vulnerable. We also count a bonus of 500 above for the slam. (g) We bid 1NT, are doubled, and make three. This gives us 2 × 40 below the line, plus 200 above for the (doubled) overtrick made when vulnerable, plus 50 'for the insult' (making any doubled game). (h) We bid and make 2♡ for 60 below, giving us the second game and 500 for the rubber. Our margin of victory is 1210.

Notes on bidding and play

Bridge is essentially a partnership game and this is nowhere more apparent than in the auction. In the play of the cards, Declarer becomes the lone and star performer, and, while there is scope for co-operation between the defenders, much of that is founded on information co-operatively exchanged during the auction – whether their own if they had a chance to bid, or, if not, by inference from that of the declaring side.

Bidding is a means of communication between partners. Its primary purpose is to ensure that they reach the best possible contract for the 26 cards held between them. This involves conveying as much information as possible to each other about their respective hands. The potential of bidding as a language derives from the fact that specific information can be conveyed by means of artificial bids, or 'conventions'. Whereas a natural bid is one you would be quite happy for the partnership to engage in as a contract, a conventional bid merely requests or conveys information. It rarely represents a serious contract, which could well be disastrous if played.

The standard British bidding system, called Acol, is widely used by both home and tournament players, and has considerable currency outside its country of origin. It has the advantage of being based on natural bids, but easily incorporates conventions and bidding sequences originally devised for other systems. It is important to note that the laws of the game forbid either partnership to use any system or individual convention which is unknown to the other side. Before play, both partnerships must state which system they are using (Acol, etc.) and with what artificial bids and conventions.

Strength and distribution

The most basic information you want to communicate about your hand is its *strength*, in terms of high cards such as Aces and Kings, and its *shape*, or relative distribution of the four suits.

Strength is measured in 'high card points', abbreviated to hcp. Each Ace in your hand counts 4 hcp, each King 3, Queen 2, and Jack 1. As there are 10 hcp in each suit, and 40 in the whole pack, a hand counting 10 hcp is about average.

Shape, or distribution, denotes the relative numbers of cards you hold of each suit. If your 13 cards are divided 4–3–3–3 or 4–4–3–2, your hand is described as balanced, even, or 'flat', and suggests a no-trump bid. If it contains a long suit of five or more, your hand is unbalanced, and suggests a bid in the longest suit. Distributions of 4–4–4–1 and 5–3–3–2 are borderline cases. The first is not balanced but contains no obvious long suit. Whether it better suits a trump or no-trump contract depends on its hcp and how it fits in with your partner's hand. The pattern 5–3–3–2 contains a long suit, but if this is a minor suit you may consider it as potential no-trump material. This is because, at lower bidding levels, you score more for a no-trump contract than for a minor suit contract requiring a greater number of tricks.

High card points should not be counted too rigidly, as they can be affected by distribtuion. For example, a hand consisting of all 13 cards of one suit counts only 10 hcp, but is as good as 40 since it will win every trick in a contract based on that suit. Similarly, you should deduct a point if your hand contains a singleton King, or has no Aces. When you and your partner have agreed a suit, you can also add points for short side suits of two or fewer cards. But distributional points must be considered with caution, as they don't become a fixed quantity until a suit is agreed. Once added, you may subsequently have to remember to subtract them again.

Bidding

The aim of the auction is for the side with the best potential contract to discover and bid it. What you and your partner are looking for is a fit, which means either the suit in which you hold between you the greatest number of cards, or a complementary distributional pattern between both hands more suited to a no-trump contract. The minimum comfortable trump requirement for a one-in-suit contract is eight cards of that suit between you. Seven is feasible and even fewer may be playable, though with fewer than seven you will certainly be in the wrong contract. For no trumps, a fit means having all four suits stopped between you. A suit is stopped if headed by an Ace or a guarded honour – that is K x, Q x x, or even, at worst, J x x x. ('x' means anything lower than a Ten, its precise numerical rank being irrelevant to the point at issue.)

In bidding towards a contract, you will be considering whether to aim for a part-score, a game, or a slam. A part-score is one that is not enough to win you the current game. 'Game' denotes a contract that brings your score to 100 or more below the line from a score of zero – that is, 3NT (100), four of a major suit (120), or five of a minor (100). If five in a minor looks probable, you will prefer to test the possibility of reaching 3NT instead, as this requires you to win only nine tricks for game, as opposed to eleven in a minor suit.

It helps to know that a game at NT or in a major suit requires 26 or more points between you, and in a minor suit at least 28. Standing at zero, your first concern will be to go for game if possible. If you already have a part-score, you will be looking for another part-score sufficient to complete the 100 points, and need not bid any higher than absolutely necessary to achieve this object and overcall your opponents' bids.

The following table of points actually scored by all possible contacts, including slam bonuses but disregarding the effects of doubling and vulnerability, is worth examining for the light it throws on their relative values.

	♣	♦	♡	♠	NT
1	20	20	30	30	40
2	40	40	60	60	70
3	60	60	90	90	100
4	80	80	120	120	130
5	100	100	150	150	160
6	620	620	680	680	690
7	1140	1140	1210	1210	1220

This makes it very clear that at lower levels, where the bidding mostly takes place, minor-suit contracts are hardly worth pressing if there is any chance of a major-suit or no-trump fit, even at a lower level, except for the purpose of overcalling the other side's bids. It is only at slam levels that this discrepancy is wiped out and minor suits come into their own.

The time to be more ambitious is when you gather from the early auction that a slam may be in the offing. A slam brings huge rewards if successful but does not lose any more than usual if unsuccessful – unless you are vulnerable, when you must bid more cautiously. A small slam normally requires about 31–33 points in a suit or 33–34 at no trump, and a grand slam 37 points.

This leaves a dead zone of rather unrewarding contracts between the levels of game and a small slam, i.e. four or five no trumps and five of a major suit. As we shall see later, this dead zone offers a patch of bidding space in which to exchange useful information about the possibility of attempting a slam.

We must, however, start at the beginning, which means with mundane low-level bids designed to convey preliminary information to one another about the nature of your hands. Here it is necessary to distinguish four types of bid as follows:

- An *opening bid is* the first one of the auction. Dealer has the first opportunity to make the opening bid, but, if he passes, the right to do so passes round the table until someone exercises it. Beginners sometimes fail to grasp the fact that the opening bid is by definition the first one of the whole auction, regardless of who makes it.

- *A responding* bid, or response, denotes, for our present purposes, the first bid made by the partner of the player who opens the bidding.

- *A rebid,* apart from its obvious general meaning, specifically denotes the second bid made by the opener in the light of his partner's response.

- An *intervening bid,* or overcall, is one made by either opponent of the opening bidder. Most significantly, it denotes the first bid made by an opponent of the opening bidder. It may intervene between the opening bid and the response, or between the response and the opener's rebid.

We can ignore intervening bids to start with and assume that the opening bidder and his partner make all the running. This does happen often enough to be realistic – perhaps not half the time, but not far off.

The first thing you and your partner need to discover is how many points you hold between you. If it's around 26 points, you should expect to make a game contract (that is, worth 100 below the line). If the points are divided 13–13, it is the responder's responsibility to make sure game is reached (for example, $1\heartsuit - 4\heartsuit$, or $1\heartsuit - 3NT$). If they are divided 16–10, the opener will make an intermediate rebid to show that his hand is not minimum and responder will then bid game (for example, $1\diamondsuit - 1\spadesuit$, $3\diamondsuit - 3NT$). When the points are divided 19–7, it will be the opener's responsibility to make sure game is reached once his partner makes a response ($1\diamondsuit - 1\spadesuit$, $4\spadesuit$) or ($1\diamondsuit - 1\spadesuit$, 3NT).

Opening one in a suit

The commonest opening bid is one in a suit. You make it with a hand containing 13 to 21 points and a reasonable rebid in case partner responds by bidding in your weakest suit. If you have six or a good five of the suit you bid, you can reduce the minimum requirement to 12 or even 11, but you must have a sensible rebid available because of the 'unlimited' nature of this opening – that is, your partner won't know whether you have a few as 12 or as many as 21, or something in between, and whatever it is makes a big difference to how your partner assesses his hand. The very fact of opening invites partner, if strong enough, to respond in his best suit, and your sensible rebid will be necessary in case his best suit is your worst.

Given the minimum requirement, open with your longest suit. For example, in the left hand, below, open one diamond. This gives you a sensible rebid of two diamonds over any response except one heart, which you can raise to two. With two 5- or 6-card suits start with the suit higher in bidding value, for example hearts in the right-hand example. This enables you to show your lower suit (clubs) at the 2-level, thereby conveying useful information about your hand and keeping your options open.

♠ x x   ♠ x
♡ Q J x x   ♡ K Q J x x
◇ A Q J x x   ◇ K x
♣ K J   ♣ A K x x x

Which to open of two four-card suits depends on whether or not they are 'touching', i.e. adjacent in bidding value, such as hearts and diamonds. Textbook procedure is to open the higher suit first. This enables you to name the lower suit if your partner responds, leaving either of you the possibility of going back to the first suit without having to raise to the level of three. Naming the lower first, then the higher at the next level, is a 'reverse' bid suggesting a high point-count (16+) and demanding a response. (Some players now tend to bid the lower suit in any case. Either way, the important thing is that you and your partner should stick to whatever system you have agreed upon.)

Of non-touching suits, bid clubs first if the other is spades. Otherwise, the choice is less easy. You may want to bid spades before diamonds in hope of finding a major suit fit first, or clubs before hearts in order to keep your exploratory opening bids at a safe level. If in doubt, the mechanical answer is to bid the four-card suit ranking immediately beneath the shortest suit held. A more creative guideline is to consider all the probable responses to either bid and make whichever of them will not give you a rebid problem.

If you want a rule for two 4-card suits that is both easy to remember and likely to be safe whether the suits are touching or not, I suggest the following: bid hearts first if this is one of them, otherwise diamonds, otherwise clubs.

With three 4-card suits, bid the one below the singleton, or hearts if the singleton is clubs.

Responses to 1 in a suit

Now swap positions and suppose you are responding to an opening bid of one in a suit.

With fewer than 6 points, pass. Your partner could have a minimum 13, and will not thank you for your support if you turn out to have 18 or fewer between you. If he has substantially more, he can always bid again.

With four or more cards of the suit bid, raise it to two on 6–9 points, three on 10–12, four on 13–15.

Without a fit, but with a biddable suit of your own and up to 15 points, bid it at the lowest possible level. If the lowest level is one, 6 points will do; if two, at least 8 are needed. With 16 or more points, jump to one level higher than necessary. This is forcing to game: it shows you have enough strength between you for a contract worth at least 100 and possibly a slam, and tells your partner not to pass before reaching game level at least. You may also jump with slightly fewer points if your suit is six or more cards long.

With neither a fit nor a distinctive suit of your own, but with a balanced hand suitable for no trump, offer one no trump on 6–9 points, two on 10–12, three on 13–15.

Opening two clubs

The two-club opening is a convention which has nothing to do with your actual holding in clubs but denotes any hand counting at least 23 points and 5 quick tricks (qt). Quick tricks are ones you can expect to make in the first two or three rounds of each suit. A suit headed by A K = 2 qt, A Q = 1½ qt, A = 1 qt, K Q = 1 qt. K x = ½ qt. It forces partner to keep bidding to game (unless you yourself stop it at 2NT).

The following hand, counting 23 points and a total of 5 qt, demands a two club opening:

♠   K Q x
♡   A K J x x
♢   A Q x
♣   K J

Partner must respond positively to this opening if he has at least 1½ quick tricks or a good 8–9 points, and can offer a major suit or no trumps at the two level, or three of a minor suit. As it is a forcing bid, however, which prevents him from passing, he must have access to a conventional negative response in case he has nothing to declare. In this case the negative reply is (logically enough) the lowest he can possibly make, i.e. two diamonds. If then you see no prospect of game, as here, you can sign off by bidding a perfectly acceptable 2NT.

If partner does respond, however, you can start developing the auction in other directions. For example, a response of two hearts would offer prospects of a slam in hearts, which you would explore by methods of slam bidding (see below). Two spades would be worth raising to four for an immediate game, and two of a minor suit would give you a safe rebid of three no trump. Either of these might then prompt your partner to start looking for a slam.

Opening two in a suit other than clubs

The so-called 'strong two' opening also has a special meaning, but, unlike two clubs, it is natural rather than conventional, in that you name a genuine prospective trump. It doesn't require any particular number of points, but indicates strength in one of the following respects:

■ Eight or more playing tricks and a long major suit headed by at least A–Q, such as:

♠   A Q J x x x x
♥   x
♦   A J
♣   A x x

■ Two long suits, worth exploring for a possible fit, such as:

♠   —
♥   A Q J x x
♦   x
♣   A K Q x x x

■ A point-count almost high enough to open 2♣ but lacking the requisite five quick tricks, such as:

♠   K Q J
♥   K Q x x x x
♦   Q
♣   A K x

You must be prepared to bid again, as a strong two opening is forcing for one round. The negative response, in case partner has nothing to offer, is 2NT, which you can leave as the final contract.

What happens if you feel your only natural suit bid is two clubs, which you can't make because it doesn't qualify for the two-club convention? Well, you only have two choices. If the suit is long enough, open three clubs as described below. If not, open one club, and hope the auction stays open so you can repeat the suit at a higher level next time round.

Opening three in a suit

Open three on a weak hand containing one suit of at least seven cards, which, so far as you can see, is useless for anything but a bid in that suit, such as:

♠ x
♡ J x x
♢ K Q J x x x x x
♣ x

A three-bid is 'pre-emptive', in that you don't normally expect to make such a contract, but would rather try it and go down than allow the other side to open up communications and possibly make a high-scoring contract cheaply. The main requirement is that you should expect to win six tricks in your own hand, or seven if vulnerable. It is best made from third position after two passes, thus discouraging the fourth player, who probably has a biddable hand, from opening except at a dangerously high level. You don't make it from fourth position yourself, of course, as you have no one to pre-empt. In this case a bid of 'one' will suffice after three passes. It isn't usual to open more than three in a suit, since strength is indicated by opening at the two level, and a three-bid specifically implies weakness in all but one quarter. An opening bid of four may be regarded as the same as three, but stronger by one trick.

1 No Trump opening and response

No-trump openings are made on balanced hands (4–3–3–3, 4–4–3–2, or 5–3–3–2 with a long minor suit), with stops (defensive tricks) in at least three suits, and, unlike one-in-suit openings, falling into a precise and narrow range of high card points. The main reason for this is that if your partner has an unbalanced hand, with a good prospective trump, he will want to know early on how much support he can expect from you in side suits in order to judge how far to go with his own suit in case a slam is on. Alternatively, he may also have a balanced hand, in which case, since no-trump contracts earn more points for fewer tricks, it is particularly desirable to bid to the most accurate level. For these reasons it is essential that you open in no trumps only within the agreed range of points for the level at which you bid, never so much as one point below that range or, even more importantly (since the temptation is greater), above it.

One no trump may be opened 'weak' on 12–14 or 'strong' on 16–18 points. Which it is must be agreed between you and your partner beforehand. Some partners agree to play a 'variable' no trump, opening strong when vulnerable and weak when not. Some prefer a strong no-trump regardless of vulnerability, but the modern tendency is to prefer 'weak' throughout. A weak no trump has the advantage – except after three passes – of a pre-empt, in that it prevents the other side from opening communications below the level of two. At the same time, its limited nature enables your partner to assess more accurately how safe it is to respond at that level himself.

The following hands may be opened at 1NT (weak):

♠	A K x	K x x x	x x x
♡	x x	A Q x	K J x x
◊	Q x x x	K x x x	K Q J x
♣	Q J x x	J x	Q J x

The following should not:

♠	x x x	K J	A x x
♡	K J x x	A J x x	K x x
◊	J x	x x	K Q J x
♣	A K J x	K x x x x	Q x x

The first should be opened one club, having two weak suits but the possibility of a major suit fit. The second should also be opened one club, being wrong in shape: 5–4–2–2 is acceptable for no trump, but not when one of the doubletons is unstopped and the other ill-headed against a bad break (of A–Q). The third counts 15, which is too many. Open one diamond and switch to no trump next time round.

In responding to a NT opening, your options are to pass, to raise the NT bid, or to try a suit take-out.

Given a balanced hand, raise 1NT (weak) to 2NT on 11–12 points, 3NT on 13–17, 4NT on 18–19, 6NT on more. The 4NT response invites opener to go for the small slam (6NT) if he bid on not less than the maximum 14 points. However, points are not everything, especially at low levels, and hands counting less than 13 should be passed if they contain an obvious weakness. Raise 1NT (strong) to 2NT on 10–12 points, 3NT on 13–18, 4NT on 19–20, 6NT on 21–24.

Given an unbalanced hand with a long major suit in the range of 0–7 points (or 0–10 if vulnerable), bid two of that suit. This is a 'weak take-out': it means 'I can't support no trumps, but your hand will support a contract in this suit, so pass and leave me in it' – which your partner is then obliged to do. You can take-out into diamonds, but as two of a minor suit scores no more than 1NT, only do this if you are sure the suit contract is safer than one in no trumps. As for two clubs, this has a special meaning.

A response of 2♣ to an opening 1NT is the Stayman convention. It means 'I have enough points to look for a game, but would prefer it in a major suit, as I hold at least four cards in both of them. Which one can you best support?' If partner cannot support either, he gives the (equally conventional) negative response of 2◇, enabling you to remove to 2NT if need be. If he can, he will bid two of his major suit, and you can take it from there, in whatever direction seems best. The Stayman convention can be extended into a response of 3♣ to an opening 2NT. Stayman is extremely useful if you play a lot. The only problem with it otherwise is that the appropriate situation may occur so infrequently that you forget to use it, or don't recognize it when you partner does.

2NT opening and responses

Open two no trumps on a balanced hand containing 20–22 points. Partner should pass with 0-3 points, but with a balanced hand should reply 3NT on 4–10, 4NT on 11–12, 6NT on 13–14, leaving you to raise any of these if your count was maximum. Alternatively, he may take you out into three of a suit in which he holds at least five cards.

There is no point in opening a balanced hand at more than 2NT. If the hand is worth 3NT, indicate your strength by opening with a conventional two clubs. This is forcing to game level anyway, while allowing you plenty of bidding space in which to explore the possibility of a slam.

Intervening bids

We have so far taken it for granted that only one side is doing the bidding, their adversaries meanwhile respectfully murmuring 'no bid' and touching their forelocks from time to time. What often happens, however, is that one side starts the auction, the other side immediately intervenes, and a period of interaction at the one and two levels (or even higher, given freakish distributions) eventually results in one of the partnerships dropping out of the auction. An intervening bid is what you may make if the bidding has been opened by the player on your right, or on your left followed by two passes.

An intervening suit bid at the one level requires length rather than strength. A 10-point count suffices with a five-card suit, and you can deduct a point for each card in excess. Thus

    ♠   x
    ♡   K Q x x x x
    ◇   x x x
    ♣   A x x

while not qualifying for an opening bid in first position, would rate a bid of one heart over a minor-suit opening from your right. With 13–15 points you can overcall at the two level. For example, change a minor-suit 'x' to a King on the above hand and you could overcall an opening one spade. With no long suit but 16 or more points you could overcall with 1NT.

Informatory or 'take-out' double

An intervening bid may take the form of a purely conventional double. This is typically made when the player on your right deals and opens one in a suit. A double in such a position cannot possibly arise from a genuine expectation that the auction will stop there and the contract be beaten. It therefore has a special use, indicating (in effect) 'My hand is strong enough to open but weak in the suit bid. Show me a suit and I will support it or make some other constructive response.' Partner should then respond as he would do if you had opened the bidding.

Slam bidding

When you obviously hold between you a lot of points and have agreed a suit with a good fit, the player who took the initiative will want to find out whether his partner has enough of the outstanding Aces and Kings for a playable slam. He will usually do this by means of the Blackwood convention, whereby bids of 4NT and 5NT ask about Ace and King holdings respectively.

Suppose you deal and find yourself with this:

- ♠ K Q
- ♡ A Q J x x
- ◊ A K x
- ♣ K J x

With 23 points, you open two clubs. Your partner replies two hearts. Good! He has at least 1½ tricks and you have a fit in hearts. Translating his tricks into at least 6 or 7 points, you have at least 29–30 between you and will be thinking of a slam. The quick way of doing this is to bid a 4NT immediately. Since 3NT would suffice for game, 4NT should be interpreted as agreeing the heart suit and seeking further information by means of the Blackwood convention.

Blackwood asks your partner to say how many Aces he holds by responding to 4NT as follows:

5♣ shows no Aces held (or all four)
5◊ shows 1 Ace
5♡ shows 2 Aces
5♠ shows 3 Aces

Suppose partner replies five hearts, showing two Aces. With four between you, a small slam is likely. Whether or not you can bid a grand slam depends on who holds the heart King. You therefore launch into phase 2 of Blackwood by bidding 5NT, asking for Kings on the same scale (except that four Kings is indicated not by 6 but by 7 clubs). If partner replies six diamonds, he has the King, and you can finally call seven hearts – not 7NT, as you could lose a trick in a minor suit.

If he replied six clubs, you would know the trump King to be off-side and would therefore sign off at six hearts. Similarly, if in response to your 4NT partner had shown only one Ace, you would have left it at five hearts. To have asked for Kings with 5NT, and got a negative response, would have left you in the impossible situation of having to bid the small slam lacking both an Ace and the trump King.

Blackwood need not be employed as precipitously as this. Given an agreed suit and the chance of a slam, bidding space can often be used to convey information to prevent the uncertainty described in the preceding paragraph. But this takes us beyond our brief and into books devoted specifically to Bridge, of which there are more than a few.

Declarer's play

The unique challenge of Bridge lies in planning, and then putting into operation, the line of play which will yield all the tricks you need from the two hands you can see. Even when it is obvious that there are enough trick-winners between them, it is not always obvious without careful examination exactly how the cards should be played and in what order. One permanent occupational hazard of Declarer is that of taking a trick in the wrong hand so as to make it impossible to get back into the other hand to win subsequent tricks. The other is that of not having enough obvious tricks, and having to work out ways of gaining the one or two extra you may need to make the contract.

In a trump contract it is usually right to attack and draw trumps as soon as possible, especially if you haven't as many of them as you would like and therefore need to establish winners in your long side suits without risking their being ruffed. As to side suits, it is often important to avoid cashing your immediate winners, but to keep them as defensive strongholds while you attack the suit or suits in which you have top card weakness. In other words, hang on to the suits headed A–K until you have driven out the adverse cards from those headed K–Q, Q–J–10, and so on. Always calculate how many tricks you can afford to lose, and lose them earlier rather than later as part of a constructive strategy to establish future winners, trusting that those you were dealt originally will not have walked away in the meantime.

Let's apply this to the following grand slam in hearts with dummy sitting west and yourself east.

♠	K Q	A x x
♡	A Q J x x	K x x x
◊	A K x	J x x x
♣	K J x	A x

First, count your tricks. In spades, three, but remember to keep back the Ace until the King and Queen have made. In diamonds, two, and you must find a way of losing the 'x' in dummy to a trick won in hand, perhaps by ♠A. In clubs, two. In trumps, assuming the worst case that they fall two to a trick, five. Total twelve. One missing. Where is the thirteenth coming from? The only safe answer is to ensure that one of the trumps from the shorter holding – the one in your own hand – can be used to ruff a lead from dummy. At some stage in the proceedings, you will want to lead ♣A from hand, followed by a low club to the King, followed by dummy's third club for you to ruff.

How is this hand likely to go? If clubs are led, which seems likely, you will take with the Ace, return a club to the King, lead your last club, and ruff it in hand, leaving you three tricks up with ten to go and clubs safe. Next, draw some trumps by leading a low one to the Jack followed by a low one to the Queen. At this point, being in dummy, win tricks six and seven with the spade King and Queen. Now get back into hand with dummy's last low trump to the King, and play off the ♠A, to which you can now discard the dummy's useless diamond. This leaves you with only diamonds in hand, enabling dummy to take the remaining four tricks with the two top diamonds and two outstanding trumps.

Sometimes, when your initial survey reveals a trick short, you may find the only chance of developing another trick is to risk a finesse, which may be defined as an attempt to win a trick with a lower card when a higher one is held (or accessible). Suppose, in the above contract, dummy's diamond holding were A–Q–J and yours 10–8–6–3. You might decide that the only way of getting home is to go for a second trick in the suit against the King. A finesse always depends upon the critical card lying in one rather than another of the adverse hands. For it to work here, the King must be in South's hand and you approach it by leading low. If South plays the King, you win with the Ace; if not, you hope he held it up and go for a win with the Queen. If North has the King, the Queen will lose, and the finesse will fail. Situations do occur in which you can theoretically finesse against either defender, but you still have to choose which one to attack, as you can't take on both at once. Whichever way you look at it, a finesse is a 50–50 chance, and should be avoided if there is any safer way of winning the trick you need.

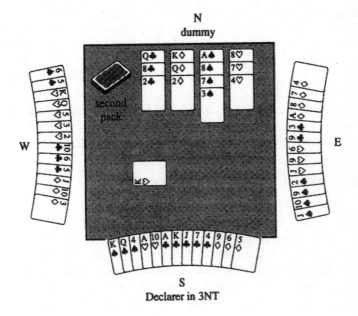

S

Declarer in 3NT

Figure 10.1   Bridge

South, with 17 points and long clubs, opens 'one' of that suit. West intervenes with 1♡. North, after some thought, rejects No Trump and spade responses in favour of three clubs. East passes. South now counts at least 27 points between the two hands which is borderline for a game in clubs, but safer at no trump. This is duly bid; North passes, West attacks hearts by leading the King, dummy goes down, and the situation is as illustrated. It is usual for trumps to be set out to the left of dummy as seen by the Declarer, or clubs in a no-trump bid, as here. Declarer will probably make five clubs, one diamond, three spades and a heart, scoring 100 below the line and 30 above for the overtrick.

Defenders' play

Experience of Whist and other partnership trick games will be of value to your play as a defender. The main problem is knowing what to lead first before the dummy has gone down. It's usually desirable to avoid leading a suit mentioned by either opponent in the auction, and to lead one mentioned by your partner, unless you have a long suit of your own headed by the Ace, which you will want to make before it can be ruffed.

If your partner hasn't mentioned any suit, a standard opening lead is the fourth highest card (i.e. fourth from the top) of the longest non-trump suit in your hand. (This can give your partner maximum information about the lie of the suit by applying the old 'rule of eleven' – see Whist.)

Another satisfactory lead is an honour heading a sequence of three or more, such as Jack from J–10–9, etc., or a low singleton so that you can trump that suit when your partner returns it.

Four-deal Bridge ('Chicago')

As a home game, Chicago has two advantages. One is that a rubber is always four deals, so if two or more tables are operating it is possible for players to swap tables and partners without too much hanging around. The other is that its scoring system, essentially that of Duplicate (Tournament) Bridge, encourages players to bid up to the full value of their hands, so there is no question of 'Why bother to bid up to five clubs if we only need 20 for game?'.

The scoresheet needs only five rows divided into two columns, one for each side. There is no distinction between above- and below-line scoring: if a partnership makes its contract it scores in its own column; if not, the defenders score in theirs. Part-scores are not carried forwards from deal to deal (though they were originally, and many Americans still play this way).

In deal 1, neither side is vulnerable. In deals 2 and 3, non-dealer's side is vulnerable. (A modern development. Originally, dealer's side was vulnerable.) In deal 4, both sides are vulnerable. If a deal is passed out, the cards are gathered and (after the shuffle and cut) re-dealt by the same dealer, instead of being passed round to the next as in Rubber Bridge.

The score for a successful contract is the sum of two parts:

■ The natural score for the number of tricks actually made, including overtricks, and with any doubling taken into account;

■ If the contract value was less than game (100), add 50 for a part-score. If it was 100 or more, add for game 300 if not vulnerable, 500 if vulnerable.

The defenders' score for defeating a contract is the same as in Rubber Bridge. There is no score for honours, nor extras for the rubber.

11 | CANASTA

A game of basket-weaving

Canasta, the Bridge of the Rummy family, is a partnership game developed in Uruguay and Argentina some time around 1940. In 1949 it swept its way across the United States and became for a while the most preferred second-fiddle game of previously dedicated Bridge addicts. Just as it reached craze proportions in 1950s Britain, the American version started developing even more complex varieties such as Samba and Bolivia. These have long since passed, and Canasta itself has now settled down into the relatively quiet life of a card game classic.

Its name is Spanish for 'basket'. According to the author of *Culbertson on Canasta* (London, 1950): 'The Spanish word for "weaving" is *teniendo. Teniendo gas cartas,* that is, "weaving the cards", is a colourful Spanish way of saying that a meld of three of a kind, or more, is being "woven" together. And when the biggest meld of all, the canasta, is completed, you naturally have woven a "basket".'

But enough of colourful Spanish phrases. (Have you ever met a black and white one?) It's time to get weaving.

How to play

Cards. 108, consisting of two standard 52 packs plus jokers. They needn't all be of the same back design and colour, but must be of the same size.

Game. Partners sit opposite each other, North-South versus East-West. A game may consist of one or more deals and is won by the first side to reach or exceed 5000 points. If both sides reach it on the same deal the one with the higher total wins. Scores are recorded at the end of each deal.

Deal. Decide first dealer by any agreed means; thereafter the turn to deal passes to the left. Deal eleven cards each, in ones. Place the undealt cards face down and squared up in the middle of the table to form the *stock*. Turn up the top card of the stock and lay it face up beside the stock. This starts the discard pile – best referred to as the *pack* – which must also be kept squared up throughout the game. The card on top of the pack is known as the *upcard*. If the first upcard is a Joker, a Two or a red Three, it must immediately be covered by the next card of the stock, and so on until the upcard is of some other rank or a black Three.

With the stock and the first upcard settled, any player who has been dealt a red Three must place it face up on the table before him and is then dealt the top card of the stock to bring his hand back to eleven cards.

You are now ready to start play, but should first note the following basic facts about the game, which will give you an initial sense of direction.

Object. The object of the game is to collect and display on the table batches of three or more cards of the same rank, such batches being called melds. A meld of seven or more cards is a canasta, and no one can end the game until their side has made at least one canasta.

Jokers and Twos are 'wild' cards: they cannot be melded, but can form part of melds based on 'natural' cards by themselves (i.e. ranks from Four up to Ace). Threes have special powers, as outlined below.

All meldable cards have a melding value, which at the end of the game counts to your credit if they are lying in melds, but against you if still left in hand. The set values are:

Jokers	50 each
Aces and Twos	20 each
High cards (K Q J 10 9 8)	10 each
Low cards (7 6 5 4 and black 3)	5 each

In addition to the melding value of individual cards, each completed canasta carries a bonus of 500 if it consists entirely of natural cards, or 300 if it contains one or more wild cards. (These are known respectively as a 'natural' and a 'mixed' canasta.)

Black Threes may only be melded when you are going out, as explained later.

Red Threes are bonus cards. Every time you get one you must lay it face up on the table before you. They are worth 100 each (doubled if you get all four) and count in your favour if you have made any melds, but against you if you have not.

The game normally ends when one player 'goes out' by melding in one turn all the cards left in his hand.

Finally, you must be aware that Canasta is essentially a partnership game. Partners keep melds made by both of them together in one place on the table, not separately in front of each. And it is sometimes inadvisable to end the game by going out without first asking your partner's permission.

Play

Starting with the person at dealer's left, each player in turn does one or more of three things in the following order:

- ■ Draw (top card of stock, or discard pile if permitted);
- ■ Meld (if any possible, and subject to certain restrictions);
- ■ Discard (unless gone out by melding all cards left in hand).

Draw. You may always take the top card of the stock and add it to your hand. If you draw a red Three, you place it face up before you and draw again.

Instead of drawing from stock, you may take the whole of the pack, provided that you immediately meld the upcard – either by laying it off to one of your existing melds on the table, or by using it to start a new meld in conjunction with two or more matching cards from your own hand (for which purpose a matching natural card plus one wild card is sufficient, though some insist that you must hold a natural pair to start a new meld with the upcard).

But you may not take the discard pile in this way if it is *frozen,* which it is in the following circumstances:

- ■ It is frozen to you and your partner until your side has made its first meld.

■ It is frozen to everybody whenever it contains a wild card (or a red Three as the result of the initial turn-up).

In these cases you may only take the pack if you can immediately use the upcard to start a new meld in conjunction with at least two matching natural cards from your own hand. (If you have none on the table already, this may count as your initial meld provided it meets the initial meld scoring requirement described below under 'melds'.) Furthermore:

■ The pack is frozen to you personally if the upcard is a black Three. In this case you may not take it at all but can only draw from stock. (The pack is said to be stopped, rather than frozen.)

Melds. All melds made by you and your partner are kept together in one place. Subject to rules governing composition and value of melds, you may in your turn start one or more new melds, and/or lay off one or more natural or wild cards to any of your partnership's existing melds. Cards once melded cannot be retrieved for further play.

A meld must contain three or more cards, of which at least two must be natural, and not more than three may be wild. All natural cards in a meld must be of the same rank.

A canasta is a meld of seven (or more) cards, and may be melded outright or gradually built up by laying off additional cards to smaller melds. Once completed, the cards of a canasta are squared up in a pile, with a red card face up on top if it is a natural canasta (containing no wild cards), or a black card if it is 'mixed' (containing one or more wild).

A canasta must contain at least four natural cards, but there is no limit to the number of wild cards that may belong or be subsequently added to it. As soon as any wild card is laid off to a natural canasta, remember to replace the top red card by a black one.

Red Threes are not melded. Black Threes may only be melded if you go out on the same turn (see below).

Initial meld. The first melds or melds made by a partnership must total not less than a certain minimum value. This value depends on your partnership's cumulative score in the current game, as follows:

Score so far	Minimum meld
A minus figure	15
0 to 1495	50
1500 to 2995	90
3000 plus	120

You may count the combined values of more than one meld towards this minimum requirement, but you may not count the 500 or 300 point canasta bonus towards it, nor any bonus deriving from red threes.

Although the pack is frozen to you and your partner until one of you has made an initial meld of sufficient value, the initial meld does not have to be made entirely from the hand. Provided it meets the minimum requirement, you can make it by melding the upcard with at least two natural cards from your hand.

Discard. Having drawn a card or taken the pack, you complete your turn (whether you melded or not) by taking a card from your hand and placing it face up on the pack, unless in your turn you go out and have nothing left to discard. In discarding, note that:

- You may not discard a red Three.
- If you discard a black Three, you thereby freeze the pack to your left-hand opponent for one turn only.
- If you discard a wild card you thereby freeze the pack to everybody, and it remains frozen until taken.

To show that the pack is frozen, place the wild card crosswise on top of the pack, so that it will remain projecting from the pack in future turns, signalling the fact that it is frozen.

Ending by going out. The game normally ends when one player goes out by melding, laying off or discarding the last card from his hand. Going out is subject to certain rules and restrictions.

You may not go out unless your side has made at least one canasta. But you can meet this requirement by melding or completing a canasta on the turn in which you go out. It is only when you are going out that you may meld three or four black Threes.

If after drawing from stock you are in a position to go out, you are permitted (but not required) to ask your partner's permission. If you do ask, you must do so before melding any card at all. The correct wording is 'May I go out, partner?', to which he must reply either Yes or No. You are then bound by his reply. In fact, if he says Yes and you find that you cannot go out after all, you are penalized 100 points.

You get a bonus of 100 for 'going out blind', that is, if you personally have not previously melded anything during the course of the current deal. But you only qualify for the bonus if all your cards are meldable in their own right – you don't get it if you lay off cards to your partner's melds.

Ending by exhausting stock. Somebody usually goes out before the stock is used up, but in case they don't, this is what happens. If you draw the last card from stock and it is a red Three, turn it face up, make whatever melds you can, but don't finish with a discard. That ends the deal.

If it isn't a red Three, play in the usual way and finish with a discard. The next in turn must then take the pack (by melding the upcard) if legally able to do so. If he can't, the deal ends.

If he can, he makes his play and then discards. From now on the 'pack' will only ever consist of the previous player's discard. If on your turn the previous discard matches one of your melds, you are obliged to take it, lay it off, and then discard. If it doesn't match, but can still be melded with the aid of cards from your hand, you may either take no action, in which case the deal ends, or you may make your meld(s), in which case you must discard unless you go out.

This continues until any player in his turn either goes out or fails to take the previous player's discard because unable or unwilling to do so.

Scores. Each side reckons its score first for bonuses and then for cards. Note that if your side has melded nothing at all then any red Threes you have drawn don't count as bonuses but as penalty cards additional to all unmelded cards remaining in you and your partner's hands.

Bonuses

For going out	100
or, for going out blind	200
For each red Three	100
or, for all four	800 (total, not each)
for each natural canasta	500
for each mixed canasta	300

To these bonuses, each side adds the total face value of all the cards they melded, counting:

Cards

Joker	50
Ace, Two	20
High card (K Q J 10 9 8)	10
Low card (7 6 5 4 and black 3)	5

From the combined total for bonuses and cards, each side now subtracts the total meld value of all cards remaining unmelded in the hand. The side that went out, of course, will have cards left only in one hand; the other side will have two handfuls to count against them. If a player proves to have a red Three in hand, having failed to expose it on the table, it counts 500 against his side.

Notes on play

Canasta is not one of those Rummy games in which the main object is to go out for a quick bonus, but one in which the main object is to build up a large score by making as many melds as possible. The side that melds first gains an immediate advantage, having, as it were, hatched the goose that lays the golden eggs, and they should go on exploiting this advantage for all it is worth. As soon as the other side has caught up, the first side should be in or approaching the position at which it has the minimum canasta requirement for going out – not for the sake of using it quickly, but for its power as a threat to the opponents.

When you get a real chance of going out, you should wait until you have a good reason for doing so. For example:

■ Despite your lead and initiative, your opponents are now beginning to catch up or even threatening to overtake you;

■ Your opponents are so far ahead that going out is your best defence against a huge loss.

■ You may have been dealt the sort of hand on which a 'quick out' will produce a small profit without your having to work too hard for it. But this does not happen very often, and you needn't go out of your way to look for it.

Otherwise, your main aim should be to break into a scoring vein as soon as possible, get as much out of it as you can while the going is good, and pull out when your advance begins to lessen – or, if you find yourself on the wrong side, to prevent your opponents from doing the same thing, even to the extent of pulling out prematurely if you consider the task hopeless.

How to set about this? Inevitably, this aspect of the game revolves around the taking of the pack (the discard pile). Even if it contains no more than three or four cards, it is nearly always advantageous to the player who takes it, and most of your play will be directed towards this end. Usually the first side to take the pack is then able to seize the initiative and dictate the course of the game. If your opponents get it first, you must be prepared to play defensively until you can afford to meet them on their own ground.

Initial meld

At start of play your immediate aim is to make the initial meld that will set you off on a scoring spree. So strive for it – but not at the expense of all other considerations. In particular, try to meld as economically as possible. The fewer cards you keep in hand, the less chance you have of taking the pack, so it can be self-defeating to use up too many in making an initial meld. For this reason you should also prefer not to make your initial meld entirely from the hand: wait until you can meld by taking the pack, so as not to deplete your hand unnecessarily.

In subsequent rounds of play, when your initial meld requirement advances to 90 or 120, you may have to accept the sacrifice of more cards in order to compensate for the extra difficulty of meeting the minimum value. Even so, you should try not to spend more than four cards for the 90, or six for the 120.

Further melding

Having started, make as many melds as you can, in order to keep the pressure up and increase your ability to take the pack. The more melds you can lay off to, the greater difficulty your opponents have in finding safe discards. Don't hesitate to devalue natural canastas by adding wild cards to them, and don't cripple yourself for the sake of working towards the bonus for going out blind. The bonus is fine if your hand happens to lend itself to that fortunate prospect; but if not, forget it.

There are times when you can usefully exercise restraint in making melds. The question of economy is one of them, as it was in the case of the initial meld: don't part with too many cards, and in particular don't part with any which may be of use in capturing the pack later. For the same reason it is also sensible to refrain from melding when the discard pile is large: the more cards you keep in hand the more chance you have of taking the pack. A good time to do your melding is when the pack has just been taken, even if not by yourself.

The importance of completing your first canasta is obvious, as it puts you in a position of constant threat (to go out). It is also important throughout the game not to fall behind in the completion of canastas, for which purpose mixed canastas, though less profitable than natural ones, are infinitely better than none at all.

Freezing the pack

It is a beginner's irritating habit to freeze the pack for no better reason than that he happens to be able to, and can't think of anything else to do. So when is it right and when is it wrong to freeze?

The most important time to freeze the pack is when your opponents have started melding and you have not, as it is your only effective defence against their ability to keep on recapturing it for continual rewards. Freezing is also a good defensive move when your opponents have too many cards in hand and melds on the table, as it enables you with relative safety to discard their players (cards which match their melds and would otherwise enable them to take the pack) and improve the overall meldability of your own hand.

When the pack is frozen it helps to have a hand containing many pairs, as they give you more chance of capturing it. But this doesn't mean that a hand full of pairs is a good excuse for freezing the pack. You obviously don't want to freeze it when it seems highly probable that the other side can easily take it. Finally, avoid freezing for no better reason than that you can't decide what to discard. In the long run this can do you more harm than good.

Black Threes

If you can find a better discard than a black Three, make it, and save the Three for the time when it's the only solution to an otherwise impossible position. Given a black Three early in the game, a good time to discard it is often when you have just made an initial meld. Since it freezes the pack to your left-hand opponent only, it prevents him from taking the pack before your partner has a chance to take advantage of the position.

Wild cards should be put to work, not hoarded. Each one added to a meld is a bird in the hand when it comes to the score. The same goes for Aces.

Discarding

Discard low in early rounds, as such cards are not suitable for initial melds. Watch the discards made by your left-hand opponent and try to match them for as long as you feel he is genuinely throwing away unwanted cards. Since your right opponent will be watching you with the same objective in view, don't make things easy for him by automatically throwing out singletons. There are times when you can quite happily discard from three or more, so that when he subsequently discards the same rank you can capture the pack and meld. The only time to concern yourself seriously with your partner's discards is when there is a real danger of your opponents' going out. By matching your partner's discards in this situation you may save yourself a lot of penalties.

The time to throw out cards matching your opponents' melds is when the pack is frozen and they appear to have little chance of capturing it. Any cards that are of no use to you but possibly of use to them are best reserved for discarding until the pack is small.

Going out

We have already noted that going out is more of a defensive measure than anything else, either because you are too far behind and want to cut your losses, or because your opponents are beginning to catch up and you don't want to cut your profit margin. Watch the timing. A good time to go out is when your opponents have too many cards in hand.

Sample game

All Rummy games are difficult to notate and inconvenient to play in sample form, but Canasta, with 108 cards, is virtually impossible. Here instead (Figure 11.1) is an illustration of the end position of a game, showing how the score is calculated.

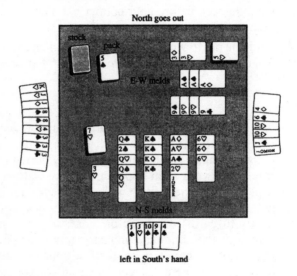

Figure 11.1 Canasta

You have just given your partner, North, leave to go out. Your side scores 100 for going out, 100 for the red Three, 300 for the mixed canasta (black Seven on top) and 90 for its component cards, 245 for melds on the table, total 835 less the 45 in your own hand, total 790. East-West score 200 for the red Threes, 500 for the natural canasta (red Five on top) and 35 for its component cards, 100 for melds on the table, total 835, less 160 for cards left in both hands = 675.

12 | EUCHRE

A Country and Western game

A partnership trick-taking game that is older than Bridge, Euchre is played in the West Country of England on a highly organized league and championship basis ranging from Bristol to Taunton to Exeter, where its popularity is equivalent to that of Cribbage in other parts of England. Judging from references to it on the Internet, its popularity seems to be spreading throughout southern England. It also has many followers on the other side of the Atlantic, and throughout the latter part of the nineteenth century was one of the most popular home and social games of the United States and Australia. Nowadays, the Australians play a hybrid of Euchre and Bridge known as Five Hundred, which you will find in Chapter 16.

Euchre's chief claim to fame is the fact that it is the game for which the Joker was invented. Here's how it came about. In Euchre, the two highest trumps are the Jack of the trump suit and the other Jack of the same colour, known respectively as the Right Bower and the Left Bower. Bower doesn't mean 'one who bows': it comes from German *Bauer*, meaning (literally) 'farmer' and (secondarily) 'Jack'. In the 1860s American players started adding to the game the blank card that was customarily included in every pack, counting it as the highest trump of all, or Best Bower. Playing-card manufacturers responded to this use by overprinting this card with the phrase Best Bower, accompanied by an arbitrary pictorial design, such as an eagle. The design that eventually won out was that of a jester, and it seems quite likely that the word Joker was suggested by the name of the game. Here it is necessary to note that 'Euchre' is a bizarre spelling for a word pronounced Yooker and deriving from a German game originally spelt Jucker (which also means Jack). In short, the Joker amounts to a highly glorified Jack.

In England, the Best Bower is often represented by the ♣2, and is called (the) 'Benny'.

The following description is of the modern English game, which differs in slight respects from the nineteenth-century American game still recorded in most card-game books. The old version was played with 33 cards, including Sevens and Eights, which meant that virtually two-fifths of the pack was out of play. The modern reduction to 25 cards has halved this chancy aspect and resulted in a more skill-rewarding exercise. It remains to add that not all schools follow exactly the same rules (and the British Euchre Association now appears to be defunct), so be prepared to encounter local variations.

How to play

Players. Four, in fixed partnerships.

Cards. Twenty-five, consisting of A K Q J 10 9 in each suit plus one Benny, which may be a Joker or the ♣2.

Game. In home play, a game is won by the first side to reach a previously agreed target score, traditionally 5 points. In tournament play, the first side to reach 21 points wins a leg, and a match is won by the first side to make two legs.

Shuffle and deal. The cards are shuffled before each deal and cut by the player at Dealer's right. Deal five cards each in two rounds of three and two respectively. Place the undealt five face down to one side and turn the top card face up. The suit of this card is the suit of preference for trumps.

Object. Players bid for the right to go for game with the turned suit as trump, or, if all pass, with a trump suit of their own choice. Game is three or more tricks. Winning all five scores double, and losing the contract loses double. The bidding player has the further option of playing 'alone', without any contribution from his partner, for a double score.

Rank of cards. The three highest trumps are:

    1. The Best Bower, or Benny (Joker or ♣2);

    2. Right Bower (Jack of trumps);

    3. Left Bower (other Jack of the same colour as trumps);

followed by Ace, King, Queen, Ten, Nine. In non-trump suits the cards rank A K Q (J) 10 9. Note that the suit of the same colour as trumps will be one card short because its Jack belongs to the trump suit and not to the suit it depicts.

Bidding. Each in turn, starting with the player at Dealer's left, must either pass or 'order it up', i.e. go for three or more tricks using the turned suit as trump. Ordering it up is so termed because, regardless of who makes it trump, the Dealer is entitled to take the turned trump into his own hand in exchange for any unwanted card, which he discards face down. A player intending to play alone must announce 'Up, down' without a pause. Ordering up ends the auction.

If all pass, the faced card is turned down and there is another round of bidding. This time each in turn has the right to bid game by announcing a different trump suit, and Dealer does not have the privilege of taking the originally turned card. The first to make trumps ends the auction. If the maker intends to play alone he must announce this as part of his bid, e.g. 'Alone, spades', or 'Spades, down' without a pause.

If all pass again the cards are bunched and the deal passes to the next player in turn.

If the faced card is the Benny, Dealer announces what suit he wishes it to represent *before* looking at his own hand. The auction proceeds as normal, except that there is only one round. If all pass, the cards are bunched and the deal passes on.

Going alone. If the maker announced 'alone' or 'down', his partner lays his hand of cards face down before the first trick is led and takes no part in the play.

The maker's partner may turn his partner down and play alone himself, but Dealer cannot be turned down if he has taken the turned trump.

If the maker (or his partner) plays alone, either member of the opposing side may then also elect to turn his partner down and attack the contract alone. As before, Dealer cannot be opposed alone if he has taken the turned trump.

Play. The opening lead is made by the player to the left of the lone player, if any, otherwise to the Dealer's left. Normal rules of trick-play apply. Follow suit if possible (remembering that the Benny and left bower belong to the trump suit), otherwise play any card. A trick is taken by the highest card of the suit led, or by the highest trump if any are played, and the winner of each trick leads to the next.

Score. The maker's side, if successful, scores:

for winning three or four tricks	1 point
for winning all five tricks	2 points
for winning all five alone	4 points

The score of 4 does not apply if the originally turned card was the Benny. The maximum score is then 2 points.

If the maker's side wins fewer than three tricks it is 'euchred', and the opposing side scores 2 points if both played, or 4 points if one played alone.

Revoke. A revoke (and, in tournament play, a misdeal) incurs a penalty of 2 points.

Notes on play

Euchre takes some getting used to if you approach it from Nap, Whist or Bridge. The main point of difference is the fact that the trump suit is longer than any individual non-trump suit, and in assessing your hand you can count Jacks as potential trumps. For example, suppose the turn-up is ♣9 and your hand is:

$$♠A Q ♡A J ◇J$$

If spades are trump your hand is worth about two half-tricks. You might win a trick by trumping a club lead, but your trump Ace is only fourth highest in its suit, being covered by three bowers. You might win a trick with the red Ace, but, with only four outstanding hearts against you, it is more likely to be trumped. Your Jacks and Queen are pretty useless.

If the turn-up were ◇K, your hand would be stronger. Your red Jacks are now second and third best trumps, and, if you dealt, you can take the trump King in exchange for the weak Queen. The hand is now worth at least three tricks.

If the turn-up were a heart, your hand would be strong enough to play alone, as you have the second, third and fourth highest trump, the turned trump itself, and an outside Ace. Whether it is worth playing alone is a moot point. It only nets a worthwhile bonus if you win all five tricks, which is unlikely as you lack the Benny. The chances are normally 50–50 of its being either with your partner's hand or in the undealt cards, but if your partner has already passed you had better reckon without it. You might just play it as a loner on the off-chance that it lies among the four unknown cards.

With a club turned, your hand is hopeless unless everyone turns the preferred trump down and you are able to choose your own suit. Obviously you will go for hearts, hoping to make three trumps, or two trumps and the ♠A, or two trumps and a trick from your partner.

As may now be obvious, skill at Euchre lies almost entirely in the bidding: in deciding whether to order up the turned suit, whether to name one of your own, and whether to play alone. With so few cards in play, it is hardly possible to exercise much strategy, as even the opening lead of a singleton Ace stands a good chance of being trumped. There is also little opportunity for communication between your own and your partner's hand.

Position is of particular importance in Euchre. In first or second position you should order it up if you have two good tricks and a possible third in your own hand, and have no especially strong suit that you would wish to call in the event that all should pass. In third position you need three good possibilities, as your partner has already shown weakness by passing. The same applies in fourth position, except that, as Dealer, you will reassess your hand more favourably by reference to the turn-up and the effect of your discard. In a second round of bidding, the non-dealing side should prefer to entrump the suit of the same colour as the turn-up ('make it next', in traditional terms), and Dealer's partner one of the opposite colour ('cross it'), for reasons which, if not obvious, should emerge from the following deal:

West deals and turns up ♠Q. (B is for Benny):

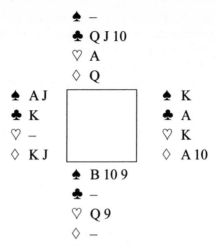

North passes, having nothing but the left bower (third highest). East passes, knowing that successful bids require trumps rather than the Aces and Kings which pass for strength in other games. South hesitates: he has three trumps, of which the Benny is unbeatable but the other two feeble. We will suppose he passes. West, also with three trumps after the exchange, orders it up and discards ◊J. North leads ♡A, and, although this is trumped by West, North-South defeat the contract by three-two. Post mortem examination shows that South, though right to hesitate, could have bid and made the contract.

Let's change the turn-up to ♣9. North, now with three good trumps and a singleton Ace, orders it up. West takes the turn-up in exchange for his red Jack, giving him three trumps including third best. By most lines of play, North-South win.

Change the turn-up, again, to ♡J. North and East unhesitatingly pass. South holds three trumps, including the Benny, and orders it up, though not without hesitation. West takes the red Jack turned up in exchange for his black Jack, and leads it to force out the Benny and weaken the contracting side in trumps. This deal could go either way. So far as I can make out, differing lines of play variously enable either side to win by one trick.

Finally, let's make the turn-up ◊9. The first three players again unhesitatingly pass. In West's position I would do the same. In the event, he would almost certainly win four-one by ordering it up, but he couldn't be expected to know about his partner's two helpful trumps. Suppose instead he also passes (by 'turning it down'). Has anyone now got a biddable hand? West's pass suggests weakness in red suits, so North and South will be looking to their red cards and East to his black. North and East will pass again. We have seen above that South could successfully bid hearts. Whether or not he would do so in actual play is more a question of psychology than strategy.

13 | DON

Latest version of a good Old English game

This increasingly popular partnership game, widely played on a league basis in England and Wales, is a modern development of the old English game of All Fours and the American game of Pitch. The following is the Lancashire version followed by the Bolton Don league.

How to play

Preliminaries. Four play in partnerships. The aim is to win counting cards in tricks. Scores for cards won are pegged on a cribbage board both during the play and at the end of each hand. Game is 91 points (one-and-a-half times round the board.)

Cards. Cards rank A K Q J 10 9 8 7 6 5 4 3 2 in plain suits, but in trumps the Five is highest and Nine the second-highest, producing the order 5 9 A K Q J 8 7 6 4 3 2.

Counters. The following cards are scored as and when captured in tricks during the course of play:

trump Five	10
trump Nine	9
trump Ace	4
trump King	3
trump Queen	2
trump Jack	1
each non-trump Five	5

Deal. Deal nine cards each in ones and stack the rest face down. The player at Dealer's right may not touch his cards until his partner has pitched – just to prevent any possibility of indicating which suit to pitch.

Play. The player at Dealer's left pitches a card to the first trick. 'Pitching' means leading a card of the suit he is making trumps. Whatever card he pitches establishes trumps, even if he pitched the wrong one accidentally. Players must follow suit if possible, otherwise may play any card. The trick is taken by the highest card of the suit led, or by the highest trump if any are played, and the winner of each trick leads to the next.

Score. Each side sorts through its tricks and pegs the appropriate amount for the counters won. The side winning a majority of card-points in that deal adds a bonus of 8 points. In case of a tie the bonus does not apply.

Play out of turn. A player who plays out of turn leaves the offending card face up on the table and must play it as soon as he legally can. In League play, the offending side also deducts 19 points from their score.

Revoke. Failing to follow suit when able to do so results in abandonment of the game and a redeal by the same dealer. In League play, the offending side also deducts 52 points.

14 | SPADES

The latest American craze

This relatively recent American Whist derivative is sufficiently popular and widespread to have become the subject of numerous clubs, tournaments and websites, so it is probably only a matter of time before it sweeps the rest of the English-speaking world. It is usually played by four in partnerships, but is easily adaptable for other numbers. It is full of variations and not subject to universally accepted official rules.

How to play

Preliminaries. Four play crosswise in fixed partnerships, using a 52-card pack ranking A K Q J 10 9 8 7 6 5 4 3 2 in each suit. Deal 13 each in ones.

Trumps. Spades, always.

Object. Each side's object is to win at least as many tricks as it bid.

Bidding. There is no competitive auction. Instead, each partnership contracts to win a certain minimum number of tricks.

First, the members of the non-dealing partnership discuss how many tricks they think they can win between them. You and your partner, in this situation, may tell each other how many tricks you can certainly win, how many you will certainly lose, and how many uncertain possibilities you have, but you may not give specific information about which cards you hold in any particular suit.

When you have agreed on how many tricks you are prepared to contract to win between you, this number is noted down, and the dealer and his partner then engage in a similar discussion.

Bidding 'nil'. If you think you can avoid winning a single trick in your own hand, you may declare 'Nil'. In this case your partner announces how many tricks he proposes to win. This establishes your side's contract, which will be lost if you, having bid nil, win any trick. Only one player per side may bid nil.

Play. To the first trick everyone must play their lowest club, so it doesn't really matter who leads. Anyone void in clubs must play any heart or diamond, but not a spade. Whoever plays the highest club wins the trick and leads to the next. Play as at Whist or Bridge, but with the restriction that trumps (spades) may not be led until the suit is broken – that is, until a player has used a spade to trump a trick when unable to follow suit. This does not, of course, apply to a player who has only spades in hand to lead.

Score. A side that takes at least as many tricks as its bid scores 10 times its bid, plus 1 per overtrick. There is a penalty, however, for consistent underbidding. When, over a series of deals, a side's overtricks total 10 or more (as witnessed by the final digit of their cumulative score), their score is reduced by 100, and any overtricks above 10 carried forward to the next cycle of ten. This is called sandbagging. (*Variant*: Each overtrick counts minus 1 point and there is no sandbagging.)

For example, a side has a score of 488, and on the next deal bid five and win nine tricks. This brings them to 538, plus four for overtricks, making 542. For the excess of 12 overtricks they deduct 100, bringing them to 442 and leaving them with an excess of two towards the next cycle.

For a failed contract, a side loses 10 points per trick bid.

For a successful nil bid, the nil bidder's side scores 50 points, in addition to the score won (or lost) by his partner for tricks made. If it fails, the nil bidder's side loses 50 points, but any tricks taken by the nil bidder may be counted towards the fulfilment of his partner's contract. Blind nil scores on the same principle, but doubled to 100.

Game. This is 500 points.

Part Four

GAMES FOR
THREE OR MORE

15 | HEARTS

Trying to lose tricks can be as tricky as trying to win them

Since its first appearance in America just over a century ago, this game has gained a new lease of life – a hearts transplant, so to speak – from its popularity as computer software. In its simplest form, the aim is just to avoid winning tricks containing hearts. Each player counts a penalty point for each heart taken in tricks, and the winner is the player with the lowest score when one player reaches a critical maximum of penalties. Probably no one, however, plays the purest form. Described here is the computerized variety derived from an early twentieth-century development called Black Lady Hearts. There are many local variations, but the following four-player game contains probably the best balance of common features and can reasonably be regarded as standard. The three-hand game (appended) also works well.

Hearts for four players

How to play

Cards. Standard 52-card pack ranking A K Q J 10 9 8 7 6 5 4 3 2 in each suit.

Deal. Deal 13 cards each, in ones.

Game. The game ends when at least one player reaches a total of 100 penalty points.

Object. To avoid winning tricks containing hearts or ♠Q. Alternatively, you may aim to capture all 14 penalty cards (a slam, or 'hitting the moon'), but need not announce this beforehand.

Exchange. Each player first passes three cards face down to his left-hand neighbour and receives the same number from his right. On the second deal, cards are passed to the right and received from the left. On the third they are passed between players sitting opposite each other. On the fourth, there is no exchange, the hands being played as dealt. The same sequence is repeated thereafter. Players may not pick up the cards passed to them until they have passed their own three on. There is no restriction on which cards may be passed.

Play. Whoever holds ♣2 leads it to the first trick. Players must follow suit if possible, otherwise may play any card. The trick is taken by the highest card of the suit led, and the winner of each trick leads to the next. There are no trumps. Two special rules apply:

- ◼ You may not play a penalty card to the first trick, unless you have no choice.
- ◼ You may not lead a heart until the suit has been 'broken' by somebody having discarded one to a previous trick. *(Exception:* You may do so if you have nothing else, or your only alternative is ♠Q.)

Unless otherwise agreed, it is acceptable to throw all non-penalty cards won in tricks to a common wastepile, and for players to leave the penalty cards they have won face up on the table before them so that everyone can see which are yet to come.

Score. At end of play each player counts 1 penalty point for each heart taken in tricks, and 13 for ♠Q. For taking all 14 penalty cards, however, you may either deduct 26 from your total, or add 26 to everyone else's. The winner is the player with fewest penalty points when one or more players reach 100. A tie-breaker may be played if necessary.

Sample game

Here is an amusing deal that demonstrates some of the problems and pitfalls the game can give rise to.

As dealt:

North	♡10 9 3	♠10 9 7 3 2	◇7 4	♣K 7 6
East	♡K 7 6 4	♠A J	◇10 8 5	♣Q J 5 2
South	♡A Q 8 5 2	♠K 6	◇Q J 9 6	♣10 8
West	♡J	♠Q 8 5 4	◇A K 3 2	♣A 9 4 3

After the exchange:

North	♡J 9 3	♠10 9 7 3 2	◇K 4	♣K 9 6
East	♡K 10 7 6 4	♠J	◇7 5	♣Q J 7 5 2
South	♡A Q 8 5 2	♠A 6	◇Q J 10 9 8 6	♣–
West	♡ –	♠K Q 8 5 4	◇A 3 2	♣A 10 8 4 3

Passing to the left, North gave East ♡10 ◇7 ♣7, getting rid of some indeterminate cards and keeping his safe run of spades – safe indeed, as you will see from the exciting finish. East discarded his eminently unsafe ♠A (trusting to luck not to be given the King or Queen), plus ◇10 8. South, similarly embarrassed in spades, unloaded its Ace, together with two useless but dangerous clubs. West, facing the awful four-spades-to-the-Queen prospect, decided to hope for an extra covering spade from North, and got rid of ♡J ◇K ♣9, leaving an ideal position in the minor suits. East, holding ♣2, kicks off with it.

	E	S	W	N	
1.	♣2	♠A	**♣A**	♣K	North would have kept the King had South not shown out of clubs
2.	◇7	◇Q	◇A	◇K	North seems unnecessarily cautious about diamonds
3.	◇5	◇J	◇3	◇4	
4.	♠J	♠6	**♠K**	♠10	West, by playing ♠K second, makes it pretty clear he holds ♠Q safe
5.	♡10	◇10	◇2	♡J	East holds up ♡K in case it encourages anyone into a slam bid
6.	♡K	♡8	♣10	♡9	Now East can play it and lose the rest
7.	♡7	♡A	♣8	♡3	
8.	♡6	♡5	♣4	♣9	
9.	♣5	♡Q	♣3	♣6	North beats West in spades . . .

At trick 6, with ♡8 led, North 'sacrifices' with ♡9, planning to win the trick and lose the rest, thus preventing anyone from making a slam. East, however, with the same object in view, 'over-sacrifices' with the King.

At trick 4, West could (and perhaps should) have unloaded ♠Q before it was too late. He reckoned, however, that his five-card holding would save him from being forced to take a trick with the

Queen, and embarked on the not infrequent dodge of letting everyone know he held the Queen and winding up the suspense by withholding her for the last trick. Unfortunately for him, however, North also held five spades and got rid of the King early on. Coming in at trick 9, North plays from ♠9 7 3 2 against West's ♠Q 8 5 4, and West finds himself, at the last trick, hoist by his own petard.

Result: North 2, East 5, South 6, and West 13 penalty points.

Partnership Hearts

Played by four with either fixed or (my invention) floating partnerships. Each partnership, or each member of a partnership, scores the amount taken by the partnership as a whole.

Fixed partnerships

The players facing each other across the table are partners for the whole game, and the passing cycle is left, right, across, none.

Rotating partnerships

In the first deal, North-East oppose South-West, and each player exchanges three cards with his neighbouring opponent. In the second, North-South oppose East-West, and each exchanges cards with his partner. In the third, North-West oppose South-East and each exchanges with his neighbouring opponent. In the fourth, there is no exchange and the first two players to win a trick become partners. A slam requires all penalty cards to fall to one player, not just to one partnership.

Ad hoc partnerships

The passing cycle is left, right, across, none. The first two players to win a trick – whether or not either trick contains a penalty card – become partners for the rest of the hand, and the other two play in partnership against them. If only one player wins tricks he will, of course, score a lone slam.

Hearts for three players

Remove the ◊2, deal 17 cards each, and play as described above. In the first deal you pass three cards to your left, in the second to your right, in the third not at all, and then repeat the cycle.

In a version called Widow Hearts, the full pack is used, four cards are dealt face down as a widow, each player receives 16 cards, there is no passing of cards, and the player at Dealer's left leads to the first trick. The widow is added to the last trick, and any penalty cards it may contain count against the player who wins it.

16 FIVE HUNDRED

The wizard game of Oz

Five Hundred, devised around the turn of the twentieth century as a cross between Euchre and Bid Whist, is a good game for three. It is also a good game for two, four, five and six. It was invented in the USA and is still played there, widely if patchily; but its real home has since become Australia, of which it may now be said to be the national card game. For this reason the following description is that of the Australian version rather than the American, which has since developed along lines of its own, exhibiting different rules of play in different localities.

Five Hundred involves tricks and bidding. It was originally played as a three-hander with the 32-card Euchre pack plus Joker, each player receiving 10 cards and three being laid aside as a widow. As this basic format applies regardless of the number of players, it follows that four play with 43 cards, five with 53, and six with 63. For the latter purpose, the Australian '500' pack contains 10 extra cards in the form of Elevens and Twelves in each suit, Thirteens in hearts and diamonds, and one Joker, known as 'the Bird', since it depicts a kookaburra. You can get genuine '500' packs outside Australia through specialist dealers such as Somerville of Edinburgh, and they are well worth having if you like tinkering about with card games for peculiar numbers of players such as five and six.

However, they are not absolutely essential to your enjoyment of Five Hundred, as I am told by the natives that very few people bother to play the game six up – in fact, it is most often played by four in partnerships. Nevertheless, I will start with the three-hander and progress to the others, largely because there is no shortage of partnership games, but there are few good three-handers that do not involve complicated card-point counting.

As noted in the chapter on Euchre, 'Bower' rhymes with 'power' and derives from a German word for Jack.

Five Hundred for three players

How to play

Cards. Thirty-three, consisting of one Joker plus A K Q J 10 9 8 7 in each suit.

Game. Scores are noted at the end of each deal and kept accumulatively. They may be plus or minus and it is possible for a score to sink below zero. The game ends when one or more players reach 500 points, either plus or (more rarely) minus, and the winner is the player with the highest score.

Deal. The turn to deal and play passes to the left. Deal cards in batches as follows: three to each player, three face down to the table, four to each player then three again all around so that each player has 10 cards. The undealt cards form the 'kitty'.

Object. The highest bidder takes the kitty, discards three in its place, and aims to win at least as many tricks as stated in the bid after declaring a trump suit or no trump. A player may also bid misère, i.e. to lose every trick, playing at no trump. Opponents also score for any tricks they take individually.

Rank of cards. When there is a trump suit, cards rank from high to low as follows:

Joker (best bower)
Jack of trumps (right bower)
Other Jack of same colour as trumps (left bower)
A K Q (J) 10 9 8 7 in each suit (except where Jack promoted).

Note that the left bower is the third highest card of the trump suit and does not belong to the suit marked on its face. The trump suit is therefore one card longer (nine) than plain suits of the opposite colour (eight each), while the suit of the same colour as trumps is one card short (seven).

In a so-called no-trump game, all Jacks revert to their normal position between Ten and Queen, and the Joker is the only trump.

Auction. Starting with the player at Dealer's left, each in turn must pass or make a higher bid than any gone before. Passing does not prevent you from bidding again later. (It did originally, forcing players to make their highest bids immediately; but this restriction has largely been dropped.) When two players pass in succession, the third becomes the declarer and the last-named bid is the contract. (It may not be increased.)

If all pass without bidding the game is played at no trump and each player aims to win as many tricks as possible.

The lowest bid is 'six spades', i.e. an offer to win at least six tricks with spades as trump. This can be overcalled by bidding six in a higher suit, for which purpose they rank spades, clubs, diamonds, hearts, no trumps (or 'no-ees'), or by increasing the number of tricks. Alternatively, bids may be made by announcing their scoring values as shown in the table. Thus a bid of 'six spades' may be announced simply as '40'.

Number bid→	6	7	8	9	10	
in spades ♠	40	140	240	340	440	
clubs ♣	60	160	260	360	460	
diamonds ♦	80	180	280	380	480	
hearts ♡	100	200	300	400	500	
No trump	120	220	320	420	520	
Misère			250	*or*	520	*open*

Misère is a bid to lose every trick at no trump. Though worth 250, it is overcalled by any bid of eight or more tricks, including eight spades for 240. Open misère, played with Declarer's cards face up on the table, overcalls everything, including the equally valued ten no trump.

Kitty. Unless everybody passed without bidding, in which case the kitty is left out of play face down and untouched, the highest bidder takes the kitty and adds it to his hand without showing it. He then throws out any three cards face down in its place.

Play. Declarer leads first, or, if all passed without bidding, the player at Dealer's left. If playing open misère, Declarer lays his cards face up on the table before leading.

Suit must be followed if possible, otherwise any card may be played. A trick is taken by the highest card of the suit led or by the highest trump if any are played. The winner of each trick leads to the next. Everyone keeps their own won tricks separate from everyone else's.

In any no-trump contract, including misère, the Joker is a trump and belongs to no suit of its own. Its holder may not play it if able to follow suit to the card led. If he leads it, he names a suit which others are required to follow if possible. This must not be one in which he has already shown himself void.

Score. If you make your contract, you score its value. There is no bonus for overtricks, unless you win all 10, in which case you score either 250 or the value of your contract, whichever is higher. If you lose, you deduct the contract value from your current total. The opponents each score 10 for each trick they won individually, or, in a failed misère, 10 for each trick taken by Declarer. (Misères must therefore be played through to the bitter end.) If all passed without bidding, each player scores 10 per trick won.

The winner is the player with the highest score when someone reaches 500 points plus or minus. If two or more players reach 500 simultaneously, and one of them is the Declarer, Declarer wins the game.

Notes on play

The first thing to be aware of in Five Hundred, if you are already used to other trick-taking games with bidding, is that of the 30 cards in play no fewer than 10 are trumps – that is, one-third of the pack as opposed to only one-quarter in other games. Usually, five or six of the ten tricks are won by a trump (whether to a trump or a plain suit lead).

Assessing the hand

No-trump hands are somewhat exceptional. A solidly reliable no trumper does not often appear, and can hardly be missed when it does. Certainly you should not attempt it without the Joker, as that is the one and only way of getting back into a suit in which you have a high gap. You will need strength in all four suits besides, since once you allow someone else to establish their suit your good cards will simply be whisked out of your hand before you get back in.

There being ten trumps and only two 'sides' to the game – you versus them – it follows that your minimum requirement is five trumps, together with strength in at least one other suit, in order to establish your 'book' of five tricks (i.e. the basis on which your actual bid must be built). You can consider bidding with only four trumps, provided that at least two are in the top three. And don't forget that the top three are the Joker and Bowers: the Ace of trumps is only the fourth highest of its suit.

Strength in side suits means at least an Ace or a high-guarded King. The high guard (Queen, or either Jack or Ten depending on the bower situation) is necessary for you to be able to make the King by leading from below and forcing out the Ace. A side suit headed by a guarded Queen is almost certain not to make a trick; in any case, the three cards involved in a guarded Queen are better discarded to the kitty to leave a void in hand. Which brings us to the second indicator of strength in a side suit, namely, a void or the possibility of creating one by means of the discard. Finally, a long side suit, one with four or more cards, is very desirable.

The kitty

The main purpose of exchanging through the kitty is not so much to draw good cards from it as to improve the balance (or imbalance) of your suits by creating a void and/or a long suit. This is not to say that it will contribute nothing useful to the hand – you can often rely upon it to produce an extra trick if you are already sure of seven, and perhaps two if you are sure of six. But the important thing is not to rely on it to provide a single specific card (such as the Joker) without which a risky bid may be lost as a foregone conclusion. Holding four of a suit, the chances of finding a fifth in the widow are 5 to 3 in favour; holding five, the chances of finding a sixth drop to 5 to 4.

Bidding

The method of bidding allows no room for manoeuvre. With most hands you will have only one potential trump suit; only occasionally will you have the luxury of switching to another suit in order to overcall on the same number of tricks. Furthermore, once you have made your bid you must lie on it – you can't increase it for a higher score. If, therefore, you have a probable eight hearts don't bother to sneak up on it by starting at six. That being the highest suit, neither of the others may wish to raise you to seven, in which event they will pass and leave you to make a certain 100 instead of a probable 300. You must start by bidding the highest you dare, and know in advance whether or not you will allow yourself to be forced up.

Note carefully what the others bid, as this can give you a good idea not only of their strong suits but also of the distribution of the Joker and Bowers.

Discarding rarely presents problems. Retain all trumps, consecutive top cards, and a suit of four or more – in that order. Create a void if possible. And do make sure to keep the kitty separate from your win tricks, just in case you mistake it for a trick.

The play

As declarer you will want to lead trumps first in order to draw your opponents' teeth, so that you can later succeed in establishing a long suit of four or more. If you have no long suit, you will gain greater control over potential trick-winners in other suits by letting the player on your left gain the lead rather than his partner. In other words, if not leading, your best position is playing third to a trick. At No Trump, lead from your longest rather than your strongest suit, and return to it whenever possible.

As an opponent of the Declarer, your primary objective is normally to defeat the contract rather than make tricks of your own. (Unusually, you might find yourself playing to the score. Thus, if Declarer is unable to make game – i.e. reach 500 points – on succeeding at his contract, but your temporary partner is not only well ahead of you but also only ten or twenty points off target, you will obviously prefer to prevent your partner from taking tricks wherever possible.)

When Declarer leads trumps, prefer to play low if your partner will win the trick, since Declarer's chief preoccupation is to leave himself holding the highest trumps in play. In fact, you can nearly always afford to duck his lead as second player if it is obvious that Declarer is trying to force out a higher trump, since, if it isn't in your own hand, it must be in your partner's.

When leading, generally try to avoid opening up new suits, and stick by preference to your own longest or strongest.

Sample game

Connie deals the following hands:

Annie	♠7 ♡A 10 7 ♣K 10 8 7 ◊J 10
Benny	♠K J 9 8 ♡K 9 ♣J 9 ◊9 7
Connie	Joker ♠Q 10 ♡Q J 8 ♣A ◊A K 8

Annie starts by making an optimistic bid of 6♡. Her ◊J would be the Left Bower with that suit as trump, making a better set of four trumps than the unbiddable alternative in clubs.

Benny, strong in spades and holding both Bowers, overcalls with ♠7, hoping to improve his scrappy side-suits by taking the kitty.

Connie bids seven of her higher-ranking diamond suit, which is well supported by the Joker and ♡J (Left Bower).

Annie and Benny pass, and Connie takes the kitty, consisting of ♠A ♣Q ◊Q. This excellent draw increases her trump holding, adds a side-suit Ace, and enables her to void a suit by throwing out three hearts. Her playing hand is now:

$$\text{Jo } ♡J \ ◊A K Q 8 \ ♠A Q 10 \ ♣A Q$$

She leads the Joker and the Left Bower, thus drawing all the outstanding trumps. Annie, who had the Right Bower (◊J), returns ♡A, believing Connie to be more probably void in clubs than hearts. Not so. Connie ruffs it, cashes her ♣A, plays her remaining trumps, and loses two spades to Benny.

Result: Connie scores 180 for her contract of 7◊, leaving Annie and Benny to score 10 and 20 respectively.

Five Hundred for two to six players

The cards used for each number of players, in addition to the Joker, are as follows:

Two players: 24 cards – A K Q J 10 9 in each suit.
Four players: 42 cards – A K Q J 10 9 8 7 6 5 in each suit, plus both red Fours.

Five players: The standard 52-card pack.

Six players: The full Australian '500' pack, with Elevens and Twelves in all four suits, and Thirteens in red suits.

In each case each player receives 10 cards and three form a kitty, though in serious four-hand partnership play it is common to omit the Joker and make only a two-card kitty. Four and six players play in respectively two or three partnerships, the members of each partnership sitting opposite each other. For example, if six play, the rotation of players around the table is A–B–C–A–B–C.

In all partnership versions, it is only the declarer who takes the kitty.

Five play on an 'optional call' basis. That is, after taking the kitty and discarding, the declarer must either announce that he is playing alone against four, or else call for a partner by naming a card not in his own hand. Whoever holds that card becomes Declarer's partner and immediately identifies himself. The plus or minus score made by the partnership is awarded equally to both members of it.

There is no reason why four should not also play on the optional call basis.

American Five Hundred

American Five Hundred is usually played by four in fixed partnerships, with a 45-card pack consisting of A K Q J 10 9 8 7 6 5 4 in each suit, plus Joker. Deal 10 each and a five-card kitty called the 'middle' as follows: 3–(3)–2–(2)–3–2, the figures in brackets being those of the middle.

17 | NINETY-NINE

Almost the game of the century

I invented Ninety-Nine some years ago in response to the need for a three-player trick-taking game with simple rules but strategic depth. The heritage of British card games has so long been dominated by Whist and Bridge, which are essentially partnership games not satisfactorily adaptable for three, that games for this number have never had a chance to blossom. Not that there is any shortage of good three-handers: many major national games of Europe are designed for three, notably Skat in Germany; but they are mostly card-point counting games, very arithmetical, that take some getting used to if you have not been brought up on them. Besides, over the centuries have developed so many refinements and complications as to render them indigestible to Westerners accustomed to the relatively plain fare of traditional Whist, Bridge and Solo.

The basic idea of Ninety-Nine is that all three players bid to take a precise number of tricks, neither more nor less. Compared with other bidding games it has the advantage that most hands can be bid in several different ways, and that all three can bid and even win their contracts in every deal, so you don't have to hang around waiting for a good hand to come up before you can bid. In this respect, at least, it beats even Bridge.

Though originally designed for three, Ninety-Nine plays very well with other numbers, and versions for two and four players follow the main description.

Ninety-Nine for three players

How to play

Note: The following version of the game is a revision of the 1983 version. It dispenses with the original method by which a trump was randomly determined with the aid of a Joker.

Cards. Thirty-six, ranking A K Q J 10 9 8 7 6 in each suit.

Game. A game is 100 points over as many deals as it takes. It is possible for more than one player to win a game. A match is won by the player with the highest total when at least one player has won three games.

Deal. Deal twelve each, one at a time, face down.

Trumps. The first deal is played without trumps. In subsequent deals, the trump suit is determined by the number of players who fulfilled their contracts in the previous deal, as follows: if all three succeeded, clubs; if two, hearts; if one, spades; if none, diamonds.

Object. Each player discards three cards face down and plays out the other nine to tricks. Your three discards are called 'bid-cards', and by means of a code explained below they are selected to represent any number from nought to nine. This number constitutes your bid, and your aim is to win *exactly* the number of tricks your bid-cards represent.

Bidding. Herein lies the point of the game. You can bid anything from nought to nine tricks by discarding three bid cards in accordance with the following code:

Any ♣ represents	3 tricks
Any ♡ represents	2 tricks
Any ♠ represents	1 trick
Any ◇ represents	0 tricks

For example, you can represent a bid of three by any of the following discards: ♣ ◇ ◇ (3 + 0 + 0), ♡ ♠ ◇ (2 + 1 + 0), or ♠ ♠ ♠ (1 + 1 + 1). Similarly, there are three different ways of bidding 3, 4, 5, 6 or 7 tricks, two ways of bidding 2 or 8, and one of bidding 0 (◇ ◇ ◇) or 9 (♣ ♣ ♣).

Note that it is only the suit that counts for bidding: the ranks are entirely irrelevant.

Figure 17.1   Ninety-Nine
Each suit represents a number of tricks related to its shape. Thus a club has three bobbles, a heart has two cheeks, a spade has one point, and a diamond is a zero with straight sides (more or less).

Having decided on your bid cards, lay them face down on the table before you, slightly spread so as not to get confused with won tricks. Normally, bids remain secret and are not revealed until the end of the game. But you do have the option of making a premium bid for a higher score, which involves giving certain information about your cards, as follows:

■ *Declaration*: Before play, you can turn your bid cards face up so the other two players know how many you are aiming for.

■ *Revelation*: For this, you not only reveal your bid but also spread your hand of cards face up on the table before the first trick is led to.

Each of these bids carries a bonus, which goes to the bidder if successful, otherwise to each opponent (regardless of whether or not they succeed).

Only one player may make a premium bid in any round. If more than one player wishes to declare or reveal, priority goes to the revelation over the declaration. If equal, the player at Dealer's left has greatest priority and Dealer least.

Tricks. The first lead is always made by the player left of dealer. Normal rules of trick-taking apply. Follow suit to the card led if possible; if not possible, either trump or discard from side suit. The trick is taken by the highest card of the suit led or by the highest trump if any are played. The winner of a trick leads to the next.

Score. When the last trick has gone, anyone who succeeded in their bid must turn their bid-cards face up to prove their entitlement to a bonus. Anyone who failed, however, is under no obligation to do so.

Each player scores 1 point per trick won, regardless of their bid, plus (if applicable) a bonus for succeeding.

This bonus depends on how many players succeeded, as follows: if all three succeeded, add 10; if two succeeded, they each add 20; if only one succeeded, he or she adds 30.

A declaration carries an additional bonus of 30, and a revelation one of 60. This goes to the bidder if successful, otherwise it is credited to each opponent, in addition to any other score they may have made on their own account.

Examples:

	A	B	C			A	B	C	
bid	4	3	1	dec		4	3	2	rev
won	5	3	1			5	3	1	
success bonus	–	20	20			–	30	–	
premium bonus	–	–	30			60	60	–	
total	5	23	51			65	93	1	

The highest possible score is 99, attained when one player bids nine tricks revealed and is the only one to succeed.

Game score. A game ends when one or more players reach or exceed 100 points. Anyone who did so adds a game bonus of 100, provided that they succeeded in their last bid. For example, if A and B reach 100, and A and C succeed in that deal, then only A gets the game bonus – not B, who failed to make his last contract, nor C, who failed to reach 100.

When one or more players have won three game bonuses, the match ends and the winner is the player with the highest score.

Notes on play

A critical feature of the game is that the cards you use to bid with, when removed, alter the hand you are left to play with. This makes for scope and variety. Almost any hand of cards at Ninety-Nine is biddable, since there are ten different numbers of tricks to bid and no fewer than 220 different ways of discarding three cards from twelve. Not all the possibilities make sensible bids, of course, but more often than not you will find yourself confronted with a choice of two or three different bids to make and two or three different ways of representing each bid. Deciding between them is where the basic strategy of the game comes in. You must be guided by various considerations, such as who has the lead, what suit is trumps (a factor which is more significant to the play of Ninety-Nine than of any other card game), what the other players are likely to bid (observing which cards are lacking from your land helps here), and, above all, which of your cards are to be regarded as trick winners and which as trick losers.

This is the point at which you must begin to assess the hand. In Ninety-Nine, you are required to win an exact number of tricks. This means that you are also required to lose a corresponding number of tricks. Thus a bid to win three tricks is the same as a bid to lose six. It follows that your first task is to classify your cards as probable winners (certain Aces, Kings and trumps), probable losers (Sixes and Sevens), and 'incalculables' – those of middle ranks, and especially Jack Ten, Nine, any one of which is likely to win a trick when you want it to lose, or lose when you want it to win.

What you must aim to do, therefore, is as far as possible to retain extreme cards (winners and losers) and get rid of incalculables by using them to represent the bid. Choosing between several likely bids will often be controlled by the suits – that is, the bid values – of the cards you can most do without. You must enter the play with a clear idea of the intended destination of each card – which are to win tricks, which are to lose tricks, and which can be switched from winner to loser, or vice versa, when something goes wrong.

Curious imbalance of suits

The fact that suits have bidding values is unique to Ninety-Nine, and has a unique effect on the relative strength in play of the four different suits. In most card games there is a trump suit and three side suits. Apart from the fact that they have different symbols, there is no essential playing difference between one side suit and another. Similarly, one trump suit is as good as another. A game with spades as trumps may score higher than one with clubs (as in Bridge), but this has no effect on those suits' relative strength as trumps once the game is under way. The same does not apply in Ninety-Nine. In Ninety-Nine, clubs are nearly always a strong suit, and diamonds nearly always weak. Here's why.

Not surprisingly, the commonest bid is that of three tricks. ('If in doubt, bid three' is a fundamental principle of Ninety-Nine.) This can be represented in three different ways: ♣◇◇, ♡♠◇ or ♠♠♠. From this bid alone it is apparent that spades and diamonds are *more likely* to be laid aside as bid cards than hearts or clubs. Statistics compiled from actual games confirm that – again, *on average* – the nine cards out in bids, and therefore missing from play, are: three diamonds, three spades, two hearts, and one club. In addition, there is a slightly greater tendency for diamonds to be out than spades, as zero is the second commonest bid.

It follows that, in play, clubs and hearts tend to be long suits (eight and seven respectively), spades and diamonds short (six and five). Players are more frequently void in diamonds than any other suit, but only rarely void in clubs. In side suits, therefore, given a normal distribution of cards, you can usually expect ♣A K to be trick winners, and probably also ♡A, but ♠A is not certain, and ◇A is positively risky, standing the most chance of being trumped.

Similarly, at the opposite extreme, if you have the lead and want to lose it, ♣7 is a much safer card than ◇7 – the latter can so easily be undercut by ◇6 and followed by a discard when the third player is void.

Thus in assessing your hand you are concerned not only with the suit of cards, in deciding which to keep and which to use as bidders, but also with their ranks. The ◇10 is from all points of view the likeliest candidate for discarding, as it is the most incalculable rank of the most unreliable suit.

This imbalance of suits also has its effect on trumps. For example, if diamonds are trumps a player dealt ◇A K Q will often discard them for a certain bid of nought. In which case the player holding ◇J has the top trump and may well be forced to take an unwanted trick with it. Should he therefore count ◇J as a probable winner?

Not at all – for an opponent dealt ◇A K Q might equally well keep them in hand and void spades for a bid of three.

But at the other extreme of suits, clubs are reliable as trumps. If clubs are trumps and your highest trump is the Jack, you can be pretty certain that it's the fourth highest in play. The upper trumps are unlikely to be out in bids, because they imply bids of high numbers of tricks, for which purpose they would need to be retained!

It follows from the above that premium bids (declarations and revelations) tend to be safer in reliable suits (clubs, hearts) than in the others.

The play

You will normally go into play with cards already earmarked as winners and losers. Inevitably, you will have one or more of middle ranks or weak suits which are winners or losers – in other words, the incalculables. General procedure for all players is to get the lead as early as possible and lead out the incalculables. If they win, you can work out in advance which probable winners you must now reclassify as losers. If they lose, you must perform the opposite calculation.

With incalculables out of the way, or if you have none to start with, begin by making your surest non-trump winners, and then lose the lead. Trumps normally play their role as leads at the end of the round, though of course circumstances occur in which they are better led early on.

Note carefully what cards others are playing. Frequently it is possible to work out what they have bid from what they play; even if not, a great deal of scope exists for playing thwarting tactics.

For example, if one leads ◇7 and the other follows ◇6 you can be sure that neither wants the trick. If void in diamonds it may be better to discard from a side suit than trump, even if you want a trick, solely to discomfit the first player, who probably counted it as a sure loser. On the whole, if you are not sure whether or not a particular lead means a player wants the trick, it generally proves best to let him have it. The fact is – and I offer no explanation for it – that in Ninety-Nine players tend to underbid rather than overbid, and therefore more often find themselves trying to lose unwanted strong cards than win with weak ones.

If one player has declared or revealed, it will benefit you to spoil their game (working in collaboration with the other player) rather than make your own bid. If you can do both, of course, so much the better.

Length of suit

Long suits are weak; voids are strong. If you can bid in such a way as to create a void, you have splendid opportunities for either trumping or losing unwanted cards when that suit is led. This point often determines which of several possible bids is best to make.

A long suit is bad unless it contains safe low cards. Suppose you hold ♣A Q 9 8 6 when some other suit is trumps. Normally you expect to be dealt three of each suit, given an even distribution. Here you have five. This could mean that an opponent who received two or one succeeded in voiding clubs with a view to bidding high and trumping them. With this danger in mind, it is wise not to regard the Ace as a winner. A much safer procedure is to treat all five as sure *losers* and bid accordingly. This particular holding is quite safe: you can never be forced to take with a club. The situation would be different, however if the five you held were ♣A Q 10 9 8, for now you have neither a sure winner (the Ace may be trumped) nor a sure loser. Leading the Eight would be a sure signal of your intentions, and the others would, on principle, force you to take the trick.

Premium bids

For a declared bid you should have extreme cards in at least three suits and a void if possible. Remember that your bid-cards will be revealed, and that opponents can learn something from them. For example, if you bid three with three spades they may assume you have a void in that suit, and will probably refrain from leading it. This could be awkward if you were relying on the void as a means of making your trumps or losing some risky cards.

In order to reveal, you must be absolutely certain of the future destination of every card in your hand. Extreme cards or voids are necessary in every suit.

Unbiddable hands

Some hands look unbiddable at first sight. And they may so be, in the sense that you need the same cards for bidding as for making the tricks you bid. For example:

(trump ◇)A 6 ♣J 10 ♡K J 9 7 6 ♠Q 10 7

Here the only sensible bid, of one trick, can only be made by throwing out the very card (◇A) you need to make it with. You could bid two, by throwing two spades and ◇6, but would then stand little chance of taking a trick in hearts.

In this example, it is impossible to make a 'sensible' bid – that is, one that you can be sure of fulfilling. What you do instead is adopt the Technique of the Meaningless Bid (TOMB for short), which involves throwing out bid-cards solely for the surprise value of their absence from play. In this case the throw-outs are ◇A and both clubs. Your chances of making six tricks are remote, but the likelihood of spoiling your opponents' bids is most promising. See the first player's surprise when you trump his ♣A with ◇6, and the second player's astonishment when he finds you out of trumps and is forced to take with ◇7!

Fortunately, few hands are completely unbiddable in this way, and it is better to avoid the meaningless bid. But laying aside a card for its surprise absence is always good tactics. Strong Aces and high trumps are ideal candidates for this practice.

Sample game

The players are Abel, Baker and Charlotte. It is the third deal, done by Charlotte, and spades are trumps because only one player succeeded in the previous deal. The hands come out:

Abel	♠A J 10	◇J 9	♣Q 10 8 6	♡K Q 7
Baker	♠K 7 6	◇K 10 6	♣A J 7	♡A 9 8
Charlotte	♠Q 9 8	◇A Q 8 7	♣K 9	♡J 10 6

A fairly even distribution. Abel has no difficulty in assessing hearts as one trick and clubs as none. Spades is an unreliable trump suit and there is a chance that both monarchs are out in bids, leaving his ♠J second highest. He bids three, discarding ♣Q ◇J ◇9, making a void in diamonds and getting rid of two highly indeterminate cards.

Baker's hand is tricky. There seem to be three winners (Aces and
♣K) and four losers (Sixes and Sevens), giving a sensible bidding
range of three to five tricks One possibility is to discard ♣J, getting
rid of a difficult middling card, together with the two high
diamonds for a bid of three. This leaves ♡9 and ♡8 as nasty
incalculables, as a low lead once the Ace has gone could easily
spell disaster. Another possibility is to discard ♡9 ♡8 ◇10 for a bid
of four. This gets rid of the problematical hearts and calls for a
fourth trick from either the ◇K or a low trump to a heart lead once
the Ace has gone. In the event, Baker goes for a 'surprise' bid,
throwing out his three spades for a bid of three and putting his trust
in his three high cards.

Charlotte's hand looks most unpromising at first sight, as it is full of
middling ranks, especially in the unreliable trump suit. The only
sure loser is ♡6, and the nearest approach to a winner is ♣K. Her
most sensible bid is two, discarding ♡J◇A◇Q, and intending to win
with ♣K and ♠Q.

The playing hands are now:

Abel	♠A J 10	◇none	♣10 8 6	♡K Q 7
Baker	♠none	◇K 10 6	♣A J 7	♡A 9 8
Charlotte	♠Q 9 8	◇8 7	♣K 9	♡10 6

And the play goes:

A(3)	B(3)	C(2)	Commentary
♡K	♡A	♡10	Abel leads the King to draw the Ace
♣10	♣A	♣9	Baker leads the second of three intended winners . . .
♣6	◇10	◇8	. . . and leads an incalculable Ten, which makes the third.
♣8	◇6	◇7	Baker gets off play with the lowest diamond, which Charlotte is not pleased to take.
♡Q	♡9	♡6	Charlotte escapes with the lowest heart, voiding the suit and hoping to be able to throw her unwanted King to it. Abel's Queen wins, as intended from his opening lead.
♡7	♡8	♣K	Baker takes an unwanted excess trick; Charlotte throws her now unwanted King.
♠J	♣7	♠9	Baker takes the second of his three proposed tricks . . .

♠10	♣J	♠Q	. . . and, as intended, loses the trump Ten to the Queen.
♠A	◇K	♠8	Charlotte leads her last unwanted card to Abel's wanted Ace.
3	4	2	*tricks*
20		20	*bonus for succeeding*
23	4	22	*score*

South bids 6 declared

Figure 17.2   Ninety-Nine

West dealt and turned the Queen of hearts for trump. South bids six (♡ + ♠ + ♣), and, rather rashly, declares it by laying his bid cards face up. This bid might have worked if South had had the lead and neither opponent wanted to win a high diamond trick.

Ninety-Nine for two players

Deal three hands of 12 cards each face down. Separate the top three cards of the dummy hand as its 'bid'. These remain face down and unseen until end of play. Each player bids in the usual way. Either or both players may declare, but neither may reveal. After the bids and any declarations have been made the dummy is turned face up and sorted into suits. The first deal is played at no trump, thereafter, the trump suit is determined as in the three-hand game.

Non-dealer leads to the first trick, waits for the second to play, then plays any legal card from dummy. If a live player wins the trick, he leads first from hand and third from dummy. If the dummy wins a trick, the person who played from it then leads first from dummy and third from hand.

At end of play, the dummy's bid-cards are turned up and both live players score as in the three-hand game. However, because the dummy rarely makes its bid exactly, consider it to have failed if it wins more tricks than bid, succeeded if it wins fewer, and declared if it made its bid exactly. If one live player declares and fails, the other two score the bonus of 30. If both declare and fail, neither gains it but the dummy scores 60 extra.

Ninety-Nine for four players

Deal 13 cards each from a 52-card pack. Use three bid-cards to bid up to 10 tricks. A bid of three diamonds represents 0 or 10 tricks, and either number of tricks automatically fulfils the contract. The contract score is 30 if one player succeeds, 20 if two, 10 each if three, zero if all four either succeed or fail in their contract. If all four succeed, the next deal is played at No Trump, otherwise the trump suit is determined as in the three-hand game. The premium score is 30 or 60 as before.

18 | TWENTY-FIVE

The Gaelic game

Ireland's national card game sometimes appears in books under the name Spoil Five, as your aim is to prevent anybody from winning three of the five tricks played if you are unable to do so yourself. Its name got changed to Twenty-Five when the habit developed of scoring points in fives instead of ones. The game is also played by Gaelic descendants in Canada and Nova Scotia, with the target score raised to 45, producing a partnership variety called (believe it or not) Auction Forty-Fives.

All these titles emphasize the peculiar obsession it seems to exhibit for the number five: five is the best number of players; five tricks are played; the top trump is the Five (originally known as Five Fingers), and even the Irish for 'trick', *cúig*, is the word for five. Gaelic through and through, it is first attested under the name Maw as the court game of James VI of Scotland (later James I of England), and was subsequently carried to the New World, where it remains popular in Canada, especially in Nova Scotia ('New Scotland').

Newcomers may find it initially daunting because of the peculiar rank of cards and rules of play, which obviously derive from the ancient Spanish game of Hombre, and take a little getting used to. But it is well worth the effort, as much for its intrinsic interest as for its cultural and historic significance – not to mention the fact that it is one of the very few games for which five is the best number of players.

How to play

Preliminaries. From three to ten *can* play, from four to six usually do. Four may play in two partnerships of two, six in two partnerships of three or three of two. For non-partnership play, five is ideal. Each starts with 20 chips or counters, but scores can easily be kept in writing.

Cards. Fifty-two. There is always a trump suit, and three or four cards are always the highest trumps, namely (from the top down):

Five of trumps ('Five fingers')
Jack of trumps
Ace of hearts ($\heartsuit$A)
Ace of trumps (if not hearts)

The others rank from high to low according to colour:

in $\heartsuit\diamondsuit$	K Q J 10 9 8 7 6 5 4 3 2 A	'high in red'
in $\spadesuit\clubsuit$	K Q J A 2 3 4 5 6 7 8 9 10	'low in black'

Note that there are usually 14 trumps, but 13 in hearts. In plain suits, the King is always highest.

Deal. Everyone chips one to the pool. Deal five cards each in batches of two and three, or four and one. Stack the rest face down and turn the top card for trump.

Object. Primarily, to sweep the pool by winning at least three tricks, and preferably all five. Failing this, to 'spoil five' by preventing anyone else from winning three, thereby increasing the size of the pool for the next deal. If played for soft score, each trick counts 5 points and the target is 25.

Robbing the pack. If dealt the trump Ace, you may declare that fact and then 'rob the pack' by taking the turn-up and discarding an unwanted card face down. You needn't declare it if you don't intend to rob, but, if you do, you must rob before playing to the first trick. If the turn-up is an Ace, dealer may rob the pack by exchanging it for any unwanted card.

Play. The player at dealer's left leads to the first trick, and the rules of trick play are:

- To a plain-suit lead, you may either follow suit or trump, as preferred, but may only discard if unable to follow suit.

- To a trump lead, you must play a trump if possible, unless the only one you hold is a top trump (Five, Jack or $\heartsuit$A) and it is higher than the one led. In this case, you may 'renege' by discarding from another suit. In other words, you can't force a top trump out by leading a lower one, only by leading a higher.

The trick is taken by the highest card of the suit led, or by the highest trump if any are played, and the winner of each trick leads to the next.

Jinking. If you win the first three tricks straight off, you sweep the pool without further play. If instead you 'jink' by leading to the fourth trick, this counts as an undertaking to win all five, and you will lose your stake if you fail to get them all.

Score. Anyone winning three or more tricks wins the pool, and for winning all five gains an extra chip from each opponent. If nobody wins three, or a jinker fails to win five, the tricks are said to be 'spoilt'. The pool is then carried forward to the next deal, increased by one chip per player.

Game. The game ends when somebody runs out of chips (hard score) or reaches 25 points (soft score).

Notes on play

You should decide almost from the outset whether to go for three tricks or to spoil the five. Most hands are run-of-the-mill, and spoiling is the safest bet. One way of doing this is to refrain from playing a top trump to an early trick – by legally reneging – thus saving it for subsequent use against a player who has won a second trick, or is threatening to do so, with a view to a third.

To go for three you generally need three trumps, one of them a top trump. A plain-suit King cannot be counted as a winner from the outset because the rules of play allow it to be trumped even by one who can follow suit. But it becomes more promising if you can retain it while trumps are being drawn in early tricks. Many a third trick is won by leading to the last trick a plain suit that no one can either follow or trump.

In the following illustration, the turned card is ◇Q, making diamonds trump, and the hands are:

Ardal	♡9 6 2 ♠3 ♣7
Bernadette	♠J 8 ♣9 6 2
Caitlín	◇5 ♡A K ♠5 ♣A
Déidre	◇9 4 ♠Q 7 4
Eamon	◇A ♡J 4 ♠Q ♣10

Only two players can reasonably go for three tricks: Caitlín has two top trumps and a King, while Eamon's ◇A entitles him to take the turned Queen in exchange for his most worthless card, ♣10. With ♡10 led, the play might go:

	A	B	C	D	E
1.	♡10	♣9	♡K	◇4	◇Q
2.	♡6	♠8	♡A	◇9	♡4
3.	♡2	♣6	◇5	♠7	◇A
4.	♣7	♣2	♣A	♠4	♣Q
5.	♠3	♠J	♠5	♠Q	♡J

1. Déidre is obliged to trump, Eamon elects to do so and wins the trick. He leads a low heart, expecting to force out trumps so that he can come in later with his Queen and win the last trick with the Jack
2. Caitlín, unable to follow suit, is forced to trump (♡A is third highest).
3. Caitlín now leads the unbeatable Five, which must force out any top trumps still in play, as well as (she hopes) the trump Ace known to be in Eamon's hand. Eamon reluctantly complies.
4. Unfortunately for Caitlín, her ♣A falls to Eamon's Queen. Eamon, having now re-entered by another route, leads the ♡J as originally intended, and sweeps the pool.

Had Caitlín led ♣A to the thrid trick, Eamon would still have won by leading ♡J to the fourth. Caitlín would have been obliged to trump, and Eamon would have won with the last remaining trump.

Auction Forty-Fives (for four or six)

This is a partnership version of Twenty-Five for four or six players. Six play in two partnerships of three, each player being flanked by an opponent on either side.

The deal, rank of cards, and play of tricks, are as at Twenty-Five.

Auction. After the deal but before the play there is an auction. Each in turn, starting with the player at dealer's left, may pass or make a higher bid than any that has gone before, except that the dealer has the privilege of 'holding' the previous bid. (That is, making it his own by privilege of position.)

Bids are made in multiples of 5, starting at 5 and going up to a maximum of 30. The maximum is greater than 25 because, in addition to the score of 5 points per trick won, another 5 is credited to the side that was dealt the highest trump in play.

Bidding continues until three pass in succession. The last-named bid is the contract.

Discards. Before play, each in turn, starting from the left of the dealer, may make any number of discards, face down, and be dealt the same number of replacements from the top of the stock.

The opening lead is made by the opponent sitting to the left of the highest bidder.

Scoring. As stated, each trick counts 5 and the highest trump counts another 5 points. The non-bidding side always scores what it makes. So does the bidding side if successful; if not, they lose the amount of their bid.

For bidding and making 30, the score is doubled to 60.

Game. Play up to 120 points. A side standing at 100 or more points may not bid less than 20.

19 | SKAT

Germany's national card game

Skat is not only Germany's national card game but one of the world's great card games by any standard of judgement. It is unfortunate, if not entirely surprising, that the game is as yet little known in Britain, but it is by no means parochial, as versions of it are still played in the United States of America, and a dozen or so other countries have groups affiliated to the International Skat Association (ISPA). The fact that it is one of the select band of card games played annually at the Mind Sports Olympiad, first held in London in 1997, gives hope that British players may soon be able to compete in international Skat tournaments.

There is no disguising the fact that Skat is hard to get into without prior experience of card-point games – where the aim is not just to win tricks but to capture counting-cards contained in them. It is, nevertheless, one of the deepest, most varied and most exciting games ever invented, and well repays the effort of mastering its intricate scoring system. A good way of approaching it, if you don't already play card-point games of this type, is through the two-handed game of Sixty-Six. Also helpful is some experience of the use of Jacks as trumps, as, for example, through the play of Euchre and Five Hundred.

The following description incorporates rule changes representing an amalgamation of those of the ISPA and the Deutscher Skatverband, effective from 1999, in which year the DSkV celebrated its centenary.

How to play

Players. There are three active players, but usually four at a table, each in turn dealing to the other three but not taking part in that hand. The turn to deal and play passes to the left. The player at dealer's left, who will lead to the first trick, is called Forehand; the next one round is Middlehand; and the last (dealer himself if only three play) is Rearhand.

Cards. Thirty-two, omitting numerals 2-6.

Rank and value of cards. Cards rank and count as follows (from highest to lowest):

trumps	♣J	♠J	♡J	◇J	A	10	K	Q	9	8	7
point-value	2	2	2	2	11	10	4	3	0	0	0
non-trumps					A	10	K	Q	9	8	7

When there is a trump suit, the four Jacks, counting 2 points each, are always the four highest trumps. The Ace of trumps (worth 11) is then the fifth highest, the Ten (worth 10) sixth highest, and so on, making 11 trumps in all. Each non-trump suit contains seven cards, headed by the Ace. The total number of card-points is 120, equivalent to 30 in each suit.

Object. In each deal an auction determines who will play a solo contract against the other two players. The basic contracts are of three types:

> ■ *A suit contract.* Cards rank and count as shown above, and the soloist's aim is (usually) to take in tricks cards totalling at least 61 points.

> ■ *Grand.* Same object, but the four Jacks are the only trumps, forming a fifth suit of their own. The other four are non-trump suits, containing seven each.

> ■ *Null.* The soloist's aim is to lose every single trick. There are no trumps or card-points, and in each suit the cards rank in their 'natural' order A K Q J 10 9 8 7.

Each of these games may be played either *with the skat* or *from the hand.*

> ■ In a skat game, the soloist takes the skat, adds it to his hand, makes any two discards face down in its place, and then announces grand, suit or null before play begins. This enables him to improve the shape of his hand and to delay choosing a contract until he has seen all 12 cards.

■ In a hand game, the soloist leaves the skat untouched and announces grand, suit or null immediately. Not surprisingly, this carries a higher potential score.

In either case, any card-points contained in the skat will count to the soloist at end of play as if he had won them in tricks (except at null, where they are irrelevant).

The winner is the player with the highest cumulative score at the end of a previously agreed number of deals. There may be any number of deals, so long as everyone deals the same number of times. In tournament conditions, a game is 48 deals with four at a table or 36 with three.

Deal. Deal 10 cards each in batches of 3–(2)–4–3, with two face down to the table after the first round of three. These two form the *skat,* which eventually goes to the highest bidder.

Contracts and game values. Bidding is done by game valuation – that is, the soloist is the player offering to undertake the highest-scoring contract, not the one offering to win most tricks or take most card-points. Players must therefore calculate the scoring value of their proposed game before entering the auction. This is complicated by the fact that most game values are not fixed but are affected by a number of factors.

Null contracts have fixed game values as follows: null with skat 23, from the hand 35, ouvert with skat 46, ouvert from the hand 59. 'Ouvert' means that the soloist spreads his hand of card face up on the table before play begins.

All other game values are found by multiplying the *base value* of your proposed trump by a number of *playing factors* as described below. The base values are: diamonds 9, hearts 10, spades 11, clubs 12, grand 24.

To calculate the number of playing factors by which the base value is to be multiplied, work through the following checklist:

First, count your consecutive top trumps, or 'tops' (*Spitze*). If you hold ♣J, then you are playing 'with' as many tops as you hold. For example, holding ♣J but not ♠J, you are 'with one'. Holding ♣J ♠J but not ♡J you are 'with two'. Holding all four Jacks and the trump Ace but not the Ten, you are 'with five'.

If you don't hold ♣J, then you are 'without' as many top consecutive trumps as you lack – in other words, as many as outrank the highest trump you *do* hold. Thus, if your highest trump is ♡J, you are 'without two' (lacking ♣J ♠J). If your highest trump is the Ten, you are 'without five'. And so on.

Note the following consequences:

- In a suit contract, the most you can be with or without is 11, as the two cards of the skat belong to you if you are the soloist.

- In a grand contract, the most you can be 'with' or 'without' is four, as only Jacks are trumps.

- The fact that the skat belongs to the soloist means that, if you play from the hand, any Jacks found in the skat at end of play may change the number of tops you thought you held, and so increase or decrease the value of your game

Having counted your top trumps, add 1 point for 'game'. This yields the minimum number by which you can multiply the value of your proposed trump and so determine your game value.

For example, suppose you think diamond your best trump prospect, and you hold ♣J but not ♠J. Then your proposed game value is 'With 1, game 2, times diamonds 9'; and on this basis you can bid '18'. If you held ♠J but not ♣J, you would be 'Without 1, game 2, times diamonds 9', which is also worth 18. In either case you merely bid '18', without detailing how you arrive at that figure. In fact, 18 is the lowest possible bid. Or again: suppose you hold both black Jacks but not ♡J, and have enough non-trump Aces and Tens to think you can play grand, then your calculation is 'With 2, game 3, times grand 24', giving a bid of 72.

There are, however, other ways of increasing the value of your prospective game, and hence raising the figure you can bid up to. One is to bear in mind that your eventual score will include an extra multiplier if you succeed in taking 90 card-points, thereby restricting your opponents to 30 and leaving them in 'schneider' (= cut down to size). This is usually achieved by winning nine of the ten tricks played. If you win all ten, you get another 1 for schwarz besides 1 for schneider. So, if you are playing with 1, game 2, times diamonds 9, and think you will make schneider, you can add a third factor and bid up to 27 instead of a mere 18.

More valuable, however, is the possibility of playing from the hand. If, and only if, playing from the hand, you may declare in advance that you are aiming to win schneider. This entitles you to add 1 factor for declaring it in addition to the 1 for (hopefully) making it. If, and only if, playing from the hand, you may declare in advance that you are aiming to win schwarz. This entitles you to add a fourth factor (to the 1 each for the included schneider and schneider declared and the 1 for winning all ten).

Finally, and rarely, if you declare schwarz you can also play 'open', with your hand spread face up on the table, which entitles you to add yet another multiplier.

To summarize, here is a table showing how the various trump game values are reached:

base value of trump	x (a) if playing with skat	(b) if playing from hand
♢ diamonds 9	1 per top trump	1 per top trump
♡ hearts 10	+ 1 for game	+ 1 for game
♠ spades 11	+ 1 for schneider	+ 1 for hand
♣ clubs 12	(90+ points)	+ 2 for schneider declared
G grand 24	+ 1 for schwarz	+ 2 for schwarz declared
	(10 tricks)	+ 1 for open

Here are all the possible game values up to 100, including the fixed and invariable null values of 23, 35, 46, and 59: 18–20–22–23–24–27; 30–33–35–36; 40–44–45–46–48; 50–54–55–59; 60–63–66; 70–72–77; 80–81–84–88; 90–96–99–100.

The highest possible game is 264 (grand with 4, game 5, hand 6, schneider 7, schneider declared 8, schwarz 9, schwarz declared 10, open 11, times grand 24). The highest possible suit contract is 216 (clubs, with 11, game 12, hand 13, schneider 14, schneider declared 15, schwarz 16, schwarz declared 17, open 18, times clubs 12).

Examples of game valuation

(1) ♣J ♠J ♣A K ♠A K ♡Q ♢10 K 8 7

The obvious contract is diamonds, and the skat is needed to get rid of the two useless singletons. Count, therefore: With 2, game 3, times diamonds 9 = 27. If the hand is played and takes in 90 or more card-points, it will gain an extra multiplier for schneider and so score 36. On these cards Forehand, having the lead, might bid up to 72 with a view to playing grand (3 × 24).

(2) ♡J ◇J ♣10 Q 8 ♠A 10 9 ♡– ◇–

Here the obvious contract is clubs from the hand: Without 2, game 3, hand 4, times clubs 12 = 48.

(3) ♠J ♡J ◇J ♣10 ♠A 7 ♡A 10 9 ◇7

Now the obvious contract is hearts – without 1, game 2, times hearts 10 = 20. If pushed, you might go to 30 in hope of taking the skat and either making schneider (without 1, game 2, schneider 3 × 10 = 30) or, with a good draw, playing grand (without 1, game 2 × 24 = 48). It doesn't look safe enough to bid hearts hand for 30.

(4) ◇J ♣– ♠A 10 Q 9 8 7 ♡– ◇A K 7

This is certainly spades from the hand, and probably good for schneider. Count, therefore: Without 3, game 4, hand 5, schneider 6, declared 7, times spades 11 = 77.

(5) ♣K 10 8 7 ♠8 ♡A J 9 7 ◇Q

A probable null contract worth 23 – note that Jacks and Tens rank in their so-called natural order. If pushed by the bidding, you would reject null from the hand for 35 because of the singleton Queen, but might risk taking the skat, burying the Queen and playing open for 46.

The auction. Bids are made only by stating genuine game valuations, and without any further details – for example, '18', '20', etc.

Theoretically, Forehand has a prior right to declare a contract. The purpose of the auction is to see if either of the others wishes to take it off him by making successively higher bids. Middlehand starts by either passing or making a bid. If he passes, Rearhand does likewise. If he also passes, Forehand wins the auction and becomes the soloist – unless he also passes, when the hands are thrown in and the deal passes round to the next dealer.

Assuming Middlehand does not pass, he bids by stating successively higher game values, such as '18, 20, 22, 23 . . .', and so on. He may go up value by value, or in irregular jumps, or may jump immediately to his maximum bid, so long as every figure he quotes is a genuine game value (see table)

To each of these Forehand replies 'Yes' if he is willing to play a contract worth at least that amount, or 'Pass' if not. This continues until one of them passes – either Forehand because he cannot accept the value proposed by Middlehand, or Middlehand because his last bid was accepted by Forehand and he will not go higher. Rearhand may then continue the auction by bidding the next higher game value against the survivor, or may pass.

This continues as before, until one of them passes. The survivor becomes the soloist, and is obliged to play a contract worth not less than the amount of the last bid.

Declaring the contract. If playing from the hand, the soloist immediately announces the trump suit, or grand or null if applicable, and adding, in this order, whichever of the following may apply: hand, schneider declared, schwarz declared, open. If playing open, he simultaneously spreads his hand face up on the table.

If not, the soloist picks up the skat, adds it to his hand without showing it, makes any two discards in its place, and then announces the trump suit, or grand, null, or null open as appropriate. No other announcement is required or permitted.

Conceding. The soloist may throw his hand in before playing to the first trick. This usually happens when he takes the skat and finds it useless. He must, however, name a contract, however unsuited to his hand, in order to determine what game value is to be deducted from his score.

Play. Forehand always leads to the first trick. Suit must be followed if possible, otherwise any card may be played. The trick is taken by the highest card of the suit led, or by the highest trump if any are played. The winner of each trick leads to the next. The two partners pile all their won cards together in a single heap: there is no need to separate them into tricks.

It is important to note that Jacks belong to the trump suit and not necessarily to the suits they display.

■ At grand, the lead of a Jack calls for Jacks to be played if possible, and the highest Jack wins the trick. If a plain suit is led, a player unable to follow may trump by playing a Jack if able and willing.

■ In a suit game, the lead of any trump calls for the play of any other trump, regardless of whether or not either is a Jack.

■ At null, there are no trumps, and cards rank A–K–Q–J–10–9–8–7 in all suits.

All ten tricks must be played, unless the soloist concedes before playing to the first trick, or takes a trick in a null contract.

Score. At end of play, the skat is turned up (except at null) and counted as part of the soloist's won tricks.

To fulfil his contract, the soloist must have taken at least 61 card-points in tricks, or 90 if he declared schneider, or ten tricks if he declared schwarz, or no trick if he bid null. If so, the game value of his contract is recalculated in retrospect by the base value of the trump times the number of applicable game factors, including those for schneider and schwarz if made but not declared. If this game value is not less than the amount he bid, he scores it in full. If less, he loses.

If the soloist fails to make his contract, he takes the full game value as recalculated above, and loses it doubled. If he declared schneider and failed to make it, his (lost) game value is increased by one multiplier for the failed schneider as well as for the declaration. The same applies to schwarz declared. If he himself is schneidered (takes fewer than 31 card-points), his (lost) game value is increased by one multiplier.

If the game value of the contract played is less than his bid, it must be increased by as many more multipliers as are necessary to make it equal or exceed his bid. For example, if he bid up to 45 but found his spade game contract worth only 33, the latter must be increased to 55.

Any lost game is lost doubled after being calculated in full. (Prior to the 1999 revision, games played from the hand were lost singly under the rules of the Deutscher Skatverband.) The doubling is not taken into account as a way of bringing his game value up to the level of the amount bid.

If the soloist takes the skat and concedes without play, he must nevertheless declare a contract in order to calculate the amount of his penalty score, which is calculated in the normal way as if he had played it, and then doubled.

Notes on bidding and play

Pick out any Jacks and put them together in high–low order. Sort the other cards by suit and place your likeliest trump suit next to the Jacks in the same high–low order.

If you haven't any Jacks, you are unlikely to have a game on unless you have one of the following three types of hand:

$$\clubsuit A K Q 9 8 7 \ \heartsuit A K Q \ \diamondsuit A$$

With six or more trumps and safety in side suits you can try for a game 'without four', or even five, in the long suit. With a fair break, the opposition should not make more than about 40 on this example of 'without four, game five, hand six, times clubs $12 = 72$'. But change the diamond Ace to a lower diamond or spade, and you will need a favourable skat to make the game safe.

$$\clubsuit A \, 10 \, 7 \ \spadesuit A \, 10 \, 7 \ \heartsuit A K 7 \ \diamondsuit A$$

This could be a 'grand hand without four', worth 144, if you are prepared to chance a balanced distribution of Jacks and suits in the partners' hands. One or more Jacks could be in the skat.

$$\clubsuit A \, 10 \, 9 \, 7 \ \spadesuit 10 \, 8 \, 7 \ \heartsuit 9 \, 7 \ \diamondsuit 8$$

Given the lead (the low diamond), this is virtually a cast-iron 'null ouvert, hand' for 59. Even without the lead the opponents would need a freakish distribution and clever play to beat it.

If you are holding one or more Jacks, consider whether your hand looks best for a suit bid, grand, null, or no bid. Most hands are either a suit bid or nothing; relatively few are right for grand or null. As a very rough guide:

- If about half your cards are Nines, Kings and Queens, pass.
- If about half your cards consist of Jacks and good suit, consider a game in that suit. With six or more trumps

and a void suit, consider playing it from the hand. With both black Jacks and a long suit headed Ace-Ten, consider grand.

■ If about half are Jacks and Aces, especially Ace-Tens, consider grand.

■ If about half are Sevens, Eights and Nines, and you have no more than one Ace, King or Queen, consider null. Null bids have fixed game values. If you can lose every trick with the hand as dealt, you can bid up to 35, or 59 if you can play it ouvert. If you need to take the skat in order to get rid of a dangerous card, you can play five trumps including Ace or Ten, at least two side suits which are either void or headed by an Ace, and not more than five losing cards.

Suit bids

For a safe game in suit the normal requirement is at least five trumps including Ace or Ten, at least two side suits which are either void or headed by an Ace, and not more than five losing cards. If dealt such a hand, you can reckon on playing it from the hand – for example:

$$\clubsuit J \; \heartsuit J \; \clubsuit A K 9 \; \spadesuit- \; \heartsuit A 10 8 \; \diamondsuit Q 9$$

This is a game at clubs, hand. The opposition will probably make up to 20 in clubs and 28 in diamonds, giving you a safety margin of 12 card-points to compensate for an Ace or Ten dropped on the other's winning trump. As Forehand, having the opening lead, you could play 'grand, hand'.

Given a void suit, look first for a hand game rather than reaching directly for the skat, as the latter all too often produces nothing but two useless cards of your void suit – and by 'useless' I mean King-Queen rather than anything lower, as the latter can be discarded to worthless tricks without giving anything away. Playing from hand also entitles you to declare schneider in advance. To do this, you must be sure of winning preferably nine tricks, possibly eight. It is the equivalent of a small slam at Bridge. The normal requirement for a hand game is six trumps, or five including the black Jacks, a void suit, and a suit headed Ace-Ten, or at least Ace alone.

The time to think of a skat game is when you need the draw and discard in order to produce the sort of hand on which you would have bid 'hand' if originally dealt it. For example:

♣J ♡J ♣A K 9 ♠K ♡A 10 8 ◇Q

In a hand game, the opposition could make 49 straight off in spades and diamonds, and finish you off with the trump Ten. Here, you need the skat to enable you to ditch the two dangerous singletons, or one of them if the skat offers support to the other.

Two points to watch in bidding suit games are Jacks and non-trump Tens.

The danger besetting a Ten is that of being caught by the Ace, giving the opposition, in a single trick, one third of the points needed to beat you. A Ten in hand is obviously safest when covered by the Ace, and most dangerous when held singleton. With a singleton Ten, therefore, you should only consider playing from hand if you can be sure of winning most of the other tricks. It is not unknown for the soloist, playing third to the first trick, to win it with a singleton Ten; but of course it would be unwise to count on it. A Ten once guarded (e.g. 10–9) is a natural risk. On a low lead from your right, you may play the Ten and find it captured by the Ace on your left; or you throw the Nine, and then lose the Ten to the Ace on a subsequent trick. A Ten twice guarded (e. g. 10–Q–7) is safer, as the suits rarely go three times round and you can hold up the Ten until you have drawn trumps.

If you are dealt one suit consisting of Ten and a low card, and you take the skat, it is usually acceptable to keep it; if dealt two, it is usually best to lay aside both Tens to ensure 20 towards your 61 card-points.

The point to watch about Jacks is the danger of bidding 'without' too many of them. Suppose you have only the diamond Jack and take the game at 36, bidding on the basis of 'without 3, game 4, times spades' = 44. You turn the skat and find it contains, say, the heart Jack. Now your game is devalued: you are 'without 2, game 3, times spades' = 33. Having bid 36, you are 'bust', and threatened with loss. The best thing to do is to play on, hoping to make schneider. This will give you the extra multiplier you need to justify your bid. If you turned a black Jack, you would be 'with (or without) 1, game 2, times spades' = 22 – worse still. In this case you must look for other ways of justifying your bid. can you make clubs trump and win schneider? If so, you will score 'with 1, game 2, schneider 3, times clubs' = 36. If not, can you make a brave attempt at a grand (48), or a clever discard for null open (46)? Generally, it is not wise to bid too high when playing 'without' Jacks, unless you can tell from the auction that the higher trumps are in one player's hand rather than lurking in the skat. Being double-crossed by Jacks in the skat tends to disconcert inexperienced players. Experts take this danger into account intuitively and are very rarely caught out by it.

Grand bids

American Skat expert Joe Wergin has shown that for a 'grand hand' you need at least five of the nine power factors represented by the four Jacks, the four Aces, and the lead, and should not hold more than four sure losers. You therefore bid grand hand on:

♣J ◊J ♣10 K Q ♠A 10 ♡A 9 8 and the lead
♣J ♠J ♣A 10 K 9 ♠7 ♡9 8 ◊A and the lead
♠J ♡J ◊J ♠10 Q 9 ♡A 10 regardless of the lead

If just short of these values, you may consider playing grand with the skat. For example:

$$♣J ♡J ♣A K 9 ♡A 10 8 ◊Q 9$$

This is the same as the hand which we saw earlier was good for a bid of clubs, hand. Given the lead, you have five of the nine power factors, but five probable losers – one Jack, and two each in clubs and diamonds. If the auction forces you beyond 36 for your hand game in clubs, you may make the mental switch to grand and go up to 48.

Null bids

Starting at the top, for a bid of 'null open hand', worth 59, it goes without saying that any void suit is an unbeatable advantage. Any other suit must be bottomed on a Seven (though a singleton 8 is not bad, especially if you are Forehand and can lead it straight off), and no card above Seven should be separated by more than one gap from the one below it. Thus a holding of J–9–7 is unbeatable, and even A–J–9–7 would lose only if one opponent held the other four of that suit and was able to lead them from the bottom up. A singleton Eight is not bad, especially if you have the lead and get rid of it immediately. With only one dangerous card you can play hand, but not open, for 35. For example:

$$\clubsuit K\,J\,9\,7 \quad \spadesuit Q\,8\,7 \quad \heartsuit 8 \quad \diamondsuit 9\,7$$

The Queen is the danger card, and you could be forced to take that spade trick if you played open. An alternative approach would be to take the skat, dump the Queen, and then play open for 46. But if the skat yielded, for example, two high hearts, you could be lost. A simple null for 23, in which you take the skat and do not play open, is a very chancy business, and one you should only call as a substitute for drawing a bad skat on a lower bid.

Play

Skat is full of opportunities for clever and subtle play, but there is only space here for one or two particular points of interest.

In a suit game, the soloist should generally lead trumps at every opportunity. With five or six trumps, a good procedure is to lead high, then low, then high again, attempting to win the third trick in order to prevent the opponent who has no trump left from throwing a high counter to a trump trick won by his partner.

From a side suit headed 10–K, it is often best – sometimes even vital – to play the Ten at the earliest opportunity. This forces the Ace out, leaving your King in command of the suit, at a time when the other opponent is still able to follow suit and hence unable to fatten the 21-point trick by discarding another Ace or Ten. If you play the King, and the Ace-holder ducks, you could lose 31 or more card-points ('half the rent', as they say) on the next round.

Always keep track of the number of card-points currently won by yourself and your opponents. This takes practice, but soon becomes second nature, and is well worth while. For example, when a suit is led which you cannot follow, don't automatically trump. It may be worth throwing useless Kings and Queens to dud tricks in order to void your side suits without giving too many away, and you can only do this with safety so long as you know the score.

At grand, don't hesitate to use a long suit to force Jacks out if your own Jacks are either vulnerable or needed for a later purpose. For example:

♡J ◇J ♠A 10 K 8 7 ♡A 10 7

Given the lead, this is a 'grand, hand, without 2'. Don't lead a Jack: it could lose you the contract. Instead, play spades from the top down. If the Ace is trumped, re-enter with a top heart or a red Jack, and lead the spade Ten. If this also is trumped, you are left with the only Jack in play and certainly five, probably six remaining tricks. (You will try to get rid of the heart loser cheaply, rather than rely on clearing the suit with your Ace-Ten.)

The main thing for the partners to do is to take advantage of every opportunity for larding tricks being won by each other with high-counting cards – especially vulnerable Tens. A typical suit-game opening sees the soloist leading a red Jack and the second dropping a black Jack in case his partner can lard it with the Ace or Ten of trumps, which might otherwise be lost. Alternatively, the second to play, having no black Jack, will himself drop the Ace or Ten, hoping his partner can play a high Jack. If not, they are both in the soloist's hand (or hand and skat, same thing), and the fat trump would probably have been lost anyway, so there was no harm in trying.

One of the most important rules of play for the partners is to keep the soloist in the middle, i.e. playing second to a trick, whenever possible. Therefore, when you are leading to a trick to which he will be playing third, and have nothing positive to contribute, lead low in a suit which your partner either heads or can trump, in order to get him into the lead.

Sample deal

Rearhand deals as follows:

Forehand	♣J ♠J ♣10 K 9 8 7 ♡10 Q 7
Middlehand	♡J ♠10 K Q 8 7 ♣A Q ◇A 8
Rearhand	◇J ◇10 K 9 7 ♠A ♡A K 9 8
In skat:	♠9 ◇Q

Middlehand, to bid first, is looking at a prospective spade from the hand, having six trumps, a void suit, and two side Aces. He starts bidding '18', '20', '22', etc, and continues up to 44 (without 2, game 3, hand 4, times 11). Forehand accepts all these because he has prospective clubs from the hand worth 48 (with 2, game 3, hand 4, times 12). So when Forehand accepts '44', Middlehand passes, as there is no chance of making schneider and so increasing his game value to 55. Rearhand now takes over the bidding against Forehand, and tries '45', looking at a possible 'diamonds, hand, without three' (game 4, hand 5, times diamonds 9).

Forehand accepts '45'; Rearhand passes; Forehand announces 'Clubs, hand', and leads. The play runs as follows:

	FH	MH	RH	soloist	partners
1.	♠J	♣Q	◇J	7	
2.	♣J	♡J	◇7	+4=11	
3.	♣7	♣A	♠A		22
4.	♡7	◇8	◇K		+4=26
5.	♡Q	◇A	◇9		+14=40
6.	?	♠10	♡9		

At trick 4, Middlehand avoids leading ◇A in case the soloist trumps it, but leads a low diamond in an attempt (successful) to put his partner in the position of leading through the soloist. Forehand's ♡7 is the typical throw of a worthless card to cheap (4-point) trick. Middlehand's next lead, ♠10, which he knows to be best now the Ace has gone, ruins Forehand's solo. It is true that he has the four remaining trumps, but his ♡10 is now unguarded and cannot fail to be lost to the Ace, giving the partners a win by at least 61-59. Forehand will in fact play on, just in case the ♡A is in the skat; but loss is inevitable. The actual loss is 96 points – the value of the bid, doubled.

If Forehand had passed earlier, and either opponent had played his hand game, it is still likely to have been lost. Middlehand or Rearhand could, however, have played a successful skat bid. Middlehand would have gained an extra trump (♠9) and probably have discarded the two non-trump Queens, laying 6 points aside and nursing a nice singleton Ace. Rearhand would have gained an extra trump (◇Q) and probably discarded the two non-trump Nines.

20 | RUMMY AND KALUKI

One-pack and two-pack varieties of a long popular game

Since its first appearance in the USA in the late nineteenth century, the game called Rum or Rummy has spread throughout the western world and even reconquered the Orient, where it appears to have originated in the form of the tile game, Mah Jong.

The basic idea – that of drawing and discarding with a view to collections, sets or 'melds' of matched cards – is so simple that it has given rise to countless variants by way of elaboration. These include Gin Rummy, for two players, and Canasta, which for a brief while came to rival Bridge as a sociable partnership game, and itself spawned such offspring as Samba and Bolivia.

The simplest member of the family is basic Seven-Card Rummy, played with a single pack plus Joker(s), which reached its heyday in the 1920s and 1930s. Most Rummy players nowadays play with a doubled pack and call the game Kaluki, or Kalookie. The precise rules of Kaluki vary from school to school. It is important to understand that in card games generally, and in Rummy games especially, both the rules and the names of popular games are constantly shifting, evolving, and changing places with one another.

Described below is the basic Seven-card Rummy, which forms a good introduction to the Rummy family for children and beginners. It is followed by the two-pack game of Kaluki. Both are suitable for three or more players. Gin Rummy for two and Canasta for four have chapters of their own.

Before we begin, here are some essential Rummy terms common to all varieties.

The general idea is to collect groups of three or more matched cards. Such a group is called a *meld,* and *to meld* is to lay it face up on the table.

A meld is either a *set* or a *sequence.* A set is three or more cards of the same rank, regardless of suit, such as A–A–A, 7–7–7–7, etc. A sequence is a series of three or more cards of *the same suit* and in numerical sequence, such as ♠2–3–4, ♡J–Q–K, etc. Whether Ace counts low (A–2–3) or high (Q–K–A) varies from game to game.

Jokers are *wild* – that is, you can use one to stand for any 'natural' card missing from a meld. For example, you can meld ♣3–4–Joker, counting the Joker as ♣5.

Exposed melds may be extended by the addition of extra cards one or more at a time. This is called *laying off.* For example, with ♢5-6-7 on the table you could lay off ♢8 to one end of it, or ♢4 to the other, or both. Some games only allow you to lay off cards to your own melds, not other players'.

Note that since all Rummy games by nature put the cards very much in order, it is essential to shuffle thoroughly between deals.

Basic (seven-card) Rummy

How to play

Players and cards. Two to five players (three best) use a single 52-card pack without Jokers. Ace counts low in a sequence: A–2–3 is valid, but Q–K–A is not. (Unless otherwise agreed – see Scoring.)

Deal. Deal seven cards each in ones. Stack the rest face down. This is called the stockpile. Turn the top card of the stock and lay it face up to start the wastepile. Throughout play, the current top card of the wastepile is called the upcard.

Object. The aim is to be the first to go out by melding, laying off or discarding the last card from one's hand.

Start. The player at Dealer's left either passes or takes the upcard in exchange for any unwanted card from his hand. If he passes, the next in turn has the same option. This continues until someone starts the game by taking the upcard. If no one takes it, the player at Dealer's left starts the game by drawing the top card of stock, adding it to his hand, melding if possible, and discarding one card face up to the wastepile.

Play. Thereafter, each in turn from the left of whoever started plays as follows:

- Draws either the upcard or the top card of the stockpile and adds it to his hand;
- (If able and willing:) Lays a meld face up on the table in front of himself, and/or (provided he has already made a meld of his own) lays a card off to anybody's meld already made;
- Ends his turn by discarding one card face up to the wastepile. If he drew from the wastepile, he may not discard the card he drew in the same turn.

End of stock. If a player draws the last card of the stockpile and does not go out in the same turn, then, after he has discarded, Dealer gathers up the wastepile, shuffles it thoroughly, lays it face down as a new stock, and turns the top card face up beside it to start a new wastepile.

Going out and scoring. Play ceases the moment one player goes out, whether by melding, laying off or discarding the last card from his hand. He scores or is paid by each player, according to the total value of cards left in their hands, counting Ace to Ten at face value and courts 10 each. (If it is agreed to allow runs ending in –Q–K–A, so that Ace counts high or low, then unmelded Aces left in hand count 11 against instead of 1 point.) This amount is doubled if the winner went 'rummy', that is, disposed of all his cards in one turn without having previously made any meld.

Kaluki

How to play

Players. Two to six, best for four.

Cards. 108, consisting of two 52-card packs and four Jokers. Ace counts low or high, enabling sequences of A–2–3– or –Q–K–A. Jokers are wild. For scoring purposes, Aces count 15 each, courts 10 each, numerals at face value. Jokers count 25 against if caught in hand at end of play.

Deal. Deal, one at a time, 15 cards to each player, or 13 if five play or 11 if six. Stack the rest face down as a stockpile. Turn the top card of the stock and lay it face up to start the wastepile. Throughout play, the current top card of the wastepile is called the upcard.

Play. Thereafter, each in turn from the left of whoever started plays as follows:

- Draws either the upcard or the top card of the stockpile and adds it to his hand;
- (If able and willing:) Lays a meld face up on the table in front of himself, in accordance with the rules of melding below, and/or (provided he has already made a meld of is own) lays a card off to anybody's meld already made;
- Ends his turn by discarding one card face up to the wastepile. If he drew from the wastepile, he may not discard the card he drew in the same turn.

Melding. You may not lay off cards to other players' melds before you have made a first meld of your own. Furthermore, the first time that you meld, you must dispose of cards with a total face value of not less than 51, for which purpose Jokers count as the cards they represent.

For example, ♡10–Joker–♡K–♡A may be melded first, being worth 55. This value may be made up from one or more melds, or a meld and lay-offs to those of other players. For example, you could meld ♠6–7–8–9 for 30, ♠4–♡4–♣4–♢4 for 16, making 46, and lay off ♢5 to another player's ♢A–2–3–4 to make up 51.

A meld may contain one or more Jokers, and it must be clearly stated what cards they represent. No meld may contain two identical cards, whether wild or natural. This means, in particular, that a set may contain not more than four cards of the same rank, and they must be of different suits.

Taking Jokers. If any meld contains a Joker, and you hold the natural card that Joker represents, you may, on your turn to play, take the Joker into hand in exchange for the natural card.

End of stock. If a player draws the last card of the stockpile and does not go out in the same turn, then, after he has discarded, Dealer gathers up the wastepile, shuffles it thoroughly, lays it face down as a new stock, and turns the top card face up beside it to start a new wastepile.

Going out. Play ceases the moment one player goes out, whether by melding, laying off or discarding the last card from his hand.

Soft score. Each player except the winner is penalized by the total value of cards left in hand, counting Jokers 25 each, Aces 15, courts 10, and numerals at face value. The game ends when a player's penalty total reaches 150, and the winner is the player with the lowest penalty scare.

Hard score. The winner receives from each opponent two units for each Joker left in hand and one for every other card.

21 | THE BUM GAME

For the player who always comes bottom

This amusing but skill-rewarding game for two to five players (four best) is basically a Chinese game that started spreading to the west in the 1970s. The Chinese call it 'Climbing Up', in the sense of climbing up to a higher position – social climbing perhaps. The Japanese version is called Dai Hin Min, meaning 'Very Poor Man', or possibly 'Drop-out'. In the west it is widely known as Arsehole, of which the French equivalent is Trouduc and the American is Ass-hole, though in American books it bears the alternative title 'President' – whether from prudery or irony is anyone's guess. The London Card Club refers to it as 'Pits', and in my own circle we play a modified version which we call the 'The Bum Game'.

All this should give you an idea of the general sociological flavour of the game, and may even put you off by its unsavouriness. But persevere! It is not only great fun to play, and unlike anything you've played before, but also, when you once get into it, turns out to call for unusual elements of skill.

The most novel feature of the game is that it is the only one in which players physically change positions from deal to deal. If you want to play it properly, you should even provide four different types of chair for them to sit on. The basic idea is that players race to play out all their cards. For the first deal it doesn't matter who sits where. The first to get rid of all his cards is designated 'the Boss', and takes his position on a dignified but comfortable chair at the head of the table. The second to go out becomes 'the Foreman', and moves to a more functional office chair placed to the left of the Boss. Third out becomes 'the Worker', and occupies a hard wooden chair to the left of the Foreman and opposite the Boss. The last player left with cards in hand is the Bum, or Dogsbody, referred to in the title. He sits on a broken stool or creaky packing-case at the fourth side of the table. Subsequent deals may produce different results, causing players to occupy higher or lower positions in the hierarchy. But, as you will see, the game is so designed as to favour the current Boss and Foreman at the expense of the Worker and Bum, so that it is not so easy to make your way up the ladder if you have the misfortune to find yourself at the bottom at the end of the first deal.

The following member of the social climbing family is the way it has evolved in my group of players, but different schools have different rules and it is easy to ring changes on the basic scheme.

How to play

Cards and positions. Use a 52-card pack plus two Jokers. Draw for initial positions, the lowest taking the Bum's place, the highest sitting at his left in the Boss's chair, and the others following the same principle.

Deal. The cards are always shuffled and dealt by the current Bum, or, in the first deal, by the player occupying that seat. Deal all the cards out as far as they will go, so that two players receive 14 to the others' 13 each.

Rank of cards. The two Jokers are the highest cards. They are followed by the Deuces (Twos), Aces, Kings, Queens and so on down to the Threes, which are lowest of all. Suits are irrelevant. Jokers and Deuces are wild in certain circumstances, as explained below.

Object. The aim of the game is to get rid of all one's cards as soon as possible by playing them out to rounds of pay which may be called 'tricks' for convenience.

Play. The opening lead is made by the player at dealer's left (the Boss), and the winner of each trick leads to the next. Won tricks are worthless in themselves and are thrown face down to a common waste pile. The advantage of winning a trick is the quite powerful one of being able to lead to the next. The leader may lead:

- a single card, or
- two or more cards of the same rank, such as K–K, 4–4–4, etc., or

■ a run of three or more cards, such as 3–4–5 (the lowest possible), 9–10–J–Q–K, K–A–2–Joker, etc.

Each subsequent player must either pass or else play the same number and combination of cards as the previous player, but higher in rank.

Thus if a single card is led, each must play a higher card, and a Joker is unbeatable.

If a pair is led, each subsequent pair must be higher, and a pair of Jokers is unbeatable. If a triplet or quartet is led, such as 7–7–7(–7), each must play the same number of a higher rank, for which purpose 2–2–2(–2) is unbeatable. You cannot beat three of a kind by playing four of a kind, or a pair by playing three of a kind, as it is always necessary to play the same number of cards as the leader.

Similarly, the lead of a three-card sequence, such as 8–9–10, can only be beaten by a higher three-card sequence, such as 10–J–Q: it cannot be beaten by, and indeed may not be followed by, a four-card sequence.

Wild cards. Jokers and Deuces may be used as wild cards in sets of matched cards. For example, 7–7–7–7 is beaten by 8–2–2–Joker, representing four Eights, and A–2–2 (three Aces) by 2–Joker–Joker (three Deuces). With the aid of wild cards it is possible, and permissible, to lead five or more of a kind. Jokers and Deuces may be used in runs, but only in their normal positions (e.g. K–A–2–Joker), not as wild cards.

Winning a trick. Play continues with each in turn either passing or playing higher than the previous player. The turn may go round several times, and a player who has passed once is not debarred from playing again if able to do so. However, the same player may not play twice in succession. Three consecutive passes end the trick, and the person who played last must then turn it down and lead to the next. If he ran out of cards on his last play, the lead passes to his left.

End of deal. A player who runs out of cards ceases play. The first out of cards scores 3 points and becomes the next Boss, changing places if not already in that position. The second scores 2 and becomes the Foreman, the third 1 point and becomes the worker. The last player, or Bum, scores nothing, but bunches and shuffles the cards and deals to the next round, starting with the Boss and ending with the Foreman.

Card exchanges. Before play, the Boss must remove the two lowest-ranking cards from his hand and pass them face down to the Bum receiving in return the Bum's two highest-ranking cards. Similarly, the Foreman passes the Worker his lowest card – one only – in exchange for the Worker's highest. The purpose of this rule is to give the Boss and the Foreman an unfair advantage. The only consolation for the Bum and the Worker is that if either is dealt a Joker he is not obliged to give it away in the exchange, but may hang on to it.

When cards have been exchanged, the Boss leads to the first trick.

End of game. The game ends when one player wins by reaching a target score, say 20 for about three-quarters of an hour's play. One's final position in the hierarchy, whether Boss or Bum, is of no particular significance but may be used to break a tie.

Variants. Many variations are recorded in respect of scores and allowable combinations. As a matter of particular interest, the Chinese game also includes multiple sequences so that (for example) 6–6–7–7–8–8 is beaten by 7–7–8–8–9–9 or higher. In the Japanese game, if both Jokers are dealt to the Worker or the Bum, he may declare a revolution. The Boss then changes places with the Bum, and the Worker with the Foreman, with all the advantages of the exchange appertaining thereto.

The game may be played with varying numbers of Jokers. If they are distinguishable from one other, for example by colour, it may be agreed that they beat one another in a particular order when played as singletons. In some versions of the game, Jokers may be used to represent Deuces but not to beat them in their own right.

It may be agreed that, in runs, Jokers may be used as wild cards, and Deuces as natural low cards, so that 2–3–4 . . . etc. is a valid run.

If, like my group of players, you are too lazy to keep changing places, you can instead prepare four place-cards labelled with the four titles, and simply shift them about at the end of each deal. In this case, however, you should ensure that when a player goes out, the next lead is made, not necessarily by the player on his left, but by the player occupying the highest hierarchical position from the previous deal.

Other numbers of players

Five players. The third to run out of cards occupies a position between the Foreman and the Worker, and does not exchange any cards.

Three players. The positions are Boss, Middleman, Bum. The Boss passes his lowest card to the Bum and second lowest to the Middleman. The Bum passes his highest to the Boss and second highest to the Middleman. The Middleman passes to the Boss the highest card, and to the Bum the lowest card, from the hand originally dealt to him (before receiving a card from each other player).

Two players. Deal 14 cards each and stack the rest face down. The first to run out of cards scores one point for each card remaining in the other's hand. The remaining cards are then dealt out and the Boss and Bum exchange their lowest and highest cards respectively. The Boss then leads from 13 cards and the Bum starts with 13 plus those remaining from the first deal. The same scoring applies at the end of the second deal.

Notes on play

It is best not to arrange your cards in suits, which are irrelevant, but in ranking order, e.g.

Jo–2–A–K–J–9–9–9–7–6–5–5–3 (Jo = Joker)

The first thing you must do is to plan how to make the best of your combinations and how to get rid of your lowest-ranking cards, which are always the most difficult. In the hand shown, for example, you must decide whether to play the two Fives as a pair at the earliest opportunity, leaving you with two middling and one low singleton to dispose of (7–6–3), or to play 7–6–5 as a run, leaving you with two low stragglers (5–3). An advantage of the run 7–6–5 is that if the turn comes round again you can play your unbeatable Jo–2–A, or, with slight element of risk, your 2–A–K, enabling you to lead your Three upon winning the trick.

Having made a decision, it is usually best to stay with it. If the person on your right plays a pair of Threes or Fours, you should resist the temptation to play your Fives. If a single Five precedes you, the best response is the straggler Jack, which belongs to no set or sequence, rather than break into your three-card sequence or trio of Nines. Following a Three or Four, however, you would promptly throw a Five, as your decision to retain the sequence has turned it into a straggler.

You will aim to get rid of low cards as soon as possible and at every opportunity. For example, it is nearly always better to lead one Three than three Fives. If you lead four Threes early in the game you may well find opponents unable to follow to quadruplets, thus putting you well ahead; but if you get stuck with only Threes in hand, whether one or all four, and haven't got the lead, you'll certainly finish bottom. A minor exception is when you hold one very low rank and a lot of high ones, when you can sometimes bank on winning a round with a bunch of high cards and then going out by leading the low one – or pair, or however many you have of it.

If your highest card is, say, an Ace, you should, unless you can see a quick way of going out by playing it, hang on to it until you have counted out all the Deuces and Jokers, so that you can be sure of its winning a trick on a singleton lead. If you play it early and have it overtaken, you may never come in at all. If you have nothing higher than, say, Jacks, don't panic: just wait, and play carefully. You can hardly expect to win on such a hand, but it is by no means a foregone conclusion that you will come bottom. The all-important skill factor is a sense of timing.

Sample game

After several rounds, Bum deals the following hands (Jo = Joker)

Boss	Jo	2	A	Q	J	J	10	9	8	8	7	4	3	3
Foreman	2	2	A	J	10	10	9	9	8	7	7	5	5	3
Worker	A	K	K	K	Q	J	10	6	6	6	5	4	4
Bum	Jo	2	A	K	Q	Q	9	8	7	6	5	4	3

After the exchange of high and low cards, these become:

Boss	Jo	2	2	A	A	Q	J	J	10	9	8	8	7	4
Foreman	2	2	A	A	J	10	10	9	9	8	7	7	5	5
Worker	K	K	K	Q	J	10	6	6	6	5	4	4	3
Bum	Jo	K	Q	Q	9	8	7	6	5	4	3	3	3

The Boss kicks off with his long sequence of Seven to Queen, which no one can follow, and leads his singleton Four to the next trick. Foreman plays an Ace, Worker passes, Bum wins with his

Joker, and leads his long sequence from Three to Nine. After three tricks the hands are:

Boss	Jo 2 2 A A J 8
Foreman	2 2 A J 10 10 9 9 8 7 7 5 5
Worker	K K K Q J 10 6 6 6 5 4 4 3
Bum	K Q Q 3 3

Bum now leads his pair of Threes, which are followed by Eights from the Boss (the natural Eight and a wild Deuce), Tens, Kings, pass, Aces, and finally Deuces from the Foreman.

This leaves:

Boss	Jo J
Foreman	A J 9 9 8 7 7 5 5
Worker	K Q J 10 6 6 6 5 4 4 3
Bum	K Q Q

The Foreman, after much thought, leads his pair of Fives rather than 7–8–9 which would leave four straggly cards. These are followed by Sixes, Queens, and the Boss's unbeatable Deuce-Joker. The Boss now exits with his Jack, to which Foreman plays an unbeatable Ace to find himself on lead again from this position:

Foreman	J 9 9 8 7 7
Worker	K Q J 10 6 5 4 4 3
Bum	K 3 3

This time he opts for the three-card sequence, 7–8–9. The Worker overtakes with 10–J–Q, wins, leads 3–4–5–6, which no one can follow. Neither can they follow his King, and he goes out second with the Four. Bum thereupon goes out with his King, leaving Foreman with J–9–7 and changing places with him in the hierarchy.

Had Foreman led his pair of Sevens from the above position, he would have held the trick, led Nines, held it again, and led the Eight, leaving himself with an odd Jack. He would then only have lost if Worker had been concentrating enough to realize that his King was now unbeatable and should be played. Otherwise he would have played the Ten (keeping J–Q–K intact), and Foreman would have dropped by only one position instead of two.

The more you play this unusual game, the more fascinating it becomes.

CRAZY EIGHTS (AND SUCHLIKE)

A selection of going-out and adding-up games suitable for younger players or lighter moments

Crazy Eights is one of several names for one or more of a group of similar games and based on the idea of being the first to get rid of all your cards by discarding them one by one to a wastepile. The catch is that you may only discard by matching the previous player's discard by rank or suit. If you can't, you have to draw more cards, thereby enlarging your hand and taking longer to go out. Games of this type have increased in popularity since the 1960s, mainly through the introduction of ever more elaborate and tricky rules about how cards are required to match one another. These rules get shunted around from game to game, as do the various names they go under, making it very difficult to keep track of exactly what is meant by which. So we will start with a basic version, and then add some of the extras.

Crazy Eights

Players and cards. From two to seven play. Use a single 52-card pack for up to five players, doubled to 104 if there are more than five. Deal five cards each, or seven if only two play, and stack the rest face down. Turn its top card face up and place it next to the stock to start a wastepile. If it's an Eight, bury it in the stock and turn the next instead.

Play. Play goes in rotation starting with the player at Dealer's left. On your turn to play you can make one discard face up to the top of the wastepile, provided that it matches the previous discard by rank or suit. For example, if the previous upcard is the Jack of spades, you can play a spade or a Jack.

Object. To be the first to play off all your cards.

Play. The player at Dealer's left goes first. On your turn to play, you may discard one card to the wastepile provided that it matches the previous discard by either rank or suit. Eights are wild: you can play one whenever you like, and nominate a suit for the next player to follow, which needn't be that of the Eight itself. If you are unable (or unwilling) to match, you must draw cards from the top of the stock and add them to your hand until you do make a discard, or the stock runs out. If you can't play when no cards remain in stock, you can only pass.

Ending. Play ends as soon as someone plays their last card, or when no one can match the last card. The player who went out collects from each opponent a payment equivalent to the total face value of cards remaining in the latter's hand, counting each Eight 50, courts 10 each, others face value. If the game blocks, the player with the lowest combined face value of cards remaining in hand scores from each opponent the difference between their two hand values. In the four-hand partnership game both partners must go out to end the game.

Note. Some play with Aces wild instead of Eights. This is the original version of the game, and is properly called Rockaway.

Two-Four-Jack

This game, also called Switch, or Black Jack, became popular in the 1960s, and gave rise to a successful proprietary version called Uno™. Play like Crazy Eights or Rockaway, except that a player unable to follow draws only one card from stock, and with the following special rules.

Aces are wild.

Twos. Playing a Two forces the next in turn either to play a Two, or, if unable, to draw two cards from stock and miss a turn. If he draws, the next in turn may play in the usual way; but if he does play a Two, the next after him must either do likewise or draw four cards and miss a turn. Each successive playing of a Two increases by two the number of cards that must be drawn by the next player if he cannot play a Two himself, up to a maximum of eight.

Fours. have the same powers, except that the number of cards to be drawn is four, eight, twelve, or sixteen, depending on how many are played in succession.

Jacks. Playing a Jack reverses ('switches') the direction of play and forces the preceding player to miss a turn, unless he, too, can play a Jack, thus turning the tables.

Twos, Fours, and Jacks operate independently of one another. You cannot escape the demands of a Two by playing a Four instead, or of a Jack by playing a Two, and so on.

The game ends when a player wins by playing his last card. A player with two cards in hand must announce 'One left' or 'Last card' upon playing one of them.

The penalty for any infraction of the rules (including playing too slowly) is to draw two cards from stock.

The winner scores the face value of all cards left in other players' hands, with special values of 20 per Ace, 15 per Two, Four, or Jack, and 10 per King and Queen.

Go Boom

A simpler relative of Crazy Eights, suitable for children.

Deal seven cards each (but some prefer ten) from a full pack – or, if more than six play, a doubled pack of 104 cards – and stack the rest face down. The player at dealer's left plays any card face up. Each in turn thereafter must play a card of the same suit or rank if possible. A player unable to do so must draw cards from stock until able, or, when no cards remain in stock, must simply pass. When everyone has either played or passed, the person who played the highest card of the suit led turns the played cards down and leads to the next 'trick'.

Play stops as soon as someone plays their last card. That player scores the total values of all cards remaining in other players' hands, with Ace to Ten at face value and face cards 10 each.

One Hundred

Another group of simple games suitable for younger players or lighter moments is based on the idea of adding up the face value of cards played as you go along, and trying to make or avoid certain totals. Games of this sort have only recently made their way to Western Europe from Eastern Europe. It is an odd fact that the only Western card game with anything like this feature is the peculiarly English game of Crib.

One Hundred is the simplest of several games. You can easily make up others of your own.

Divide a 32-card pack between from two to seven players so that all have the same number of cards. If any are left over, deal them face up to the table and announce their combined face values, counting as follows:

Rank	A	K	Q	J	10	9	8	7
Value	11	4	3	2	10	9	8	7

Each in turn plays a card to the table and announces the total of all cards so far played. For example, if five play and the two undealt cards were a Jack and a Nine, the dealer would announce 'Eleven', and if the first to play added an Ace, he would announce 'Twenty-two'.

Keep adding cards one by one, in turn, and announcing the new total. If you make the total exactly 100, you win. If you bring it to more than 100 from a figure below 100, you lose.

Obstacle Race

Divide a 32-card pack evenly between from two to seven players and play as above (One Hundred), except that cards now have these face values:

Rank	A	K	Q	J	10	9	8	7
Value	1	4	±3	2	10	9	8	7

Note that, if you play a Queen, you can either add or deduct 3 from the current total, whichever you prefer.

The 'obstacles' in this race are 55, 66, 77, 88, 99 and 111. You score 1 point if you bring the total exactly to an obstacle number, but lose a point for causing the total to jump an obstacle number without making it exactly. Note that the play of a Queen enables an obstacle to be hit or jumped either upwards or downwards, and more than once.

When the total reaches or exceeds 120 it is re-set to zero, and play continues as before. The winner is the player with the highest score after one or more deals, or the first to reach an agreed target.

Ninety-Nine

This is said to be a Romany game.

From two to seven players receive three each from a 52-card pack and the rest are stacked face down.

The order of play runs to the left around the table to start with, but may change (as in the game of Switch).

Each in turn, starting with the player at dealer's left, plays a card face up to the table, announces the total face value of all cards so far played, and draws a replacement from stock.

Whoever brings the total over 99 ends the round and loses a life. Another deal follows, and the first player to lose three lives is the overall loser.

The cards have the following face values:

Black Ace	*any*	Seven	7
Red Ace	1	Eight	8
Two	2	Nine *makes*	99
Three	0	Ten *minus*	10
Four	0	Jack	10 *and switches*
Five	5	Queen	10
Six	6	King	10

Playing a black Ace entitles you to make the total anything you like, from 0 to 99.

A Nine automatically brings the total to 99, and can therefore only be followed by a Three, a Four, a Ten, or a black Ace.

Playing a Jack adds 10 and reverses the order of play. For example, when the first Jack is played, the next card is played by the person to the right of the one who played the Jack, and play continues to the right until another Jack is played.

Part Five

GAMBLING GAMES

23 | NEWMARKET

An old favourite from start to finish

This popular pastime of pubs and clubs has undergone a number of changes since it first appeared in books. In various forms it goes right back to a game called Comet played at court in seventeenth-century France. Many other games of this family are also named after other racecourses, such as Epsom and the American game of Michigan.

The following rules are typical of the modern game (South London, 1990s), but variations in detail may be encountered from place to place.

How to play

Cards. Standard 52-card pack. Cards run from low to high as follows: A 2 3 4 5 6 7 8 9 10 J Q K

Players. Three to eight; ideal for four.

Deal. Remove the four Kings and set them out face up on the table. Deal all the cards out one at a time, the last of each round going to a 'dead hand' which is left face down. It doesn't matter that some players have more cards than others.

Staking. Everybody stakes the same agreed amount to a pool or kitty, and another agreed amount on each of the four Kings.

Object. There are two aims. One is to be the first to play out all your cards, thereby winning the kitty. If no one goes out, the kitty is increased and carried forward to the next deal. The other is to win a King stake by playing the Queen of the same suit. The game ends when all four Kings have been won. This may take several deals, and sometimes many more.

Buying the dead hand. If the dealer is unsatisfied with his hand, he may exchange it for the dead hand free of charge. If he declines, the option of buying it passes to the left until someone else has exercised it or everyone has passed. Anyone who takes the dead hand, except the dealer, must pay another stake to the kitty. The two hands may not then be changed back again.

Play. Each in turn plays a card face up to the table in front of himself. Whoever holds the lowest diamond starts by playing it. The holder of the next higher diamond plays next, then of the next up, and so on in numerical order one at a time. If this sequence gets as far as the Queen, the player of that card wins the stake on the diamond King, turns the King down, and starts a new sequence as described below.

More usually, the sequence will peter out because the next diamond in sequence is lying in the dead hand so no one can play it. In this case the player of the last card starts a new sequence by playing the lowest card he holds of either black suit. If he has no black suit, the turn to start passes to the left until someone can go.

Play continues in the same way. Each sequence is continued by the player holding the other card of the same suit. Whoever plays a Queen wins the stake on the matching King (if it has not already been won in a previous deal), turns it down, and starts again. The starter of a sequence must play the lowest card he has of a suit *opposite in colour* from the one last played.

End of hand. There are two ways a hand can end.

- ■ Whoever plays the last card from their hand ends the play and wins the kitty.
- ■ If no one can start a new sequence because they can't change colour, play ceases and the kitty is carried forward.

In either case, the cards are gathered up, the deal passes to the left, and everyone adds another stake to the kitty.

Burying the Jack. When three King stakes have gone and only one remains, no one may buy the dead hand, and a new rule comes into play. The player holding the Queen matching the last King announces 'Bury the Jack' – or, if he also holds the Jack, the next

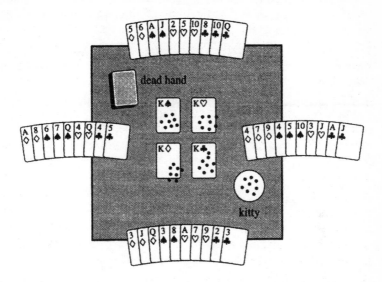

Figure 23.1   Newmarket

West leads, holding the lowest diamond (Ace). No one has the Two, so West leads again, switching colour as required. The play continues:

West	♣4–5, ♡4
North	♡5 ♣8 ♡2
East	♡3 ♠4–5
West	♠6-7
South	♠8 ♡A ♣2–3 ◇3
East	◇4
North	◇5-6
East	◇7
West	◇8
East	◇9 ♣A ♡J
West	♡Q ♠Q = out

West sweeps a King with each Queen and the kitty for going out.

This looks like the first deal played with a new pack. It is rare for the suits to be evenly distributed and for everyone who completes a sequence to be able to switch colour for a new lead. The nature of the game is such that in subsequent deals players are more likely to be dealt hands containing a void suit or dominated by cards of one colour.

card below the lowest card he holds of the sequence headed by the Queen. (Fox example, holding 9–10–J–Q he would say 'Bury the Eight'.) The holder of the card called for burial must then exchange his hand for the dead one, free of charge.

If no one holds the Queen, she being in the dead hand, play continues with the hands as dealt, and the King stake will be carried forward to the next deal.

End of game. The game ends when someone plays the Queen matching the last King. This wins both the King stake and the kitty.

24 | PONTOON

A game by any other name . . .

This gambling game is played all over the world. Its most general and accurate title is Twenty-One, but different versions of it appear in different countries and in various social contexts under a variety of characteristic names. Pontoon, probably a corruption of its older French name, *vingt-un,* denotes the informal British game played at home, in school and (if permitted) in the pub. Its American equivalent is Blackjack, which differs in certain details from Pontoon, and is the form of the game played in British gaming establishments. As a casino game, it has the remarkable, if not unique, property of enabling an intelligent and assiduous player to consistently break even against the house, if not actually to stay ahead. This can be done by means of complex computer-aided analysis, but of course this makes the game less fun to play, especially as casino proprietors are quick to spot it and keen to stamp it out.

The following rules of the common or garden domestic British Pontoon are typical rather than definitive. As with all gambling games, details vary from school to school. It is important to note that this is *not* the game played in casinos under the name Blackjack, which is well described by Belinda Levez in *Teach Yourself How to Win at Card Games.* (A slightly misleading title, as it covers only casino card games and has nothing to say about domestic card games.)

How to play

Preparation. Use a standard 52-card pack. Pontoon is played for chips, counters or other manageable objects. Agree first on minimum and maximum permitted stakes (for example, one and five chips respectively). Each deal is a separate event and is settled individually. The game ends when one player goes broke, or after an agreed time-limit. Choose first banker by drawing a card from the pack: Ace counts high, and highest banks first. The bank subsequently passes to the first punter (player against the bank) to make a winning pontoon.

Shuffling. The cards are shuffled before the game starts, and by each player upon taking over the bank. After each deal the banker returns all played cards to the bottom of the pack and cuts, but does not shuffle, before dealing. (Players may agree beforehand to dispense with the cutting rule.)

Value of cards. Cards are only of interest for their numerical values, suit being completely irrelevant. Court cards count ten each, others their face value, and Ace either one or eleven at the discretion of the holder (and he may change his mind about it as often as he likes). Cards worth ten (10 J Q K) are called tenths.

Object. To draw cards totalling more than the banker's cards but not more than twenty-one or less than sixteen. The possible hands rank as follows:

Bust (over 21)	–	always loses, but banker wins equality
A count of 16 to 21	–	wins if higher than the banker's total
Pontoon	–	a count of 21 on two cards (Ace and a tenth)
Five-card trick	–	five cards totalling not more than 21
Royal pontoon	–	21 made on three Sevens (only valid when held by a punter: in the banker's hand it is an ordinary '21').

The deal and stake. The banker deals one card face down to each player, in clockwise rotation ending with hirnself. Each punter (but not the banker) looks at his card and places a stake beside it, leaving the card face down on the table before him. The banker then deals everyone a second card face down.

Pontoons? The banker now looks at his cards, without revealing them, to see if he has a pontoon (an Ace and a tenth). If so he shows it, and each punter pays him twice his stake, unless he also has a pontoon, in which case he shows it and only loses his single stake. If the banker does not have a pontoon he leaves his cards face down and indicates his readiness to play further. In this event, any player holding a pontoon must turn the Ace up to show that he cannot lose and will be taking over the bankership.

Pairs? Anyone holding two cards of the same rank may split them, and play them as two separate hands. They must, incidentally, be of exactly the same rank, not just different tenths, like a Queen and a Jack. The player indicates that he is splitting by separating the two cards, laying the whole of his stake against one of them and placing exactly the same amount as his stake against the other. The banker then deals him two more cards, one for each hand. Again, the punter looks at his second cards, and may split again if he has another pair. In all subsequent play, a punter who has split pairs must count himself as two (or more) separate people, and concern himself with each hand individually.

Stack, buy, twist or bust. The banker now addresses himself to each player in turn, dealing him as many more cards as requested, until the punter either sticks or announces himself bust. So long as the punter's count is less than 16 he must either buy or twist another card. At a count of 16 or more he may buy or twist, or else stick, thus indicating satisfaction with his hand and his intention to compete against the bank. At a count of 22 or more he must announce himself bust and hand his cards to the banker, who returns them to the bottom of the pack and wins the punter's stake.

If the punter says 'buy' the banker deals him a card face down; if he says 'twist', the card is dealt face up. In order to buy a card the punter must first increase his stake, but he must not pay less than he did for the previous card, nor more than the total already staked. As soon as he has twisted a card, he may only acquire more by twisting and may not revert to buying. If he gets a total of four cards with a combined count of 11 or less, so that he is bound to make a five-card trick, he may not buy but only twist a fifth. In any case, even when he (legally) buys a fifth card it is dealt face up instead of down. No player may have more than five cards in any one hand.

The banker's play. If everybody busts, the bank wins all stakes and there is no further play. If any punter is left in, however, the banker now reveals his two cards and continues to deal himself more cards, face up, until he either sticks or busts. (He may not split pairs.)

If the banker busts, each punter left in the game reveals his own cards and collects from the banker an amount equivalent to his stake if he has a count of 16 to 21, or twice his stake if he has a pontoon or a five-card trick, or three times his stake if he has a royal pontoon (three Sevens).

If the banker sticks at a count of 21 he wins the single stake of any punter with 21 or less, but is beaten by and pays out a single stake to a punter's pontoon, double stake to a five-card trick, treble stake to a royal pontoon. If his count is less than 21 he pays anyone with a higher count. (With a count of 17, for example, he says 'Pay 18', and anyone with 18 or more turns his cards face up to claim payment.)

If the banker has a five-card trick he beats anything except pontoon and royal pontoon. Banker's royal pontoon (three Sevens) counts only as an ordinary 21, and loses to pontoons and five-card tricks.

Settlements at Pontoon:

Punter's hand . . .	. . . is beaten if banker's hand is:	. . . otherwise is paid as below:
bust (over 21)	anything	
count of 16-21	equal or higher	single stake
(A + tenth)	pontoon (only)	double stake
five-card trick	five-card trick*	double stake
royal pontoon	(unbeatable)	treble stake

* Not beaten by a pontoon, because if the banker had one then nobody could have drawn five cards! In some circles, incidentally, a banker's five-card trick beats a pontoon. This marginally increases the excitement on some hands, but there seems little point in increasing the banker's already generous advantage.

Notes on play

Bank take-over. The bank is taken over by any punter who wins a pontoon (not a royal pontoon or a five-card trick), but not if he does so on a split hand. If more than one has a pontoon, it goes to the first of them to the present banker's left.

Skill at gambling consists in playing systematically, though not necessarily to a 'system'; adjusting the amount of your stake to the probability of winning; and resisting the temptation to stake wildly when low on resources. The recommended one-to-five minimum/maximum stake enables you to (a) distinguish between a low, a middling and a high stake, in accordance with the probabilities, and (b) adjust this scale to your current resources. For example, when low on funds you should play cautiously and fix your stakes at, say, 1, 2 or 3; when well off you may fix them at 2, 3, 4 or 3, 4, 5; or at any other time work to a 1, 3, 5 series of gradations.

Don't underestimate the bank's advantage. Most of the banker's income derives from punters who bust, since they still pay him even if the banker busts. Another large proportion comes from the fact that he wins from equals. And, in his own play, he has an advantage in knowing how many punters are standing against him. As a player, your safest course is to stick when you can – even at 16, since the mean value of a card is seven, and the chances of your not busting are 2-1 against. The banker may conceivably stick at 16 if there is only one punter against him, but with three against him (or up to six, counting split hands) the draw of another card is more likely to win than an agreement to 'pay seventeens'.

The probability that the banker has a pontoon, or that you will be dealt one from scratch, is about 0.024, equivalent to less than 2.2 per cent, or one in every 41 hands. (Hence, in a four-player game expect to see a pontoon once in every ten deals.) The probability of being dealt a five-card trick from scratch, according to my calculations, is twice as high – amounting to about 0.045, or 4.4 per cent, or one every 22–23 hands. If fewer actually appear than this figure suggests, it is clearly because many potential five-card tricks are not filled out, but abandoned at the fourth or even third card. The probability that the banker will bust after you have stuck is about 0.3, or three in ten. This figure assumes that he follows the policy of always sticking when he can; if not, your chances improve.

The fact that an Ace may count 1 or 11 introduces some fascinating complications. In Blackjack terminology a hand containing an Ace and not exceeding 21 is described as 'soft'; if it exceeds 21 by counting the Ace as 11 it is 'hard'. It is pretty obvious that you should always stick at, say, 18 – but what about a 'soft' 18, which alternatively counts 8? Here the answer depends in part on how many cards you have – with four, for example, a count of 8 guarantees you a five-card trick; with three, you must consider the possibility of drawing an Eight or Nine, which gives you a lower stickable number, an Ace, Two or Three, which gives you a 21 or a five-card trick, a tenth, which leaves you back where you started (with 18), or one of the other four ranks, which complicate matters further.

Whether or not to split pairs is not a difficult question provided that you follow a policy in deciding which counts are good and which bad. If the individual count of each card is better than the total count of both, split them; otherwise, don't. All you need then is a good policy.

In view of the possibility of a five-card trick, the number of cards on which you reach a given count is of considerable significance. The following suggestions for strategy are therefore subdivided into the numbers of cards held.

First card

Stake high on an Ace, for obvious reasons. The probability of being dealt a tenth next is about 0.38, giving two chances in five of making a pontoon. On a tenth, stake high, but with reservations. The probability of a pontoon is less than 0.08 (12–1 against). You have a three-in-ten chance of getting a second tenth, and must weigh that against the possibility that banker will make 20 or 21. In straitened circumstances, make it a middling stake. On anything else, prefer to stake low.

Second card (no pair)

Stick on 16–20 (hard): your chances of not busting if you twist at 16 are barely two in five, and naturally worse on higher numbers. The banker will certainly beat your 16 if he sticks, but it is safer to bank on his busting than to try it yourself. On a soft 18–20, stick if you want to play it safe. Soft 16/17 is better counted as 6 or 7.

A hard count of 12–15 is the worst range of all and the safest procedure is to twist. The fact that the mean value of a card is seven doesn't mean that 14 is the most promising count: 12 is clearly better, as it gives you the smallest chance of busting. A soft count of 12–15 should, of course, be regarded as 2–5.

A count of 10 or 11 is highly favourable – see *First card* card for the probabilities. Here it is better to buy than to twist.

On a count of less than 10, buy, for a modest amount. Don't start splashing out yet against the possibility of a five-card trick.

Splitting pairs

Aces: safer to split them than to keep them and go for a five-card trick.

Tenths: the question here is whether a count of 20 in the hand is better than two chances of a pontoon in the bush. It surely is. Don't split.

Nines: your choice is to stick at 18, or to try for two slightly-better-than-even chances of not doing worse. Don't split unless you can afford to indulge a delight in gambling for the sake of it.

Eights: your choice is to stick at 16, twist to a 5-in-13 chance of improving, or split on two 9-in-13 chances of improving a count of eight. Splitting is best; sticking worst.

Sevens, Sixes: neither rank allows you to stick, and both put you in the dreaded 12–15 range. Always split. (The odds against drawing a royal pontoon to a pair of Sevens are about 24–1.)

Don't split Fives, as 10 is a good count to buy to.

Split Fours: it's true that they are of a favourable average value for a five-card trick, but the chances are not good, and 8 is a bad count to buy to.

Don't split Threes or Twos: both 6 and 4 are acceptable counts to buy to, and you may be permitted the thought of a five-card trick.

Third card

Stick on hard 16–21. If you must gamble on soft 20, twist, don't buy: you have one chance of improving, four of equalizing, eight of doing worse. Whether you count this as only a five-in-thirteen chance of not doing worse, or an eight-in-thirteen chance of not doing better, the odds are still not in your favour. Soft 18 or 19 is best left alone, but you may twist (or even buy, if you can afford it) to soft 16 or 17, either of which is at least in the running for a five-card trick.

With 12–15 (hard), twist, as for the same total on two cards. Count soft 14-15 as 4-5 and buy with a view to a five-card trick. If you have soft 13, you have been playing it all wrong, as a soft 12 on three cards is only obtainable with a card counting zero, which Pontoon has not yet invented.

Buy gladly with 10 or 11, and with a view to a five-card trick on a count of 4-7. Buy cheaply or twist, on a count of 8-9.

Fourth card

If you have from 5 to 11, you are obliged to twist, as the five-card trick is beyond question. From 12 to 20, of course, your only concern is not to bust, and the probability of doing so gradually increases as follows:

Count of   12: 0.31 probability (3 in 10 chances of busting)
                  13: 0.38
                  14: 0.46
                  15: 0.54
                  16: 0.62
                  17: 0.69
                  18: 0.77
                  19: 0.85
                  20: 0.92

In general, then, you may consider buying so long as your chances of not busting are better than even, i.e. up to a count of 14. You can't stick at 15, so whether you buy or twist is a question that must be answered by balancing the slightly-worse-than-even chance of improving against how much you can afford to gamble.

From 16 upwards the probability of making a five-card trick is exactly the same as that of improving a similar count on a smaller number of cards. However, the difference is that you now stand to win twice your stake if successful as against losing only your single stake if you bust. At 16, then, you have 62 chances in 100 of losing one stake (total: minus 62), but 38 chances of gaining two stakes (total: plus 76). This produces a balance of +8 in your favour, so at 16 it is worth buying if you can afford it, or twisting if not. At a count of 17, a similar calculation of the balance turns out to be almost the same amount against you, so it would be slightly better to stick. At 18 or more, you should stick.

Banker's play

The same suggestions as those made above for punters apply also when you are the banker, only more so, since you have a natural advantage. If you always stick when you can, you are bound to win in the long run. But, since you don't know how long a run you are going to get, you may be influenced in some of your decisions by the number of punters standing against you. For example, with three against you it is hardly worth sticking at 16; with only one against you, you will already have gained two stakes and can well afford to take another card to a count of 16.

Sample round

The players are A, B, C and D for dealer, who is also the banker, and who deals as follows:

First two cards

A gets ♣3, stakes 3, then ♣2, making 5.

B has ♡K, stakes 4, is dealt ♠2, making 12

C gets ♡8 then ♠8, and splits them, staking 2 on each. C-right gets ♢6 for 14 and C-left ♠3 for 11.

D deals himself ♠A, ♢2, counting 3 or 13.

Further transactions

A (staking 3 on 5) buys ♣10 for 2, making 5 or 15, twists ♡5, and sticks at 20.

B (staking 4 on 12) twists ♣9, sticks at 21.

C-right (staking 2 on 14) twists ♠K, busts.

C-left (staking 2 on 11) buys ♡A for 2, counts 13, twists ♢A, making 14, twists a fifth card and gets ♣4, giving him a five-card trick counting 18.

Dealer, with a count of 3 or 13, now confronts three hands with counts of 20, 21 and a five-card trick. He draws ♠Q for 13, then ♡7 for 20, and announces 'Pay twenty-ones'.

Result

A on a count of 20 pays 5 to D

B on 21 receives 4 from D

C-right (bust) pays 2

C-left, having a five-card trick, receives 8 (twice his stake of 4)

This leaves Dealer 5 down on a somewhat exceptional deal. But he's sure to make it up soon.

Variations

In some circles, a pontoon is strictly defined as an Ace and a 'royal', Ace and Ten being only an ordinary 21. The objection to this is that it increases the banker's advantage by reducing a punter's chance to take over by 25 per cent.

Some permit the banker to look at his first card before dealing out anyone's second, and to call for double stakes if he likes what he sees. In this case all players must double the stake made on their first card before seconds are dealt. Again, it may be objected that this works to the banker's advantage.

There are various ways of changing the bankership. The least satisfactory, though clearly the fairest, is for each player to deal in turn. Or the banker may offer to sell the bankership, or entertain an offer to buy it, at any time, so long as the price is acceptable. This is usually followed when the banker has been playing so badly that he can't afford to lose too heavily on the following round.

A Joker may be conveniently put to use as a marker card. Place it at the bottom of the pack before the first deal. When it appears at the top, shuffle the cards, or allow the bankership to pass to the left or be sold by auction.

25 | BRAG

Traditional British equivalent of Poker

Brag has been one of Britain's most popular gambling games for centuries, a position confirmed in a survey conducted in the 1980s which showed it to rank fourth on a list of the most widely played card games. It goes back to the Tudor game of Post, subsequently called Post and Pair until it was equipped with wild cards called 'braggers' and accordingly renamed Brag in the 1720s. Then regarded as an aristocratic pastime, it has since suffered a social decline under the assault of its richer and more sophisticated American derivative Poker.

Brag is an eminently non-standard game occurring in a variety of forms, of which the following are but a selection. All, however, are based on the same three-card combinations, namely:

■ *Prial* (= *Pair Royal*). Three cards of the same rank. A prial of Aces beats a prial of Kings, and so on down to the lowest prial (Twos). A prial of Aces, however, is not the best hand but is beaten by a prial of Threes, although in most other respects Three ranks in its normal position between Two and Four.

■ *Flush Run* (or *Running Flush*). Three cards in suit and sequence such as 2–3–4 or Q–K–A. As between flush runs, the one with the highest-ranking top card wins. The Q–K–A hand, however, is not highest but is beaten by A–2–3, which can be beaten only by a prial.

■ *Run*. Three cards in numerical sequence but not all of the same suit. The highest is A–2–3, followed by A–K–Q, K–Q–J, etc, down to 4–3–2.

- *Flush.* Any three cards of the same suit. As between competing flushes, the one with the highest top card wins, or second highest if tied, or third if tied again. Ace is highest, Two lowest, Three second lowest.

- *Pair.* Two cards of the same rank, the third one odd. A pair of Aces beats Kings, and so on down to Threes and then Twos (lowest). If two players have a pair of the same rank, the one with the higher third card wins.

- *High card.* As between competing hands containing none of these combinations, the best is the one with the highest top card, or second if tied, and so on. Ace is high, Three and Two are low.

Wild cards. One or more cards may be designated wild, standing for any card nominated by its holder. The Jack of clubs and/or any other Jack or Ace is traditional. Alternatively a Joker may be added to the pack as a wild card. Originally, a hand containing a wild card

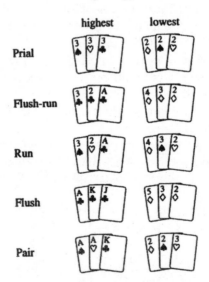

Figure 25.1   Brag

Brag hands from highest to lowest – a prial of Threes to a pair of Twos. The diagram excludes hand containing three unmatched cards, i.e. no combination at all.

or 'bragger' beat an equivalent hand consisting entirely of natural cards; but this rule has long since been reversed, probably under the influence of Poker.

Brag is played in a variety of different ways according to the number of cards dealt and various other factors.

Three-card Brag

Decide first dealer by any agreed means. A game consists of any number of deals so long as all players deal the same number of times. Cards are shuffled at the start of play and immediately after any deal won with a prial, but not otherwise. Dealer puts up an agreed stake in advance *(ante)* and deals cards face down one at a time clockwise around the table until everyone has three. Place the remainder face up to the left to show the position of the deal.

Players now look at their cards (unless playing blind, as explained below). The first player to dealer's left must either bet any amount not less than the ante, or *stack*, i.e. throw his cards in, which he does by squaring them up and placing them face up on the top of the undealt portion of the pack.

Thereafter each player must do one of the following:

Stack his cards if he does not wish to continue play;

Stay, by increasing his stake to equalize that of the previous active player on his right; or

Raise, by equalizing (as above) and adding a further amount which subsequent players must meet if they wish to stay.

This continues until only two players are left in. Either of them may then stack (in which case the other wins without showing his cards) or raise, or see his opponent by equalizing the stakes. The better hand then wins the pot, pool or kitty. If the caller admits defeat, he need not show his hand.

In case you already play Poker, you should take note of two important poins about Brag. The first is that equalizing the stakes does not cause a showdown. Thus, if there are three players and Abel stakes 3, which Baker and Charlie then match, Abel must either stack or raise again; in fact, there is nowhere else to go so long as more than two players remain in the pot. This brings us to the second difference., which is that no showdown takes place until only two players are left in. Then, and only then, can one player call to 'see' the other's hand by equalizing the stakes.

Betting blind. Some schools permit players to bet *blind,* that is, without looking at their hand but leaving their cards face down on the table. A blind player may stack, stay or raise in the usual way, and may cease to play blind at any time by taking up his cards. So long as he does play blind, however, he need only bet half the appropriate stakes, while non-blind or 'open' players must be double the amount by which he raises. In this game there is a rule that 'you cannot see a blind man'. Consequently, if one of the last two left in is playing blind the other must either keep equalizing the amount he bets, or raise it, until either of them stacks or the blind man takes up his cards.

If both continue to play blind the situation is even more amusing, though in some schools it is permitted for a blind man to 'see' a blind man. If everybody stacks, leaving a blind man to win the kitty with his unseen hand, he is permitted (if he wishes) to keep the same hand for his next deal, provided that he does not look at it until the betting is under way. In this case it is customary to deal him three cards in the usual way, but face up, in order to 'preserve the order of the cards'. These are then stacked before play begins.

Five-card Brag

Five cards are dealt to each player, who rejects any two and plays the rest in the usual way. In this version there is nothing special about Threes, but the highest hand may be agreed to be a prial of Fives.

Seven- and Nine-card Brag

In Seven-card, as the name implies, seven cards are dealt to each player. He forms six of these into two Brag hands, placing the higher of them to his left and the lower to his right, and rejecting the odd card. When ready, the player at dealer's left turns up his left (higher) hand. Each in turn after him either passes, if he cannot beat it, or turns his left hand face up if he can. When this round is complete, the player showing the highest hand then turns up his right hand, and the others then likewise if they can beat it. A player whose two hands are each highest in their turn wins the pool, to which everyone will have anted an agreed amount at the start of play. A player who wins on one hand and ties for best on the other also takes the pool, and in the unlikely event of two ties the pool is carried forward to the next deal.

Refinements: (a) there is nothing special about Threes, but a prial of Sevens is the top hand, beating a prial of Aces; (b) if anyone is dealt four of a kind among his seven cards he exposes them immediately, and the highest ranking four of a kind wins the pool. Four Aces may be beaten, in some circles, by four Fours or four Sevens (whichever is agreed beforehand).

Nine-card Brag works on the same principle. Each player receives nine cards and arranges them into three Brag hands, which are revealed in order from highest to lowest as described above. A player must win all three hands to take the pool, or at least tie best on any he does not win outright, otherwise the pool is carried forward. The highest hand is four of a kind, which wins outright if dealt originally. Four Nines (or Fours, as agreed) beats any other four, and a prial of Nines (or Three) beats any other prial.

Crash

A logical extension of Nine-card Brag, which became popular around Norwich some years ago. Four players receive thirteen cards each and form them into four Brag hands, which they place face down in a row, rejecting the odd card. Each hand is then revealed in turn, in order from left to right or right to left but not at random, and the winner marks one point on a special scoring board. In some circles the last hand only scores if it is a pair or better. The game is won – after as many deals as it takes – by the first player to mark seven points, but if one player wins all four hands in a deal it is a *crash* and he wins outright. Anyone who has made no score at the end of a game may be required to pay extra to the winner, or to ante double stakes to the next pool. (A Crash board for marking the points consists of a square of wood about five inches each side, with two lines of thirteen holes drilled from corner to corner like a St Andrew's cross, the middle hole being common to both. Each player starts with his peg or matchstick at one corner and advances it one hole per point towards the centre, which, of course, it takes seven steps to reach.)

American Brag

This is played like Poker but with three cards and Brag hands. All Jacks and Nines are wild cards (braggers). The highest hand is three braggers, since wild hands beat natural hands of the same degree.

Bastard Brag

Also known as Stop the Bus.

Everyone antes an agreed amount. Three cards are dealt to each player and three face up to the middle of the table as a spare hand. Each player in turn may exchange any or all of his cards for the spare hand, and the process of exchanging with the cards in the middle continues until one player, satisfied with his hand, ends the game by knocking. The others may then stick or make one more exchange before the showdown, at which the best hand wins. In an improved version of the game, a player may exchange either one or all three cards, but not two, and/or each player following a knock must exchange one last time. This version renders the name of the game even more appropriate.

Classical Brag

This is the old version of the game still described in the textbooks. There are no runs or flushes. The highest hand is a prial of Aces, followed by successively lower-ranking prials down to the Twos (nothing special about Threes). The next best hand is a pair, again ranking from Aces down to Twos, and with the odd card deciding in the event of a tie. Hands containing neither combination are decided on the highest cards as usual. There are three wild cards or braggers: ♣J, ◇A and ◇9. A hand with braggers beats an equal hand with none or fewer. Betting proceeds as at Poker rather than modern Brag, i.e. whenever all bets are equalized there is a showdown, regardless of how many are left in.

26 | **POKER**

The game of the Wild West (also played in the Tame East)

Contrary to the popular opinion of those who do not play it, Poker is a game of skill. It also happens to be a gambling game, but only in the technical sense of the word – that is, in the sense that it cannot be played for score-points, like Bridge, but only for hard score, i.e. cash, or at least for tokens representing cash ('chips'). It also differs from Bridge and other intellectual card games in the fundamental sense that the latter are played with cards whereas Poker is played with money. No physical card-play is involved at all in Poker. Playing-cards merely serve the purpose of providing raw material on which to exercise the skills of money management and practical psychology. In the absence of cards, which have the merit of being convenient and traditional, the play of Poker can be – and often is – applied equally well to dice, dominoes, Mah Jong tiles, Scrabble tiles, even pound notes and dollar bills. An understanding of the basic mathematical principles of probability is helpful to this game, but the skills involved are essentially psychological. It is the fact that you play the opponents and not the cards that makes Poker the great leveller.

A product of American genius, Poker is the most advanced and globally successful member of an ancient family of games including Brag and Primero. It originated around New Orleans during the 1820s, probably from a group of related games then chiefly represented by the French game of Poque. Further evolution during the course of the nineteenth century turned it into the highly sophisticated game that it is today – one not to be taken or undertaken lightly.

Like most gambling games, and unlike Bridge, Poker is played in a variety of forms. All are based on the same five-card combinations or 'Poker hands', as described below, and are best played with proper Poker chips available from any good games shop. Chips come in various colours that may be used to represent any agreed scale of values. At least three colours are required, the lowest being white, the middle red, and the highest blue (whence the phrase 'blue chip' for an investment of high value). Typical scales of value are:

white	1	1	1	1
red	2	2	5	5
blue	5	10	20	25
yellow	25	25	50	100
black	100	100	200	250

Beginners should start with Draw Poker on a scale of 1–2–5. The five-card Poker hands rank from highest to lowest as follows. Note that individual cards rank 2 3 4 5 6 7 8 9 10 J Q K A, with Ace optionally low in a numerical sequence, and that no suit is better than another. (The abbreviations in brackets are mine, there being no recognized standard.)

Straight flush (SF). Five cards in suit and sequence, Ace counting high or low. The lowest is A–2–3–4–5 of a suit. The highest, 10–J–Q–K–A of a suit, is called a royal flush.

Four of a kind, or Fours (4S). Four of the same rank, from 2–2–2–2–x to A–A–A–A–x. The fifth card (x) is immaterial.

Full house (FH). Three of a kind and a pair, from 2–2–2–3–3 to A–A–A–K–K. Of two full houses, the one with the higher triplet wins – e.g. 5–5–5–2–2 beats 4–4–K–K.

Flush (FL). Five cards of the same suit but not all in sequence. The lowest would be 2–3–4–5–7 of a suit, the highest 9–J–Q–K–A.

Straight (ST). Five cards in sequence, but not all the same suit, from A–2–3–4–5 to 10–J–Q–K–A.

Triplet, three of a kind, or threes (3S). Three of the same rank plus two of two different ranks, from 2–2–2–x–y to A–A–A–x–y.

Two pairs (2P). Self-explanatory, from 2–2–3–3–x to A–A–K–K–x. Competing two pairs are decided on the higher pair, or the lower pair if equal, or the odd card if still equal. Thus J–J–7–7–3 beats J–J–7–7–2, and either of them would beat J–J–6–6–4.

One pair (IP). From 2–2–x–y–z to A–A–x–y–z. A higher pair beats a lower. As between two hands containing a pair of the same rank, the tie is broken in favour of the highest of the three unmatched odd cards.

High card. A hand containing no pair, flush or straight is called a high-card hand because when two or more of them compete the one with the highest card wins, or second highest if equal, and so on. Thus A–7–5–4–2 (Ace high) beats K–Q–J–10–8 (King high), which beats K–Q–J–10–7.

Poker cannot be successfully played without instant recognition of each type of hand for its true worth. The following table indicates their relative value by showing how rare or common they are. The first column of figures shows how many different hands there are of each type. The second expresses the same thing as a percentage of the total number of possible hands. The third shows the odds-to-one against being dealt such a hand straight from the pack (higher figures rounded to nearest 50):

hand	how many	frequency	odds
Straight flush	40	0.0015	65,000
Four of a kind	624	0.024	4,150
Full house	3,744	0.144	700
Flush	5,108	0.196	500
Straight	10,200	0.392	250
Three of a kind	54,912	2.13	46
Two pairs	123,552	4.75	20
One pair	1,098,240	42.25	1
High card	1,302,540	50.12	1
Total	2,598,960	(100%)	

This reveals that about half the hands dealt are nothing in particular, and most of the remainder are one pair. At an evening of ordinary Draw Poker, most of the pots will be won on two pairs or threes, while anything higher than a Full House would be something of an event. In case this sounds unexciting, it may be worth noting that different types of Poker game increase the frequency of winning on higher hands – for example, by dealing seven or more cards and allowing the player to choose the best five from them.

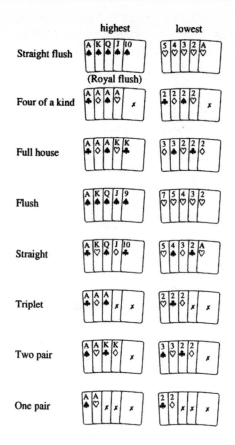

	highest	lowest

Straight flush

(Royal flush)

Four of a kind

Full house

Flush

Straight

Triplet

Two pair

One pair

Figure 26.1 Poker hands

From highest to lowest. Note that Ace always counts high except in conjunction with 2–3–4–5, forming a straight or straight flush. The top hand, an Ace high straight flush, is known as a royal flush. Cards marked 'x' are 'idlers' and count for nothing except to break a tie between hands containing equally high combinations.

Draw Poker

With slight regional variations, this is the original form of the game and the most widely played throughout the world. It differs in some respects from the form described in many English books, which I refer to as English Club Poker. It is also, but not quite accurately, sometimes known as Jackpots.

How to play

Preliminaries. From five to seven is a good number of players. With fewer, the game is dull because the average winning hand is very low; with more, there are not enough cards to go round in comfort. Each player should start with the equivalent of 200 chips in whites, reds and blues. Set a time limit on play and stop play at the end of the deal in which the limit expires. Agree on the value of the chips, the amount of the ante (ideally, one white chip), the maximum permitted raise in the first betting round (e.g. five whites or equivalent) and the maximum permitted in the second round (e.g. ten whites or equivalent). Alternatively, agree to play 'pot limits' – i. e. the maximum permitted raise is the size of the pot at the time it is made.

Shuffling the cards. Theoretically each new deal should be made from a thoroughly shuffled pack, and it is permissible to alternate between two packs so that one can be shuffled while the other is being dealt. In practice one pack is used continuously until a new one is called for – which anyone may do if he feels (rightly or wrongly) that the cards are 'running against him'. Also, in practice, there are people who prefer to play without shuffling the cards between deals, in order to produce 'more exciting hands'. There are such people who do this in all card games as a matter of course, but the practice has nothing to commend it in an honest game.

Anybody who wishes has a right to shuffle, but the dealer has the right to shuffle last. Before dealing, he should have the cards cut by the player on his right. The purpose of this is to prevent the bottom card of the pack from being seen by anyone, as may sometimes happen at the end of a shuffle. For similar but less tenable reasons, some players insist that the top card of the pack be 'burned' immediately before dealing – that is, transferred from the top to the bottom of the pack. (I suspect that 'burned' originated as a misreading of 'buried'.)

Ante. Before the deal, each player contributes to the pot by paying an ante of one white chip, placing it in the centre of the table.

Deal. Deal cards one at a time, face down, in rotation, starting at dealer's left, until each player has received five cards.

Opening. Each player in turn, starting at dealer's left, may fold, check, or bet. A player *folds* if he has bad cards and does not wish to stay in the deal, by laying his cards face down on the table and announcing that he is out of the present pot. He *checks,* by announcing 'I check' or knocking on the table, if he wishes to stay in and play the hand but is either unwilling or unqualified to make the opening bet. The opening bet may only be made by a player whose hand contains a pair of Jacks or better (unless previous agreement has been made to 'open on anything'). He does so by announcing 'Open for two', or however many chips it may be, and pushes that number forwards towards the middle of the table – though not actually in it with the antes, as it is necessary during the course of the game to be able to see exactly how much each player has so far bet, and so determine whether or not the bets have been equalized.

If no player has opened the betting before the turn comes round again to the first to speak, the cards are thrown in and the next deal ensues. The antes stay in the middle of the table as part of the next pot, to which a fresh ante is made by each player.

Continuation of first betting interval. Once somebody has opened, each player thereafter must do one of the following: drop out of play, 'stay' by increasing his stake so that it equals that of the previous player still in the game, or equal the last bet and 'raise'.

Example: Player A says 'Open for two'. Player B says 'Fold' and throws in his cards. Player C says 'Stay for two', staking two chips to equal the stake of the opener. Player D says 'Stay for two and raise two', pushing four chips towards the pot. Player E says 'Stay for four, since D has increased the amount necessary to stay in the pot and E does not wish to raise further. Back round to player A again, and he must pay two if he wishes to stay, since he is two short of the amount so far staked by E and D.

This continues until one of two things happens:

■ Somebody raises and everybody else folds. The last raiser wins the pot without showing his hand and the deal is at an end.

■ More usually, all bets are equalized between the two or more players who have stayed in the pot. Note: if one person raises and the others either fold or stay but do not re-raise, the betting interval is at an end: a player may not re-raise himself.

When all bets are equalized it is time for the draw.

The draw. The dealer now addresses everybody in turn who is still in the game, starting at his left, and asks whether they want to 'stand pat' (keep the cards they were dealt) or exchange any. If not standing pat, each player discards from one to three cards, face down, and receives the same number dealt face down one at a time from the top of the pack. When the dealer gets round to himself he must announce clearly how many he is discarding and drawing.

As it is silly to exchange more than three cards in the draw, some players insist on a rule prohibiting the exchange of more, as implied in the paragraph above. Players should agree beforehand whether or not this rule applies. Serious players rarely, if ever, draw more than two.

If the player who opened the betting did so on a high pair – Jacks or better – it is quite possible that he may want to discard one of them in the draw. This is known as 'splitting openers'. He need not announce that he is doing so, but must keep track of his discards in case he wins the pot, as he may then be required to show that he was qualified to make the opening bet.

Second betting interval. This time the first person to speak is not necessarily the player at dealer's left but the one who opened the first betting interval. He may fold, bet, or check. Checking means that he wishes to stay in the pot but doesn't want to open the betting this time round. If he checks, each player in turn after him has the same options. If everybody checks, then the original opener may not check again but must either fold or open the second period of betting.

Once the betting interval has been opened, each player in turn after the opener may fold, meet the amount of the last bet, or meet it and raise again. This continues in exactly the same way as the first betting interval. If all but one player drop out, the one left in wins the pot. Otherwise, betting continues until all bets have been equalized, at which point there is a showdown. All those still in the pot reveal their hands – they must do so, and must reveal them entirely – and the pot goes to the player with the best hand, or is divided equally if two have identical best hands. If the pot is won by the original opener and he cannot prove that he was qualified to open, it goes to the second best hand. If there is no second best (all but the opener having folded), the pot is carried forward to the next deal.

Irregularities. In the event of a misdeal, such as exposing a card, dealing in the wrong order or with an imperfect or unshuffled pack, the cards are gathered in and the same dealer deals again after shuffling and cutting. If he misdeals twice in succession he forfeits the deal, which passes to the left.

If a player bets out of order, he must do whatever he said he was going to do (fold, bet or raise) when his proper turn comes round – he may not say one thing at the wrong time and do something different at the right.

If too many players draw too many cards, there may not be enough left in the pack to go round. In this case the dealer deals cards from the pack as far as they will go short of the last card. This he keeps, and adds it to all the folded hands and discards of the other players, except the discards of the original opener in case he split openers and has to prove it later. The new pack must be shuffled and cut, after which the draw can be continued from it.

If a player runs out of chips during the course of a hand he may (by previous agreement) be permitted to 'tap out'. This means that he may stay in the pot free of charge, provided that he does not raise but only notionally meets existing bets, and may even take part in the draw. All bets made after a player has tapped out are kept slightly apart from those made previously. If the tapper-out emerges the winner, he takes only the main pot: all the bets made after he tapped out constitute a second prize which goes to the second best hand. If not, he is out of the game, unless permitted to buy himself back in.

Notes on play

Whole books can be written about strategy at Draw Poker, and have been, and pretty boring they are too. There is no substitute for experience, and in these pages no space to do more than outline the broadest of hints.

Character of the game

How you play depends largely on how everyone else is playing. A 'loose' game is one in which players fool around, take reckless chances and reach bankruptcy at great speed. A 'tight' game is one in which the participants are either mathematicians or money grubbers or both: the game is played in expressionless silence, the draws are all of one card if any, and the action is only enlivened by long periods of rumination before each player makes a move. Needless to say, a sensible game steers a middle course between two extremes. A game is a social activity and players should be sociable without being silly, otherwise it will not serve its primary purpose of generating enjoyment at the exercise of skill.

As a game progresses, it usually tends to get looser. It also gets looser if the table is a mixture of loose and tight players. In order to counterbalance this, it may be best to err on the side of tightness without going so far as to become a po-faced skinflint.

Position

Position counts. If you're first to speak in the first betting interval, you may have a hand qualified to open, but if it is only a pair of Jacks (say), the bare minimum, you have no way of knowing what the opposition is likely to hold. You could open and find yourself raised all around the table, or you might check and find the deal passed up by everybody. The dealer, on the other hand, is in the best position to make a positive decision, because he will have heard all his opponents' initial reactions to their hands before he comes to speak. It is therefore sensible for a player in an early position to open with not less than a pair of Queens, Kings or even Aces, depending on how many there are at the table.

Throughout the game, it is useful to erase from your consciousness, from your vision if possible, those players who have dropped, and see only yourself in relation to those left in the pot. Your actions may then be guided by whether the players on your immediate right and left are tight or loose players, whether they are winning or losing, and so on.

First betting interval

The first betting interval is rather more mathematical than the second. First, you must assess the strength of your hand by whether it is probably the best, or the worst, or about middling. Since about half the hands dealt are nothing, and most of the others are a pair, you can immediately assess a low or non-pair hand as worthless. On average, about half the players round the table should get a pair, which is why the minimum worthwhile opening hand is a pair of Jacks. Remember that the more players there are taking part, the more chance there is that at least one opponent has been dealt a strong hand, say two pairs or three of a kind. Mathematics also enter into it because in the first interval you are only partly betting on what your hand is – a greater consideration is what it may *become* after the draw. For this purpose the table on page 252 is worth being acquainted with. The first column shows the type of hand you may be dealt and the amount of it you would keep when discarding. (A 'kicker' is an Ace accompanying the main combination, which you may keep hold of in hope of pairing it. With three of a kind, the kicker may be any rank.) The next shows how many cards you might exchange from it, followed by the type of hand you hope to get as a result. For each type of desired result, the final column shows the odds against actually getting it.

A word about odds and probabilities. It is not worth attempting to commit them to memory if you haven't got that sort of mind, but sufficient to know which combinations are worth going for and which are very long shots. If you do remember any of the figures, one way of using them is this: if the odds offered you by the pot are greater than those offered by the draw, make the draw; if not, don't. For example, suppose there are 25 chips in the pot (including the ones you have so far staked) and it costs you five to stay in. Then the pot is offering odds of 25 to 5 or 5:1. It is therefore worth staying in on a high pair, since the odds of improving after discarding three are 3:1 against, which is shorter than the odds offered by the pot. But it is less worthwhile pursuing a two pairs hand, as the odds against improvement are 11:1. Of course, the odds are not everything – they are only a guide. Poker is primarily an intuitive game; but, just as there is no reason why intuition shouldn't enter your calculations, so there is no reason why calculations shouldn't contribute to your intuition.

Playing the dealt hand. If you are dealt a high five-card combination (straight, flush, full house or straight flush), you have no discarding problems and will stand pat. Mathematics hardly enter into it: your objective is the psychological one of betting hard enough to build up a good pot but not so hard as to frighten everybody out of it.

Four of a kind is similar, except that you have the option of standing pat or discarding the odd card just for fun. (But make sure you don't discard the wrong one or the joke will misfire.) There are those who think it immoral to discard one from four of a kind, but how often are you likely to be in the happy position of so tussling with your conscience?

Any of these combinations are likely to be winners in the first round. But what counts is not the first but the second round. Bear in mind that players with worse hands may nevertheless convert them into better as the result of the draw. You don't want to bet so hard as to drive out such speculators, but you must remember that a pat hand, though probably the best going in, is not necessarily the best coming out.

Three of a kind is a good hand. It is usually the best going in and quite often the best even after the draw. It also gives you the greatest variety of options. You may discard two, giving yourself the best chances of making any improvement, or one, which gives fair chances and has the advantage of revealing no information about the shape of your hand, since one card is the commonest and least tell-tale draw in sensible Poker. Or, if not too many remain in the pot, you may even take a chance and stand pat on it.

Two pairs, by contrast, is the most awkward dealt hand to cope with, in many ways worse than one pair. The only sensible discard from two pairs is one card, and the odds against improving (a full house being the only possible improvement) are 11:1. The only advantage is that the one-card discard at least gives nothing away. The problem, of course, is that two pairs is usually the best hand going in, but rarely the best coming out. This applies especially if the pairs are low, since an opponent who went in with a high pair may well convert to a winning two pairs. Hence the best thing to do with two pairs is to bet hard in the first round if you bet at all, in order to drive out as much opposition as possible, and be prepared to relinquish it in the second period if it then seems unlikely to be the best round the table.

If you have a pair, discarding three is a dead give-away. However, you have the consolation of the best chances of making any improvement – $2\frac{1}{2}$ to 1 according to the table, with a number of different hands as your ultimate prize. To give less away about your hand, you may keep the pair and a 'kicker' and merely exchange two. The higher the kicker, the better. With a pair and an Ace, few players would discard the Ace. If in the sort of company that invariably draws no cards or one, you could be ridiculously cheeky and discard one, keeping two kickers. The odds of making any improvement at all are about 5:1, specifically 7:1 against getting two pairs and $22\frac{1}{2}$:1 against getting threes. But don't make a habit of it.

The only combinationless hands worth taking seriously are four-flushes and open ended fourstraights, each of which is worthless in the first period and remains worthless in the second unless improved by the draw of one card, in which case they become very probable winners. If you have four cards of a suit the chances of drawing a fifth are about four to one against. If it fails you will either have to disown it in the second period or try to bluff it out, but at least it has the advantage of requiring the draw of only one card.

A hand containing four cards to a straight is only worth playing if they form an open ended sequence fillable by either of two cards, such as 7–8–9–10, which can be filled by a Six or a Jack. The odds are only 5:1 in this case, but are less worth playing in the case of an inside straight (e.g. 6–7–rubbish–4–9) or a closed straight (i.e. A–2–3–4–rubbish or A–K–Q–J–rubbish). Here only one rank will do, and the odds are 11:1 against.

Related hands are the pair-bobtail and four to a straight flush. If you have a four-card straight flush the odds against improvement are considerably shorter – 2:1 in the case of an open ended fourstraight and 3:1 if only one rank will fill the straight. In the former case, say 6–7–8–9 of spades, either of two cards will make a straight flush, and of six others will make a straight, and any of seven others a flush.

A pair-bobtail is a four-card straight or flush and a fifth card of the same rank as one of the others – for example, J–J–10–9–8 is a pair and an open ended straight, while ♠J–♡J–7–4–2 is a pair combined with a fourflush. The question in these cases is whether to keep the pair and discard the other three, or to go for the higher combination by breaking the pair up. In the first case you finish up with a pair, which is not a strong hand, but better than nothing and quite capable of winning a pot. In the second, you may finish up with a probably unbeatable hand, but only if you make it – if not, the loss of the pair leaves you worse off than when you started. The odds favour keeping the pair in most cases, and forgoing the chance of the higher hand, especially if the pair is as high as Aces or Kings.

General

The second betting period is less mathematical and more psychological. You will have seen how many cards are being drawn by your opponents, they will have seen how many are being drawn by you, and everyone will be trying to relate this to their knowledge of how everybody else thinks and behaves over the Poker table.

The two most useful generalizations that can be made for this period and for all other forms of Poker generally are as follows. First, if at any stage in the proceedings you ready believe your hand is not the best round the table, drop it. You may be able to bluff your opponents into thinking your hand is better or worse than it really is, but you can't bluff the hand itself. The other side of the coin is that, having once decided that you are going to follow a hand through, do so with inner confidence. Never just string along in the hope that everyone else will drop out first and leave you to sweep the pot without showing your hand.

Second, the most dangerous property of a poor Poker player (in both senses of the word!) is predictability. Poker gives you plenty of opportunities for varying the way in which you draw cards and play the hands. If it becomes known that you always do the same thing – such as standing pat on two pairs or betting too hard on a low straight, or holding your cards tight and close to the chest when you are sure you have a winner – then more observant players will note and remember it. I would say that the true meaning of the much misunderstood word 'bluff' lies in avoiding any sort of predictability in the way you play.

Chances of improving the hand at 5-card Draw

hand dealt	cards drawn	possible improvement	odds against*
Ace high	4	1P Aces	3
		2P inc.Aces	14
One pair	3	any	2½
		2P	5
		3S	7†
		FH	97
		4S	360
One pair + Ace kicker	2	any	3
		2P inc. Aces	7½
		2P other	17
		3S	12
		FH	120
		4S	1,080
Two pairs	1	FH	11
Threes	2	any	8½
		FH	15½
		4S	22½
Threes + kicker	1	any	11
		FH	14½
		4S	46
Fourstraight, double-ended	1	ST	5
Fourstraight, one place open	1	ST	11
Fourflush	1	FL	4
Four-card SF, double-ended	1	ST or FL	2
		SF	22½
Four-card SF, one place open	1	ST or FL	3
		SF	46

* *odds over 100 are rounded*
† *often quoted as 8:1 against, but in fact 1 in 8, or 7:1 against*

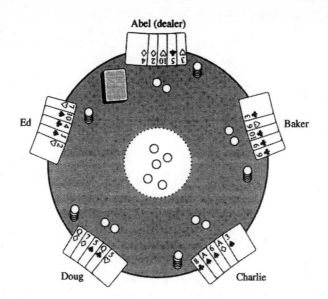

Figure 26.2 Poker

Opening deal in a five-player game to which Abel dealt. All have placed an agreed ante of 1 chip to the pot (represented here by the outlined circular area). Baker's pair of Sixes do not qualify as openers, but he may be willing to draw one to a flush, and checks. Charlie's Aces do so qualify, and he opens for two chips, which he pushes towards the pot. Doug, with a very poor two pairs, meets Baker's opening for two, but does not raise for fear of frightening subsequent players out. Ed, very properly, allows himself to be frightened out. Abel stays for 2, intending to draw one to his four-card straight, and Baker does likewise, holding four to a flush. The situation is now as illustrated, and the eight chips so far bet are now pushed into the pot with the original five. Note that these players are sufficiently experienced to hold their cards in the order dealt without arranging them by rank and suit, which would convey much useful information to the practised eye. (The cards are not exposed, of course.)

Charlie discards 3–6 and draws 2–9, making no improvement on his pair of Aces. Doug draws one – getting a Six for his Seven – not because he seriously expects to get a full house, but because his Queen-high two pairs is probably the best hand, and standing pat might frighten others out. Abel draws a Two for his Ten, giving him a pair of Twos, and Baker the diamond Three for his heart Six, giving him a pair of Threes.

Charlie checks, Doug bets 2, and Abel throws in his pair of Twos. Baker tries a bluff, meeting Doug's 2 and raising 2 as if his one-card draw had made a straight or flush. Charlie now loses confidence in his Aces and folds. Doug sees Baker for 2 and, of course, his two pairs wins. He gets 13 from the pot, 4 from Baker, and his own 4 back, yielding a net profit of 14 chips for 7 invested.

Not an exciting deal, but a typical and instructive one. Few hands at orthodox Draw Poker are won by anything higher than two pairs; the best hand going in is often the best hand going out; drawing one to a straight or flush rarely pays off; and if you (Baker) are really going to bluff, wait until you can afford to make it so big that no one dare call it.

Stud Poker

There is no draw in Stud Poker. Instead, some of your cards are dealt and kept face up, so that everyone can see part of everyone else's hand. For this reason Stud is more suitable than Draw for larger groups of players, eight being a good table. There are endless variations on the basic theme, but we will start with the simplest.

Five-card or Short Stud

Everyone antes the minimum amount before the deal, or else (and preferably) the dealer antes by putting up as many chips as there are players.

After the shuffle and cut, deal a round of one card face down to each player followed by one card face up. Each player looks at his down-card and places it face down on the table before him as him as his hole card and covering it with his up-card.

The first betting interval follows, opened by the player showing the highest ranking up-card, or, in the case of a tie, by the tied player nearest to the dealer's left (dealer himself, if tied, counting as furthest from his own left). At this and each subsequent betting interval it is part of the dealer's duties to indicate which hand bets first. The first to speak must either bet or fold. At this stage no one is allowed to check or pass. Each subsequent player then folds, pays an equal amount to stay in, or raises by increasing that amount. After any raise there must be another complete round of announcements to enable each active player to fold, equalize or re-raise. This continues until all bets are equalized, or all but one player fold, in which case the one remaining wins the pot without exposing his hole card.

If two or more remain in the pot, deal each active player another up-card. Cards should be dealt with one hand from the top of the squared-up pack, which remains face down on the table. In some circles it is customary for the dealer to announce, as he deals each card, the best hand that could be held on the evidence of the player's up-cards at that moment, e.g. 'One pair', 'Ace high', 'Possible flush', etc.

The first to speak in this and subsequent betting intervals is the player showing the greatest number or highest value of paired cards if any, or the highest-ranking individual card if not, followed by the second highest in the event of a tie, and so on. First-to-speak may now check instead of folding or betting, if he wishes, and, if he checks, each subsequent player has the same three options until someone bets, after which the others must fold, call or raise. If everyone checks the betting interval ends and the next card is dealt. A third and fourth up-card are dealt in this way, each followed by a betting interval.

A showdown is reached when the last person to raise has been called. All those in the pot must reveal their hole cards and the best hand wins the pot. If everyone checks there is an automatic showdown. If one player raises and everyone else folds he wins the pot without revealing his hole card.

Because there is no draw the winning hand is on average lower than in Draw Poker – often as low as a pair, sometimes merely a high card. Most of the action centres on paired combinations rather than straights and flushes. In practice this means you should not normally aim for, or bluff on, a possible straight or flush until you have your third up-card, unless your up-cards reveal a substantial threat – for instance, the possibility of a straight flush or at least a winning high pair.

American Seven-card or Long Stud

Long Stud is played like Short Stud except that there are five betting intervals, which follow these deals:

    1. Two cards down followed by one up

    2. A second up-card

    3. A third up-card

    4. A fourth up-card

    5. A third hole card

By the last round, then, each player has four cards visible and three hole cards. When it comes to a showdown he selects any five cards from his seven to act as his final hand.

Strategy is the least of your worries. The first thing you have to do is recognize potential hands when you see them. Not for nothing is Long Stud known as 'Down the River', as you may gather when you note that a player showing four rubbish cards may actually be sitting on four of a kind. A useful exercise is to deal out seven hands without looking at the hole cards and then make a note of what is the best hand that each player could possibly be nursing.

English Long Stud

Either everyone antes one chip, or (preferably) dealer antes as many chips as there are players. Assuming an ante and minimum bet of one chip, it may be agreed to limit raises to one chip in all betting intervals except the last, or to increase them gradually – say by one additional chip per interval until the last is reached, for which a maximum may be specified.

The difference between English and American Long Stud is that, in English, the sixth and seventh are not dealt in addition to the first five but as replacements for two discards from the first five. In effect, it is a cross between Stud and Draw, with a maximum buy of two cards.

A betting interval follows each of the following events:

- ■ Deal a first down-card to each player, then a second. When they have looked at their hole cards and placed them face down on the table, deal a third card face up to each player. Highest up-card speaks first. He may not check in this round.

- ■ Deal a second up-card. Highest visible pair speaks first, or best individual card if none. From now on first-to-speak may check, and if all players check the betting interval ends.

- ■ Deal a third up-card. At this and each subsequent deal first-to-speak is the player showing the highest number of paired cards, or highest ranking if tied.

- ■ Each player in rotation from the dealer's left now discards any one of his cards and receives a replacement from the top of the pack. The replacement is dealt face up if an up-card was thrown, down if a

hole card was rejected. A player may stand pat if he
wishes, but must then also stand pat on the next round.

■ A second discard is made and replaced, the
replacement again being dealt up or down to match the
discard. A player may stand pat if he wishes, and must
do so if he stood pat before. This inaugurates the last
interval.

As to strategy, the addition of what amounts to a two-card draw
increases the mathematical skill factor of the game (not necessarily
the psychological skill factor) and has an effect on the average final
hands. The incidence of 2P and 3S is reduced because only two can
be drawn to 1P instead of the three at Draw Poker, but that of ST
and FL increased because two can be drawn to a bobtail instead of
only one at Draw.

Flop Poker

A flop is one or more cards dealt to the centre of the table and
counting as communal cards – that is, anyone may count any one or
more of them as being part of his own hand. The original and
simplest form was a variety of Draw known as Spit in the Ocean.
The most advanced version is Hold 'em, the game now preferred by
international tournament players.

Spit in the Ocean

This is basically five-card Draw except that the fifth card is a flop
(the 'spit').

Deal four cards to each player and one face up to the table. There is
no minimum opening requirement; in fact, the player at dealer's left
may be required by previous agreement to open the betting
regardless. When bets are equal in the first round, each player may
discard and draw up to four replacements. In the event of a
showdown the pot is won by the best five-card hand, counting the
central spit as the fifth card. The average winning hand is lower than
at ordinary Draw Poker, since everybody has the same fifth card and
nobody can change it.

Hold 'em

Deal two cards face down to each player, followed by a round of betting. Deal three cards face up to the centre of the table, and bet again. Then deal two more flop cards face up, one at a time, with a betting interval after each one. When all bets are equalized, the pot is won by the player who can make the best five-card hand, counting for this purpose any five out of seven – i.e. his own two and the five flop cards. The average winning hand is in the straight-to-flush region, usually a full house if the flop include a pair.

Wild-card Poker

All forms of Poker may be played with one or more cards 'wild'. The original and dullest version involves adding a Joker to the pack and allowing whoever gets it to count it as any desired card. Any card or cards may be specified as wild, ranging from 'one-eyed Jacks' to 'all the spades'. (One-eyed Jacks are the ones depicted in profile so that only one eye is displayed – an interesting variation because of the wide variety of different designs now encountered in standard packs.)

Perhaps the most popular, and certainly the most sensible, is 'Deuces wild', in which all four Twos may count as anything specified by their holder(s).

Fun and complication is introduced by making the wild card variable. For example, in Stud Poker it may be agreed that each player's first hole card is wild for his hand only, so that he may count this and any others he receives of the same rank as wild. In varieties of Flop Poker it may be stated that the rank of the first communal card is wild, together with all others of the same rank. And so on.

The more wild cards there are in a game, the higher the average winning hand. It should also be pointed out that the highest hand is five of a kind, the best possible being four Aces and a wild card, counting as five Aces. Between equal hands containing wild cards, the one with fewest wild cards wins – unless agreed otherwise.

Dealer's Choice

If it's variety you're after in the game of Poker, the best way of introducing it is to play Dealer's Choice. This means that each player in turn, as he becomes the dealer, chooses the variety of Poker to be played, which may be a standard one or one invented on the spur of the moment.

GLOSSARY OF CARD PLAYING TERMS

Ante A fixed amount staked by the dealer, or by every player before cards are dealt.

Auction Preliminary part of a trick-taking game in which players bid for the right to specify conditions of play (such as the trump suit) in return for an undertaking to achieve a higher valued objective than anyone else.

Bid Offer to achieve a higher valued objective than anyone else in return for the right to specify certain conditions of play, such as the trump suit.

Combination A set of matching cards for which a score or payment may be due by the rules of the particular game.

Contract An irrevocable undertaking to achieve a certain objective after bidding higher than anyone else and specifying conditions of play.

Court (card) A King, Queen or Jack (originally coat card). In America it is called *face card*.

Declare Various meanings according to context, but generally either (a) to announce the conditions of the game or the objective to be achieved, or (b) to show and score for a scoring combination of cards.

Declarer The soloist in solo games, otherwise that member of a partnership primarily responsible for declaring the contract.

Defender In Bridge, the opponents of the declarer.

Discard (a) To reject an unwanted card from the hand. (b) In trick-play, when unable to follow suit to the card led, to play a card from a suit other than trumps or the one led.

Doubleton Exactly two cards of a given suit remaining in (or dealt to) a player's hand.

Draw To take (or be dealt) cards from the stock and add them to one's hand, sometimes in exchange for unwanted cards.

Eldest The player sitting immediately next the dealer (on his left if the game is played clockwise round the table, his right otherwise), who normally has the privilege of bidding or playing first. In two-player games the non-dealer is elder.

Exchange To discard unwanted cards and replace them with fresh ones. In some games the discard is made before replacements are seen: in others, replacements are taken first and may form part of the discard.

Flush Cards of the same suit.

Follow (suit) To play to a trick a card of the same suit as the one led to it.

Forehand Same as **eldest.**

Game *See also* **rubber.** (a) Complete period of play at the end of which all scores are settled – may be anything from one deal to a whole session. (b) The target score which, when reached by at least one player, terminates the period of play and settlement, e.g. a game may be described as '500 up' – i.e., played up to a score of 500. (c) The stated objective and conditions of play for one particular deal – e.g. 'game in diamonds' means diamonds are trumps. (d) In Bridge, the number of points still needed to win a game by a side that may already have a part-score. (e) In contradiction of (a) above, several 'games' may constitute a larger self-contained period of play.

Guard(ed) In trick play a card in the hand is guarded by at least as many lower cards (guards) as there are cards above it lacking from the hand. For example, if your highest spade is the Queen, you need two lower spades to guard it, so that when they have been thrown in turn to the Ace and King, your Queen will be the best in its suit (its 'master' card).

Hand (a) The cards held in a player's hand. (b) A player (as in 'eldest hand'). (c) Period of play between the point at which all cards have been dealt and the point at which all have been played.

Head In tricks, to follow suit to the card led and beat all those that have so far been played. In some games it is obligatory to head the trick if possible.

Honours Certain cards for which the rules of the game may prescribe a score of payment to their holder.

Kitty *See* **widow.**

Lead To play the first card of deal or to a trick.

Long A suit in which you hold more cards than average. For example, if four players are dealt 13 each and you have four or more of a suit, your holding of that suit is 'long'.

Make To fulfil a contract.

Meld A winning or scoring set of cards that match one another by rank and or suit. To show or declare such a set.

Misère An undertaking to lose every trick.

Numerals Cards other than court cards. (Americans call them *spot cards.*)

Opponent Sometimes has also the specialized meaning of one who is playing against a solo player or declarer. Thus the opponents of the soloist are not necessarily opponents of one another.

Ouvert (Open) In trick-taking games, playing with one's hand of cards face up on the table.

Overcall To make a higher bid than the preceding bidder.

Overtrick A trick won in excess of the number contracted.

Pass To make no bid when it is your turn to do so.

Pip(-value) Literally, a pip is a suit symbol printed on a card. The pip value of a card is its value when captured, for example in a trick. The term avoids confusion with 'points' in the scoring sense.

Plain suit One that is not trumps. (Also *side suit* or *off-suit.*)

Rank The denomination of a card – e.g. Ace, King, Two Three and so on.

Renege Often used to mean 'revoke', but actually meaning to fail to follow suit in trick-taking games where special circumstances permit you to do so (as in Twenty-Five).

Renounce Loosely, to fail to follow suit; strictly, to play a card other than a trump when unable to follow suit.

Revoke To fail to follow suit, even though able and required to do so, for which a penalty may be exacted.

Round A round of play or bidding is complete when every player has had one opportunity to play or bid. Also, for example, 'third round of trumps' means 'third occasion on which a trump has been led to a trick'.

Rubber Equivalent to a match or tournament, the winner of a rubber being the first to win a certain number of games – typically three in Whist and Bridge.

Ruff A trump. To play a trump to a plain-suit lead.

Sequence A set of cards in numerical or ranking sequence, such as A–2–3 or 10–J–Q–K. In some games a sequence only counts if the constituent cards are also of the same suit.

Singleton Exactly one card of a given suit remaining in (or dealt to) a player's hand.

Slam The winning of every single trick, called a 'grand slam' in games which also recognize a 'small slam' of every trick but one.

Solo(-ist) A solo game is one in which one player (not usually called the soloist, though it seems the best word) undertakes to win a certain number of tricks without a partner, playing alone against the combined efforts of everyone else.

Stock The undealt portion of the pack if not all cards are dealt.

Trick See Introduction.

Trump See Introduction.

Void Having no cards of a given suit (e.g. 'I am void in spades' or 'I have a void in spades').

Widow A hand of cards dealt face down to the table (also called the *talon*, *blind*, or *kitty*). These cards can often be taken up by the declarer or soloist in exchange for unwanted discards.

Wild card One that may represent any card its holder wishes.

INDEX OF GAMES